The geology of the country around Cromer. (Explanation of sheet 68 E.)

Clement Reid, Horace B. 1848-1914 Woodward

MEMOIRS OF THE GEOLOGICAL SURVEY.

·ENGLAND AND WALES.

THE GEOLOGY OF THE

COUNTRY AROUND CROMER.

(EXPLANATION OF SHEET 68 E.)

BY

CLEMENT REID, F.G.S.

(WITH NOTES BY H. B WOODWARD, F G.S)

PUBLISHED BY ORDER OF THE LORDS COMMISSIONERS OF HER MAJESTY'S TREASURY.

LONDON:
PRINTED FOR HER MAJESTY'S STATIONERY OFFICE,
AND SOLD BY
LONGMANS & Co., Paternoster Row; TRUBNER & Co , Ludgate Hill;
LETTS, SON, & Co , Limited, 33, King William Street, E C.,
E. STANFORD, 55, Charing Cross; J WYLD, 12, Charing Cross, and
QUARITCH, 15, Piccadilly ,
ALSO BY
DAY, 53, Market Street, Manchester ,
W. & A. K JOHNSTON, 4, St Andrew Square, Edinburgh ,
HODGES, FIGGIS, & Co , 104, Grafton Street, Dublin , and
A. THOM & Co , Abbey Street, Dublin.

1882.

Price Six Shillings.

LIST OF GEOLOGICAL MAPS, SECTIONS, AND PUBLICATIONS OF THE GEOLOGICAL SURVEY.

The Maps are those of the Ordnance Survey, geologically coloured by the Geological Survey of the United Kingdom under the Superintendence of ARCH. GEIKIE, LL.D., F.R.S., Director General. The various Formations are traced and coloured in all their Subdivisions

(For Maps, Sections, and Memoirs illustrating Scotland, Ireland, and the West Indies, *see* Catalogue.)

ENGLAND AND WALES.—(Scale one-inch to a mile.)
Those marked * are also published as Drift Maps.

Maps, Nos 3* to 41, 44, 47, 64, price 8s 6d each, with the exceptions of 2, 10, 23, 24, 27, 28, 29, 32, 38, 39, 58, 4s each. Sheets divided into four quarters, 1*, 42, 43, 45, 46, (48 SE*), (50 SW*), (51 SW*), 52, 53, 54, 55, 56 57, (59 NE SE), 60, 61, 82 63, 64, (66 NE*, SE*), (67 N*), 71 72, 73, 74, 75 (76 N. S), (77 N), 78, 79, 80 (NW*, SW*), 81 (NW*), 82, 87, 88 (SW*), 89 (SE*), (90 SE*, NE*), (91 SW*, NW*), (92 SW, SE), (93 SW, NW), (95 NW*, SW*), (97 SE), (98 NE, SE, SW), (101 SE), 103 (NE*, NW*), (104 SW*), 105 (SE*), (106 NE, SE), (109 SW) Price 3s Except (87 NW), 78 (N), (77 NE), (95 SE*), (104 SE*), (105 NE*), (109 SE) Price 1s 6d

HORIZONTAL SECTIONS, *Illustrative of the Geological Maps*
1 to 129, England, price 5s. each.

VERTICAL SECTIONS, *Illustrative of Horizontal Sections and Maps.*
1 to 57, England, price 3s 6d each

COMPLETED COUNTIES OF ENGLAND AND WALES, on a Scale of one-inch to a Mile

The sheets marked * have Descriptive Memoirs   Those marked † are illustrated by General Memoirs.

ANGLESEY,—77 (N), 78 Hor Sect. 40.
BEDFORDSHIRE,—46 (NW, NE, SW†, & SE†) 52 (NW, NE, SW, & SE)
BERKSHIRE,—7*, 8†, 12*, 13*, 34† 45 (SW*) Hor. Sect 59, 71, 72, 80).
BRECKNOCKSHIRE,—36, 41, 42, 56 (NW & SW), 57 (NE & SE) Hor Sect. 4, 5, 6, 11, and Vert. Sect. 4 and 10.
BUCKINGHAMSHIRE,—7* 13* 45* (NE, SE), 46 (NW, SW†), 52 (SW) Hor Sect 74, 79
CAERMARTHENSHIRE, 37, 38, 40, 41, 42 (NW & SW), 56 (SW), 57 (SW & SE) Hor Sect. 2, 3, 4, 7, 8, 9, and Vert. Sect 3, 4, 5, 6, 13, 14
CAERNARVONSHIRE,—74 (NW), 75, 76, 77 (N), 78, 79 (NW & SW). Hor. Sect 28, 31, 40
CARDIGANSHIRE,—40, 41, 56 (NW), 57, 58, 59 (SE), 60 (SW). Hor Sect 4, 5, 6.
CHESHIRE,—73 (NE & NW), 79 (NE & SE), 80, 81 (NW* & SW*), 88 (SW). Hor Sect 18, 43, 44, 60, 64, 65, 67, 70
CORNWALL,—24†, 25†, 26†, 29†, 30†, 31†, 32†, & 33†.
DENBIGH,—73 (NW), 74, 75 (NE), 78 (NE & SE), 79 (NW, SW, & SE), 80 (SW) Hor. Sect. 31, 35, 38, 39, 43, 44, and Vert. Sect 24.
DERBYSHIRE,—62 (NE), 63 (NW), 71 (NW, SW, & SE), 72 (NE, SE), 81, 82, 88 (SW, SE) Hor. Sect. 18 46, 60, 61, 69, 70
DEVONSHIRE,—20†, 21†, 22†, 23†, 24†, 25†, 26†, & 27†. Hor Sect. 19
DORSETSHIRE,—15, 16, 17, 18, 21, 22 Hor Sect 19, 20, 21, 22, 56 Vert. Sect 22
FLINTSHIRE,—74 (NE), 79. Hor Sect 43
GLAMORGANSHIRE,—20, 36, 37, 41, & 42 (SE & SW) Hor Sect 7, 8, 9, 10, 11, and Vert Sect 2, 4, 5, 6, 7, 9, 10, 47
GLOUCESTERSHIRE,—19, 34*, 35, 43 (NE, SW, & SE), 44*. Hor. Sect. 12, 13, 14, 15, 59, and Vert Secs. 7, 11, 15, 46, 47, 48, 49, 50, 51
HAMPSHIRE,—8†, 9†, 10*, 11†, 12*, 14, 15, 16 Hor Sect 80
HEREFORDSHIRE,—42 (NE & SE), 43, 55, 56 (NE & SE) Hor Sect 5, 13, 27, 30, 34, and Vert Sect 15.
KENT,—1† (SW & SE), 2†, 3†, 4*, 5†, 6† Hor Sect 77 and 78.
MERIONETHSHIRE,—59 (NE & SE), 60 (NW), 74 75 (NE & SE). Hor. Sect 26, 28, 29, 31, 32, 35, 37, 38, 39
MIDDLESEX,—1† (NW & SW), 7*, 8†. Hor. Sect. 79
MONMOUTHSHIRE,—35, 36, 42 (SE & NE), 43 (SW) Hor Sect 5 and 12, and Vert Sect 8, 9, 10, 12.
MONTGOMERYSHIRE,—56 (NW), 59 (NE & SE), 60, 74 (SW & SE). Hor Sect 26, 27, 29, 30, 32, 34, 35, 36, 38.
NORTHAMPTONSHIRE,—64, 45 (NW & NE), 46 (NW), 52 (NW, NE, & SW), 53 (NE, SW, & SE), 63 (SE), 64
OXFORDSHIRE,—7*, 13*, 34*, 44*, 45*, 53 (SE*, SW). Hor. Sect. 71, 72, 81, 82.
PEMBROKESHIRE,—38, 39, 40, 41, 58 Hor Sect 1 and 2, and Vert. Sect 12 and 13.
RADNORSHIRE,—42 (NW & NE), 56, 60 (SW & SE) Hor. Sect. 5, 6, 27.
RUTLANDSHIRE,—this county is included in sheet 64.
SHROPSHIRE,—55 (NW, NE), 56 (NE), 60 (NE, SE), 61, 62 (NW), 73 74 (NE, SE) Hor. Sect. 24, 25, 30, 33, 34, 36, 41, 44, 45, 53, 54, 58, and Vert Sect 23, 24
SOMERSETSHIRE,—18, 19, 20, 21, 27, 35 Hor Sect 15, 16, 17, 20, 21, & 22; and Vert Sect 12, 46, 47, 43, 49, 50, and 51
STAFFORDSHIRE,—(54 NW), 55 (NE) 61 (NE, SE), 62, 63 (NW), 71 (SW), 72, 73 (NE, SE), 81 (SE SW). Hor. Sect. 18, 23, 24, 25, 41, 42, 45, 49, 54, 57, 51, 60, and Vert. Sect. 16, 17, 18, 19, 20, 21, 23, 26
SURREY,—1 (SW†), 6†, 7*, 8†, 9†, 12† Hor Sect 74, 75, 76, and 79
SUSSEX,—4*, 5†, 6†, 8†, 9†, 11†. Hor Sect. 73, 75, 76, 77, 78
WARWICKSHIRE,—44*, 45 (NW), 53*, 54, 62 (NE, SW, & SE), 63 (NW, SW, & SE) Hor. Sect 23, 48, 49, 50, 51, 82, 83, and Vert. Sect 21.
WILTSHIRE,—12*, 13*, 14, 15, 18, 19, 34*, and 35 Hor. Sect 15 and 59
WORCESTERSHIRE,—43 (NE), 44*, 54, 55, 62 (SW & SE), 61 (SE). Hor. Sect 13, 23, 25, 50, and 59 and Vert. Sect. 15.

GENERAL MEMOIRS OF THE GEOLOGICAL SURVEY.

REPORT on CORNWALL, DEVON, and WEST SOMERSET By Sir H T. DE LA BECHE 14s (*Out of print*)
FIGURES and DESCRIPTIONS of the PALÆOZOIC FOSSILS in the above Counties. By PROFESSOR PHILLIPS. (*Out of print*)
The MEMOIRS of the GEOLOGICAL SURVEY of GREAT BRITAIN, and of the MUSEUM of ECONOMIC GEOLOGY of LONDON. 8vo Vol I 21s, Vol II (in 2 Parts), 42s
The GEOLOGY of NORTH WALES. By PROFESSOR RAMSAY With an Appendix, by J. W. SALTER and R ETHERIDGE 2nd Edition. 21s (Vol III. of Memoirs, &c.)
The GEOLOGY of the LONDON BASIN Part I The Chalk and the Eocene Beds of the Southern and Western Tracts By W. WHITAKER (Parts by H W BRISTOW and T McK HUGHES) 13s. (Vol. IV. of Memoirs, &c)
The GEOLOGY of the NEIGHBOURHOOD of LONDON By W. WHITAKER. 1s.
The GEOLOGY of the WEALD (PARTS of the COUNTIES of KENT, SURREY, SUSSEX, and HANTS). By W TOPLEY (3, 4, 5, 6, 8, 9, 11, 12) 17s. 6d
The TRIASSIC and PERMIAN ROCKS of the MIDLAND COUNTIES of ENGLAND By E. HULL. 5s

MEMOIRS OF THE GEOLOGICAL SURVEY.

ENGLAND AND WALES.

THE GEOLOGY OF THE

COUNTRY AROUND CROMER.

(EXPLANATION OF SHEET 68 E.)

BY

CLEMENT REID, F.G.S.

(WITH NOTES BY H. B. WOODWARD, F.G.S.)

PUBLISHED BY ORDER OF THE LORDS COMMISSIONERS OF HER MAJESTY'S TREASURY.

LONDON.
PRINTED FOR HER MAJESTY'S STATIONERY OFFICE,
AND SOLD BY
LONGMANS & Co., Paternoster Row; TRUBNER & Co., Ludgate Hill;
LETTS, SON, & Co., Limited, 33, King William Street, E C;
E. STANFORD, 55, Charing Cross, J. WYLD, 12, Charing Cross, and
QUARITCH, 15, Piccadilly;
ALSO BY
DAY, 53, Market Street, Manchester,
W. & A. K. JOHNSTON, 4, St Andrew Square, Edinburgh;
HODGES, FIGGIS, & Co., 104, Grafton Street, Dublin; and
A. THOM & Co., Abbey Street, Dublin

1882.

Price Six Shillings.

PREFACE.

The Cromer Cliffs of the Norfolk Coast are well known to Geologists as the locality of the famous " Forest-bed " and " Contorted Drift." These interesting deposits are fully described in the following Memoir from original detailed observation. Reference to the previous literature of the " Forest-bed " will be found at p: 20. The Maps, Sections, and Memoir now published by the Geological Survey are intended to be a record of the present condition of the Cliffs and of all that is known regarding their geological history up to this date. These publications will thus, it is hoped, serve as data from which to compute the future changes of the Cliffs from the encroachment of the Sea, and to mark the additions which further research at this locality may make to our still fragmentary knowledge of the Pliocene and Pleistocene History of England.

ARCH. GEIKIE,
Director General.

Geological Survey Office,
London,
9th October 1882.

R 1195. Wt. 14208.

NOTICE.

THE Geological Survey Map 68 E, of which the following Memoir is a description, includes the two Quarter-sheets 68 N.E. and S.E. of the Ordnance Survey.

The area was surveyed geologically, between the years 1876 and 1879 inclusive, by Messrs. H. B. Woodward and C Reid; the former being responsible for the south-western portion extending northwards to Wolterton, Coleby, and Suffield, and eastwards to North Walsham and Worstead, while the remaining and much larger portion was surveyed by Mr Reid under the superintendence of Mr. Woodward.

The chief interest of the district lies in the coast-section, where is exhibited perhaps the finest section of Glacial Drift in the country, and where the later Pliocene (or "Pre-Glacial)" deposits, including the well-known "Forest Bed" of Cromer, are also well displayed. The details of these beds have been carefully given by Mr. Reid in Sheet 127, Horizontal Sections, which is drawn on the scale of 18 inches to one mile. But even here the minute subdivisions cannot be separately shown, and enlarged drawings of various points of especial interest are therefore given with this Memoir. The coast-section varies greatly in appearance at different seasons, it is, also, being worn back at an average rate of from two to three yards in a year. The accurate drawings now published will, therefore, be of value for comparison in future years

Owing to Mr Reid's enthusiastic labours and to the assistance rendered by geologists resident in Norfolk, the list of organic remains from the Pliocene Beds has been largely increased; the number of species being now more than double what it was previous to the Geological survey of the district.

The Chalk fossils were identified by Mr. George Sharman, and the Vertebrata from the later Tertiary Beds have been identified by Mr E. T Newton, who, having determined several new forms, has devoted a separate Memoir to the subject.

While Mr Reid's lengthened observations entitle his theoretical conclusions to respect, it is but just to mention that he alone is responsible for the expression of such views.

H. W. BRISTOW,
Senior Director.

Geological Survey Office,
   28, Jermyn Street, London, S.W.,
     9th August 1882.

AUTHOR'S PREFATORY NOTE.

THE Geological Survey of the country around Cromer having brought me into communication with many of the geologists of Norfolk, I gladly acknowledge the kind way in which in every case they have given me information. Though I have not always been able to accept their views, the discussion of them has often greatly assisted in the elucidation of the geology of this difficult district.

To Mr. John Gunn, M.A., F.G.S., whose long and enthusiastic labours have resulted in the grand collection of fossil mammals now in the Norwich Museum, and to Mr. Alfred C. Savin, who in a few years has gathered together an extremely fine series of the remains at Cromer, I am especially indebted for numerous local details of the occurrence of fossils. In the determination of the specimens the work has been much assisted by the kindness of several naturalists, whose help has enabled me to attempt, what I have long hoped to prepare, a carefully revised list of the peculiar fauna and flora of the " Cromer Forest-bed," and associated deposits. The delay in the completion of this Memoir is due to the time needed for the determination of the organic remains. Mr W. Carruthers, F.R.S, has examined the Plants; Mr. H. B. Brady, F.R.S., the Foraminifera; Dr G. S Brady, F.R S, the Entomostraca; Mr. G. Busk, F.R S., the Polyzoa, and Mr. C. O. Waterhouse, F.Z.S, the Coleoptera The Mollusca have been revised by Mr Etheridge and Mr. Sharman, who have also determined the Chalk fossils. All the Vertebrata have been most carefully studied by Mr. E. T. Newton, whose Memoir on the subject will speak for itself.

Mr. A G. Nathorst (of the Geological Survey of Sweden) kindly instructed me on the mode of occurrence, and method of collecting, the fossil arctic plants. In the stratigraphical part of this Memoir I must acknowledge the assistance of the Rev. Osmond Fisher, M.A, F G.S, and Messrs. S V. Wood, F.G.S., F. W. Harmer, F.G.S., and Henry Norton, F.G S.; and I would especially record my obligation to the published papers of Sir C. Lyell and Prof Prestwich   In various other ways I have been helped by Mr. Edgar Smith, F Z S , (of the British Museum,) Mr James Reeve (of the Norwich Museum), Mr. Thomas South-well, F Z S., of Norwich, Mr. Robert Fitch, F S A., of Norwich, and Messrs. E. R. Priest and W G Sandford, of Cromer.

CLEMENT REID.

CONTENTS.

CHAPTER XIV.—ALLUVIAL DEPOSITS—PLEISTOCENE FOSSILS.

CHAPTER XV.—DENUDATION.

CHAPTER XVI.—ECONOMIC GEOLOGY.

LIST OF WOODCUTS.

FOLDING PLATE OF CLIFF SECTIONS.

THE

GEOLOGY

OF THE

COUNTRY AROUND CROMER.

CHAPTER I.—INTRODUCTION.

Area.

In this Memoir is described the north-east portion of Norfolk, including Cromer, North Walsham, and Aylsham, and the cliffs between Weybourn and Eccles. The maps referred to are Sheet 68 E. and a portion of Sheet 68 N.W. of the Geological Survey Maps. The total area is about 150 square miles

The chief geological interest of the district lies in the cliffs, a section of which has been published on a scale of 18 inches to the mile. For more minute details, woodcuts of typical sections have been inserted in the text, and a folding plate has been added to this Memoir.

Physical Geography.

From Weybourn to Palling the rapidly wasting coast stretches for 23 miles without a single bay or point; the cliffs of mud and sand, which face the sea for the greater part of the distance, rising near Cromer to a height of 250 feet. This high land, which forms the most marked feature of the district, ranges from east to west, from the coast at Paston, to Weybourn, and thence beyond the tract under consideration to Holt and Wells. These hills, rising to a height of 200 or 250 feet, form a bold escarpment facing the North, running nearly parallel to the sea coast, and seldom more than a mile from it. On the southern side, the escarpment, being much cut up by tributaries of the Bure and Ant, is not so marked as on the northern.

The southern portion of the area is occupied by undulating land considerably lower than the Cromer Hills, so that from the Hills one can overlook most of the country as far as the Bure Valley. On the east the high land is cut off abruptly by a tributary of the Ant, beyond which appear gently undulating fields, becoming flatter and flatter till they reach the "Broad" district.

The drainage, with the exception of a small stream flowing into the sea at Mundesley, and others still smaller at Cromer and Sherringham, is inland; the streams nearly all rising within a short distance of the coast, and flowing southward to join the

R 1195

A

Ant and Bure   " The Bure, which rises in Melton Park near
Hindolvestone, flows eastwards by Thurning into the area at
Itteringham, and thence by Ingworth, Aylsham, Burgh, Brampton,
and Oxnead.   The river was rendered navigable from Coltishall
to Aylsham Bridge, by a bill which received the royal assent
in 1773.   The Ant rises near Antingham, and has been utilized
in the formation of the North Walsham and Dilham Canal,
which occupies its course by Honing and Dilham to Wayford
Bridge   Thence it flows through Barton Broad, and joins the
Bure near St. Benett's Abbey." *

" In exceptionally rainy seasons the alluvial valleys are flooded.
In the autumn of 1878, on Nov 15, the day before the great
flood at Heigham, the Staithe at Millgate, Aylsham, was flooded,
and there was from 3 to 4 feet of water in the main road leading
to North Walsham.   The cottages known as Nash's Row had
the lower rooms filled with water; and for several days the
meadows on both sides of Aylsham were submerged " *   The
low-lying fens near Palling and Stalham are often flooded in
the winter; but the only permanent Broad now existing in the
district is that of Calthorpe   Besides floods of rain-water, the
low country at Eccles and Palling is liable to be submerged
should the sea break through the sand hills.

Formations.

The following is a table of the strata described in this
Memoir :—

Recent	Blown Sand.	
	Shingle	
	Alluvium.	
	" Submerged Forests.'	
Newer Pleistocene (Post Glacial)†	Loam or Clay.	
	Valley Gravel (Palæolithic)	
Older Pleistocene (Glacial Drift)	Boulder Gravel.	
	Gravel and Sand	(" Middle Glacial "?)
	Contorted Drift.	
	Sands	
	2nd Till	
	Intermediate Beds.	} Cromer Till.
	1st Till.	
	Arctic Fresh-water Bed.	
Newer Pliocene	*Leda-myalis* Bed.	
	Upper Fresh-water Bed.	
	" Forest Bed" (Estuarine).	} "Forest Bed" Series.
	Lower Fresh-water Bed.	
	Weybourn Crag.	
Cretaceous	Upper Chalk.	

---

* From Mr. Woodward's notes.   † In this district.

CHAPTER II—CHALK.

General Description and Details.

Chalk is the fundamental rock over nearly the whole of the district; but as this is covered by a great thickness of Glacial and Pre-glacial beds, and is either below or but a few feet above the sea-level, it can only be examined on a portion of the coast or in the Bure Valley near Aylsham.

"In the latter district Chalk with flints is exposed in the valleys in the parishes of Aylsham, Burgh, Brampton, Marsham, Oxnead, Skeyton, and Lammas, the only pits now worked being at Oxnead, whence Mr S Woodward* recorded *Lima granulosum.*"†

At Weybourn the Chalk forms a cliff rising about 20 feet above high-water mark, but towards Cromer the line sinks, till just east of that town it disappears below the sea-level. Chalk is only again seen for a short distance at Trimingham, where, however, it has been forced by glacial action much above its normal height.‡

Still further eastward, at Bacton and Happisburgh §, Eocene Strata are probably present; but there being no direct evidence, their position can only be inferred from the thickness at Yarmouth, and the general lie of the beds in the East of England. Writers on Norfolk geology mention exposures of Chalk at Mundesley and Happisburgh. There is little doubt that by Mundesley the Trimingham section was meant, for none of the fishermen have seen Chalk at Mundesley, and as they are constantly fishing and shrimping in the neighbourhood, they would be sure to find it if it were ever exposed, for the nets would catch on the flints. At Happisburgh a mass of chalk-rubble 2 or 3 feet long is included in the Boulder Clay on the foreshore; this has very probably been mistaken for solid Chalk. Another circumstance that might easily mislead is that some years ago, as we are informed by Mr. Humphreys, a vessel laden with Chalk came on shore at Happisburgh, and before she could be got off about 100 tons of the cargo had to be thrown overboard. Portion of this mass is still occasionally to be seen.

Between Weybourn and Cromer the Chalk is soft,‖ with many flints, in fact, at Runton flints are so abundant that on the foreshore they often form a nearly continuous reticulated pave-

---

* Geology of Norfolk, p 48   † From Mr H B Woodward's notes.
‡ *See* pp. 95, 115   § Pronounced Haisbro
‖ Immediately under the Crag, at one or two places near Sherringham, the Chalk is, however, very hard and splintery, like that of Antrim. This appears to be only an irregular metamorphism of Pliocene date

ment. Tabular flints are rare; **only** three or four instances were observed, all of which were vertical plates filling joints, in one case cutting through a paramoudra. From Old Hithe to Cromer paramoudras are common; and besides the ordinary flints and paramoudras there are numerous rings of flint, commonly 3 to 6 feet in diameter, often containing smaller rings, with sometimes a paramoudra in the centre.* (*See* Fig. 1.)

Fig. 1.

Plan of Concentric Rings of Flint on the foreshore at Runton.

Scale 2 feet to an inch

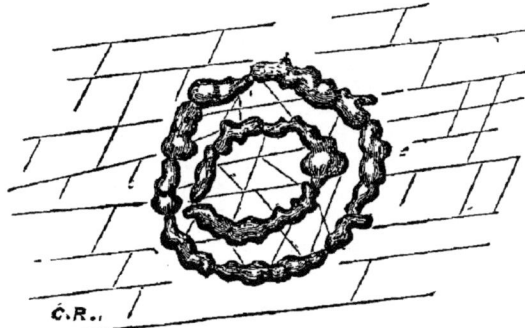

Perfect circles were measured up to 9 feet across; and one irregular oval was 15 feet. These rings, when shown in plan on the foreshore, remind one much of the so-called "fairy rings" seen in meadows. They are mere shallow rings, about 10 inches or a foot in depth, and not sections of cups, for when traced downward they never show a cup-shape or any tendency to a narrowing of the circle. Though sponges are very abundant, no definite connection can be traced between the shape of the sponge and that of the ring or paramoudra, for irregular sponges appear to occur indifferently in the Chalk or in the flint †

Fossils, except sponges, are not very plentiful, though *Belemnitella mucronata* and fragments of *Inoceramus* are common. A sponge (*Spongia* sp.) was obtained at Runton, with the horny portions replaced by pyrites, so that the external surface and roots are almost perfectly preserved. From the general character of the Chalk it appears to correspond with that of Norwich; but the Fossils have yet to be collected and compared.

As far as can be ascertained, the dip is almost due east; so that at the next exposure, at Trimingham, we ought to reach a higher zone. The Trimingham Chalk is soft, mottled grey and white,

* Mr C B Rose states that on the beach at Sherringham and Runton "there is to be seen almost a complete pavement of Paramoudras *in situ* I measured the upper extremity of one, which proved to be 5 feet in diameter." Proc. Geol. Assoc., vol 1, p. 230.

† *See also* "Geology of the Country around Norwich," by H B. Woodward, pp. 20–25.

distinctly bedded, and distinguished from the Upper Chalk of the rest of Norfolk by the absence of paramoudras, and by the peculiar porous and spongiform character of its flints,—a character which enables us readily to distinguish them when included in Glacial gravels. One bed, about a foot thick, decidedly sandy,* is important, as being the only example known in the East of England of a sandy bed in the Upper Chalk. Fossils are very abundant, the most conspicuous being the sponges, polyzoa, *Ostrea larva*, and the large *Ostrea vesicularis*, which is also often found with the spongiform flints in Glacial gravels in more westerly districts † A list from this locality is given below. All the species are Upper Chalk forms; none characteristic of higher zones, such as the Maestricht Chalk, having at present been found.

Probably the thickness of the Chalk over the whole district is nowhere less than 1,000 feet At Norwich Messrs. Colman's well showed 1,152 feet of Chalk, and it commences at the bottom of a valley cut partly through that rock; the total thickness would be nearly 1,200 feet. Between Weybourn and Runton the beds correspond with those near Norwich, and if the general dip of the Cretaceous rocks is continued to Trimingham we ought there to have a thickness of no less than 1,400 or 1,500 feet, unless, as seems very probable, the lower beds may thin out in that direction. Owing to disturbance from glacial action and other causes, no very satisfactory dips can be obtained on the coast, but probably the angle becomes less and less as we travel eastward, and 1,300 feet will be a sufficient estimate for the thickness of the Chalk at Trimingham.

Fossils from the Upper Chalk at Trimingham ‡

Spongida:
 Ventriculites alternans, Roem.
 Coscinopora globularis, D'Orb.
 Spongia, sp
Foraminifera .
 Cristellaria, sp.
 Nodosaria, sp
Actinozoa :
 Parasmilia centralis, Mant
 Trochosmilia cornucopiæ, Dunc.
Echinodermata :
 Ananchytes ovatus, Leske.
 Cidaris, plate of
 Cyphosoma Konigi, Mant.
 Discoidea cylindrica, Lam
 Echinoconus abbreviatus, Desor.
 Micraster, sp.
 Pentacrinus, sp
 Starfish, ossicles of.

* *See* Fig. 13, p 116.   † *See* p. 107.
‡ Collected by C. Reid , named by R Etheridge and G Sharman

Annelida :
> *Ditrupa,* sp.
> *Serpula granulata,* Sow.
> —————— sp.
> *Vermicularia,* sp.

Polyzoa :
> *Entalophora madreporacea,* D'Orb.
> *Lunulites regularis,* D'Orb.
> *Eschara echo,* D'Orb.

Brachiopoda ·
> *Crania Parisiensis,* Defr.
> *Magas pumilus,* Sow.
> *Rhynchonella limbata,* Schlot.
> *Terebratula carnea,* Sow
> *Terebratulina gracilis,* Schlot.
> —————— —————— *striata,* Wahl.

Monomyaria
> *Inoceramus,* sp.
> *Lima,* sp.
> *Ostrea frons,* Park
> —————— *larva,* Lam
> —————— *vesicularis,* Lam.
> *Pecten,* sp
> *Pinna sulcata,* Woodw.

Cephalopoda ·
> *Belemnitella lanceolata,* Schlot.
> —————————— *mucronata,* Schlot.

Pisces ·
> *Cimolicthys Lewesiensis,* Leidy (= *Saurodon Leanus*
> of authors)

From a single flint Professor W. J. Sollas obtained the following
species of sponge spiculæ* :—

> *Discodermites cretaceus,* Soll.
> *Rhagadinia Zittelii,* Soll.
> *Eurydiscites irregularis,* Soll.
> *Nanodiscites parvus,* Soll.
> *Compsapsis cretacea,* Soll.
> *Podapsis cretacea,* Soll.
> —————— *parva,* Soll
> *Corallistes cretaceus,* Soll.
> *Macandrewites Vicaryi,* Carter.
> *Corallistites ?*
> *Pachastrellites fusifer,* Soll.
> —————————— *globiger,* Soll.
> *Tethylites cretaceus,* Soll
> *Triphyllactis elegans,* Soll.
> *Dercitites Haldonensis,* Carter.

---

* Ann. Nat. Hist., ser v., vol vi, pp 384 and 437. *See also* remarks by
Dr. G. J. Hinde, "Fossil Sponge Spicules from the Upper Chalk," p. 82.

Geodites cretaceus, Soll.
Rhopaloconus tuberculatus, Soll.
Pachœna Hindi, Soll.
Scohorhaphis ?
Euplectella ?

A number of Polyzoa were found in the Weybourn Crag at East Runton. These were sent to Mr Busk, who has kindly looked through them, and states that they do not correspond with any known Crag forms. Mr Busk suggests that the specimens may be derived from some Cretaceous bed, but they are too worn and fragmentary for definite determination. As the forms are as yet unknown in the Chalk near Runton, it is worth placing on record the occurrence of these Polyzoa even though their original horizon is undetermined. They appear to belong to eight species, doubtfully referred by Mr. Busk to :—

Eschara cenomana ? D'Orb.
————- sp
Like *Siphonella subcompressa,* Hagenow.
Melicerita ?
Like *Membranipora cenomana,* D'Orb., but not incrusting
Cœleschara.
Vincularian (very obscure)
Something like *Vincularia Santonensis,* D'Orb.

Mr H. B Woodward has furnished a memorandum of other species recorded from Trimingham by Samuel Woodward, the Rev W Foulger, Mr Jukes-Browne, and Dr C Barrois, which include the following —

Guettardia angularis, T Smith   (Norwich Museum)
Rhynchonella plicatilis, Sow   (W F)
Baculites Faujasii, Sow   (W. F)
Bourgeticrinus ellipticus, Mill   (W F)
Cardiaster granulosus, Goldf.   (W F, S W.)
————— *rostratus,* Forbes   (W. F)
Cidaris serrata, Desor.   (C B.)
Cyphosoma elongatum, Cott.   (C. B.)
Pecten quinquecostatus, Sow   (A J. J. B)
Serpula lumbricus, Defr   (C. B)
Vermilia macropus, Sow   (W F)
————— *striata,* Woodw ?   (W F)
————— *pentangulata,* Woodw   (S W.)

Dr. Barrois also gives *Serpula heptagona ?* Hagenow, and a species allied to *Ostrea Wegmanniana,* D'Orb *

———

* " Recherches sur le Terrain Crétacé Supérieur de l'Angleterre et de l'Irlande," Mem. Soc. Géol. du Nord, 1876, p 165

CHAPTER III.—NEWER PLIOCENE.

Introductory.

Over the greater part of the district to which this Memoir refers there lies between the Chalk and the Glacial Drift a series of fluvio-marine beds belonging to the Newer Pliocene formation; none of which, with the doubtful exception of a thin bed at Burgh, appears to be as old as the Chillesford Crag. Older Pliocene strata, however, may occur beneath the sea-level in the neighbourhood of Happisburgh. These fluvio-marine beds, with regard to the correlation of which an extraordinary amount of confusion exists, have been known for upwards of 120 years, and the literature of the subject is scattered through about 100 papers and books, but, notwithstanding, or perhaps because of this, their age and order of succession are still disputed points.*

The best known member is the so-called "Cromer Forest-bed," celebrated for the number and variety of the fossil mammals which it has yielded, and for the presence in it of pre-glacial land surfaces. The relation of the "Forest-bed" to the shelly Crag of Weybourn, and to the Chillesford Crag, has been much discussed, for the fresh-water beds are unknown in the neighbourhood of Norwich, and most authors have overlooked the occurrence of the fossiliferous Weybourn Crag beneath the "Forest-bed" near Cromer. Lyell, however, as early as 1839, was aware that it occurred there, but in his later writings he makes the Weybourn Sands and the "Forest-bed" pass laterally into one another.

On the coast the beds have received a great variety of names, among which may be mentioned "Forest-bed," Weybourn Sands (Lyell), Bure Valley Beds (S. V. Wood, jun), Westleton Beds (Prestwich), Mundesley Beds (Prestwich), and Laminated Series (Gunn). But in all cases the lines of division, and in most even the order of succession adopted, are quite different from those arrived at in the course of the Geological Survey. In many instances beds of various ages have been confounded, or the same bed with changed lithological character has appeared under several heads. The succession made out is given below, established names being as far as possible used.

With regard to the terms which have been employed by different authors, it will be advisable to give a brief outline, showing which beds are referred to, and the reasons for the adoption or rejection of the names.

---

* For a complete list of papers on the geology of Norfolk, *see* "Memoir on the Geology of the Country around Norwich"; those marked † referring to Cromer and the neighbourhood.

The Norwich Crag (at Weybourn and Cromer) of Professor Prestwich and other authors is generally the horizon called the "Weybourn Sands," by Lyell; the latter name, altered to Weybourn Crag, for the sake of uniformity, and because the beds are only partly sand, has been adopted. The "Chillesford Clay" of Professor Prestwich, at Weybourn and along the coast, is at various horizons, but generally in the Weybourn Crag. The relation of the Clay at Chillesford and Aldeby to the Weybourn Crag will be discussed in the next chapter

.The term "Forest-bed" cannot be traced to any one author, but has gradually grown into use Though in many respects unfortunately chosen, it is better to accept the name than cause confusion by inventing a new one. Its application is very unsettled, almost every writer who has attempted a definition giving a different one, and differing as to the limits of the horizon. The term "Forest-bed Series" is here used to include the whole of the fresh-water and estuarine beds between the marine Weybourn Crag and the *Leda-myalis* Bed.

Professor Prestwich has classed together part of the estuarine "Forest-bed," the Upper Fresh-water bed, *Leda-myalis* Bed, and Arctic Fresh-water Bed, under the head Westleton and Mundesley Beds. This name can scarcely be adopted, for the shingle at Westleton is now believed to belong to the Glacial Beds, and at Mundesley several beds deposited under quite different conditions, and showing marked changes of climate, are included. The term "Mundesley Beds" is also of later date than any of the others brought forward.

Mr. Gunn's "Laminated Series" appears to include any laminated clays between the Chalk and the Glacial Drift.

It is not possible to follow Messrs Wood and Harmer in their use of the term "Bure Valley Beds" (on the coast) for beds newer than the "Forest-bed," and supposed to be equivalent to the Cromer Till; for their typical Bure Valley fauna occurs below and not above the Forest-bed, and there is no evidence whatever that the pebbly gravels are in any case a beach deposit of the age of the Till; on the contrary, they reach their fullest development in the same area as the Till, and vertically beneath it. Messrs. Wood and Harmer believe that the Crag of Weybourn passes over instead of under the "Forest-bed," and the former is classed by them with the Lower Glacial Beds, while the latter, though newer, is included in the Pre-glacial Series

Professor W. King's term "*Leda-myalis* Bed " (called by him *Leda-myalis* Clay)* is adopted for the marine bed above the "Forest-bed," as it is the only name which has been proposed for that restricted horizon. Various local terms have been used for single beds, but these will be discussed with the particular sections to which they apply.

---

* Geologist, vol. vi., p. 169.

The subdivisions of the Newer Pliocene Strata referred to in this Memoir are as follows.—

Leda-myalis Bed (Prof. W. King, 1863).
Upper Fresh-water Bed (C R., 1877)⎤
" Forest-bed " (Estuarine)   -   - ⎬ " Forest-bed
Lower Fresh-water Bed (C R , 1880)⎦   Series "
Weybourn Crag (Lyell, 1873).
Chillesford Crag ?

The various beds on the coast will be described in succession, commencing at Weybourn and tracing them to the east and south Afterwards the inland sections will be mentioned, about the exact correlation of which, from their isolated position, the scarcity of fossils, and the absence of intervening fresh-water beds, there is much difficulty, and, as far as possible, their relation to the coast section will be indicated.*

---

* The inland sections in the Bure Valley and south-west of the Ant have been examined and described by Mr. H B Woodward; for the notes on the remainder I am responsible —C. R.

CHAPTER IV—WEYBOURN CRAG.

Commencing with the lowest bed seen on the coast, we find resting directly on the Chalk at Weybourn, shelly sand alternating with laminated clay, and becoming more clayey as it is traced to the south-east. For this restricted horizon the term "Weybourn Crag" has been adopted. In describing this Crag it will be advisable to commence at Weybourn, where a definite base is seen, and follow it along the coast to the south-east till it is lost beneath the sea-level.

Details

Weybourn.—At Weybourn, and wherever the surface of the Chalk can be examined, there is nearly always a bed of large unworn or little worn flints at the base of the Crag. This is the "stone-bed" of Norfolk geologists, but it does not necessarily belong to any one horizon; exactly similar beds of unworn flints are now being formed from above low-water mark to about 10 fathoms, and are caused merely by the wearing away of the soft Chalk. The "stone-bed" is not formed by the subterranean dissolution of the Chalk, for among the flints we often find bivalves in the position of life, and beneath them the Chalk is here and there bored by *Pholas* and *Saxicava.**

About 30 yards east of the flagstaff at Weybourn the Crag is abruptly cut off by the Contorted Drift, which at that point ploughs into the Chalk. Here and for some yards further, sand and Chalk rubble mixed with marine shells are seen, but so much disturbed that nothing definite can be made out. At 100 yards, at the point where the Boulder Clay first appears on the top of the cliff, the base of the Crag, and the stone bed which rests on a very uneven surface of Chalk, are full of littoral shells. This is at present the most convenient spot near Weybourn for collecting, though the shells are confined to the lower 2 or 3 feet of the Crag. About 30 yards further east we have the following section, but no shells could be found:—

		Feet
Soil	- - - - - - - -	3
Valley Gravel -	Loose angular sandy gravel -	10
Contorted Drift -	{ Stony loam - - -	1
	{ Brown sandy loam - . - -	3
Upper Fresh-water Bed	Laminated sands and blue loams -	3
Land surface - -	Weathered stony loam penetrated by roots	1½
Weybourn Crag or Estuarine "Forest-bed" - -	} Disturbed sandy gravel without fossils -	5

Chalk with a very uneven surface, and occasional pipes filled with manganese.

In the neighbourhood of Weybourn it cannot be said definitely whether the whole of the beds between the Fresh-water Bed and the Chalk belong to the Weybourn Crag, or whether the upper unfossiliferous portion may not in places include the estuarine division of the Forest-bed. There is certainly here and there a line of erosion between them, but this by itself goes for nothing in such shallow water deposits; similar lines of erosion are abundant all along the coast, and generally only show contemporaneous erosion and filling up

---

* See also remarks in the Memoir on the "Geology of the Country around Norwich," by H. B. Woodward, pp. 38–40.

At 170 yards from the flagstaff the beds shown are :—

		Feet.
Soil	- - - - - - -	2
Contorted Drift	- Stony loam with thin seams of marl	11
Forest-bed ? and Weybourn Crag - -	Sandy quartzite gravel mixed with a little loam - - -	8
	Laminated loam full of marine shells -	2
Chalk with flints		

A few yards east of this section the clay with shells dies out, and the chalk shows pipes of manganese-ore

The next section of importance is shown in Fig. 2 (p. 13).

Here a marked bed of laminated loam about 2 feet thick occurs near the base of the Crag This has been correlated by Prof. Prestwich with the Chillesford Clay, but both east and west of this section it soon dies out, and is replaced by sand, other clay beds coming on at different horizons The shells, which are a good deal decayed, are at this point confined to the stone bed and sand beneath the clay

For 150 yards the gravel with quartzite pebbles appears to cut out the Crag, and rest directly on the Chalk; but about a quarter of a mile from the cliff end shelly Crag again appears, and the gravel rises till it has entirely thinned out against the Boulder Clay. At this point (about 170 yards west of the marl pit at the edge of the cliff) the following section is seen —

		Feet
Soil	- - - - - -	2
Contorted Drift	- Obscurely bedded stony marl -	14
Weybourn Crag -	Alternating thin clays and sands with seams of much decayed shells in the lower half - -	10
	Stone-bed with marine shells and a quartzite boulder about 10 inches in diameter - -	1
Chalk with lines of flints		

For a considerable distance there is no further change in the beds, and the clay-seams are evenly distributed throughout the Crag. Wherever seams of shells are divided by laminated clay, collections have been made from each and the results compared, but they all seem clearly to belong to the same horizon

Still travelling eastward, at about 170 yards east of the marl pit, the Crag has thickened to 19 feet, and may be described as false-bedded sands alternating with thin clays. Only the lower 3 or 4 feet is shelly, though it is not improbable that shells have existed in the upper part, but are now entirely dissolved away. Another 100 yards and the Crag consists of well-laminated loams and sands, with the shells confined to the base and the stone-bed A short distance further we find pebbly sands with a few seams of loam, (perhaps at this point the Forest-bed gravels come on again, but there is a good deal of talus which obscures the section,) and the beds continue with this character as far as the road to the beach, patches of shells being occasionally seen near the base.

East of the road the shells extend nearly to the top of the Crag, but there is no change in the lithological character. At one spot in the stone-bed, underneath a mass of shells, there was found an angular boulder of bedded brown sandstone, a foot long, of unknown origin. About 160 yards from the road the section shows pebbly sands, with thin seams of clay near the base, and clay mixed with the stone bed

For a quarter of a mile the cliff is hidden by talus, but the Weybourn Crag is again seen about 130 yards east of the next gap Here we have the following beds :—

		Feet.
Soil	- - - - - -	about 1
Contorted Drift	- Contorted stony loam and marl	13
Weybourn Crag -	Sand with scarcely any loam shells nearly throughout. In it a fragment of mammalian bone was obtained -	9
	Laminated clay -	1
	Stone-bed - - -	½
Chalk		

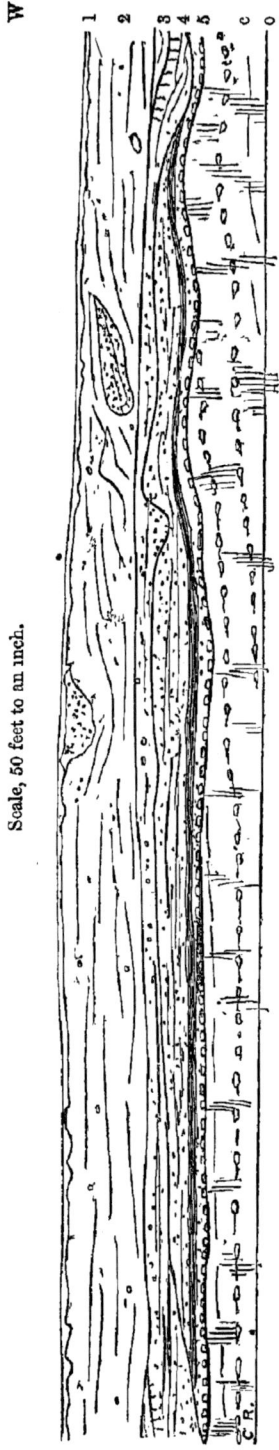

FIG. 2.

Cliff section about 300 yards east of the Coast Guard Station, Weybourn.

Scale, 50 feet to an inch.

1. Loamy soil, often filling pipes in the marly Boulder Clay.

Contorted Drift - 2 Stony loam and marl, with included masses of sand.

Upper Fresh-water Bed 3 Peaty loam, here unfossiliferous, but 100 yards further east containing *Bythinia* and *Cypris*

Forest-bed? (estuarine) { 4 Sand, laminated loam, and quartzite-gravel ; the upper part, where overlaid by the Fresh-water Bed, is weathered into a loamy soil, and is full of small roots penetrating three or four feet This has been termed the "Rootlet bed"

Weybourn Crag { 5 Alternating loams and sands, with a bed of blue clay in the lower part and unworn flints at the base. Fossils at this place only occur near the Chalk, further east they are found throughout.

c Soft Chalk with layers of black or grey flints Dip about S S E.

o. Ordnance datum (approximate).

Within 20 yards the section alters to —   Feet.
   Sand without shells   -   -   -   -   - - 7
   Sand with shells -   -   -   -   - - 3
   Laminated clay with shells   -   - - 5

But following it a few yards further the thick bed of clay has died out altogether, and under the marl pit we find alternating sands and thin clays, without fossils and without any conspicuous clay bed.

The Crag now becomes false-bedded and gravelly, and contains beds of clay pebbles at several horizons. Clay pebbles, which are very common in most shallow water and estuarine deposits, cannot by themselves be accepted as showing lines of unconformity, for in most cases they only point to contemporaneous erosion and filling up, and in several instances there are two or three beds, one above the other, separated by evenly bedded clays or shelly sands, all belonging to one horizon.

At a quarter of a mile east of the marl pit, a mass of clay is again seen a short distance above the Chalk, and the section is as follows :—

		Feet
Soil - - - - - - - -		1
Contorted Drift	{ Contorted stony loam and marl with masses of sand - - - }	26
Weybourn Crag	⎧ False-bedded sand with a little gravel and loam - - -	9
	⎨ Stiff-bedded blue clay with fragments of *Mytilus* - - -	5
	⎩ Stone-bed, full of fossils - -	½
Chalk with flints		

But the clay dies out entirely within a few yards in each direction, and 90 yards further east the Crag consists entirely of false-bedded sands with a few clay pebbles. At this point a quartzite boulder 18 inches long was found in the stone-bed.

Nothing of interest is now seen for a considerable distance; there are slight changes in the lithological character of the beds, but none of importance, and fossils are scarce and badly preserved.

Lower Sherringham.—About a quarter of a mile east of Old Hithe a clay bed is again seen near the base of the Crag, extending 150 yards, and then passing into sands. Shells are here confined to the stone bed and sandy seam beneath the clay.

Under Skelding Hill the Crag is cut out for 100 yards by the Boulder Clay, but at the foot of the eastern slope of the Hill the section is :—

		Feet.
Boulder Clay		
Leda-myalis Bed ?—Sand, gravel, and loam - -		13
Weybourn Crag	⎧ Shell bed (shells much decayed) -	½
	⎨ Ferruginous sand with loamy seams -	5
	⎩ Stone-bed cemented by iron-oxide -.	½
Chalk with the surface bored by *Pholas*		

Probably the 13 feet of sand under the Boulder Clay belongs to the *Leda-myalis* Bed, but there is so much talus that the connection cannot be traced.

Nearly under the style at the edge of the cliff, a quarter of a mile west of Lower Sherringham, a very important section is seen, but at this spot only the base of the Weybourn Crag is preserved :—

		Feet
Boulder Clay		
Leda-myalis Bed	{ Yellowish sand and a little gravel -	15
	{ Gravel - - - - -	3
Forest-bed (estuarine division)	⎧ Stiff dark-blue clay, with drift wood and small cakes of peat, bones and teeth of elephant, and antlers of deer -	3
Weybourn Crag—"Pan" crowded with shells*		1½
Chalk with flints		

* "Pan," or "Iron pan," is a local name for ferruginous conglomerate, or gravel cemented by iron oxide.

This section is only a few yards east of the bed of oysters mentioned in Chap VI.; the oysters occur in the gravel at the base of the *Leda-myalis* Bed

From this point to Sherringham the Weybourn Crag is represented only by the stone bed, and sometimes a foot or two of sand and clay, but it is very shelly, with exceptional abundance of species of *Astarte* (*A borealis*, and oval variety, *A sulcata, A compressa*)

From Sherringham to Beeston the Crag is also thin, and only contains local patches of shells. (*See* plate at the end of this Memoir) Between Beeston and West Runton Gap, for a considerable distance, it is cut out by the Contorted Drift, and where preserved it is usually hidden under the beach, but at the latter place it can often be seen on the foreshore, and is very fossiliferous

Runton —The stratigraphical relations of the Weybourn Crag at Runton will be best understood by reference to the plate at the end of this Memoir It is often very difficult to say whether an isolated exposure should be referred to the Crag or to the Forest-bed, for here they are both shelly, though the Forest-bed is the more decidedly estuarine Another difficulty is that the line of junction is usually hidden by the beach, but wherever it can be examined it shows distinct erosion In the neighbourhood of Runton there is nearly always in the stone bed on the chalk a quantity of *Mya arenaria* and *Tellina obliqua* in the position of life This bed must not be confounded with the bed containing *Mya truncata* shown at the base of the *Leda myalis* Bed in the cliff. Between East and West Runton Gaps the Weybourn Crag is represented by a few feet of shelly sands and clays on the Chalk, overlaid by the estuarine clays of the Forest-bed Opposite Wood Hill several indeterminable fragments of mammalian bone have been seen

From East Runton Gap to Cromer the Crag is generally hidden by shingle and sand, but with certain winds it is laid bare on the foreshore, and some of the most important sections on the coast are shown Commencing at the Gap, the Forest-bed there cuts down to, or nearly to, the Chalk, but it soon rises a few feet, and shelly sands alternating with clay are seen on the foreshore. For about 100 yards there is a mass of ferruginous Crag, 2 or 3 feet thick, principally composed of broken shells, and containing in extraordinary abundance *Tellina Balthica* For some yards further the Crag is very shelly, but being generally cemented into a hard mass, it is difficult to collect from it

At a quarter of a mile south-east of the Gap the character of the deposit changes to an iron-grey shelly sand, often sufficiently loose to be sifted This bed, only occasionally visible on the foreshore, is by far the most fossiliferous exposure known, it has yielded every species of marine shell known from beds of this age in the coast section, besides a number as yet only found at this locality To a large extent, however, the longer list of fossils from it is due to the facility with which it can be sifted, and to the fact that during the progress of the Geological Survey a considerable quantity of material was taken away and examined. This may be accepted as a typical section of the Weybourn Crag, for there can be no doubt as to its stratigraphical position, for when the beach is low the Forest-bed may be seen vertically above it, and separated from it by a mass of rolled clay-pebbles The section is as follows, but there is some doubt as to the exact thickness of the beds —

		Feet.
"Forest-bed"	Laminated clay full of lignite, small twigs, and occasional fir cones, and fragments of *Mytilus*	?
	Mass of rolled clay-pebbles on uneven surface of -.	?
Weybourn Crag	Grey shelly Crag, in the lower part alternating with thin loams	About 4
	Bed of unworn flints mixed with clay, and containing *Mya arenaria* and *Tellina obliqua* in the position of life	About ½

Soft Chalk with paramoudras and rings of flint

The fossils given in the table at p 18 from East Runton are all from this spot. It is noticeable that the bed indicates not only deeper water than the Crag at Weybourn, but more estuarine conditions; the characteristic Newer Pliocene fang-toothed vole (*Arvicola intermedius*, Newton) being very abundant, and land and fresh-water shells not uncommon Still further south-east, and nearly as far as Cromer Jetty, patches of this grey Crag may occasionally be seen, but it is much harder, more clayey, and does not contain such a varied fauna.

Cromer to Sidestrand.—South-east of Cromer the Chalk is lost beneath the sea level, and the lower part of the Crag cannot be seen. From Cromer to near Sidestrand, when the foreshore below half-tide is laid bare, there may be seen greenish laminated clay and clay-ironstone, with thin seams of sand and lines of marine shells, principally in the state of ironstone-casts. No measurements can be taken of the thickness of the Crag, but probably it is about 10 or 15 feet. The clay is often carbonaceous, and contains a little lignite, mammalian bones also occur now and then.

Trimingham.—At Trimingham, due north of the village, the last and one of the most important sections is seen. The exact spot can be found on the shore by the remains of an old groyne, on each side of which most of the beds can be examined. The Weybourn Crag would here normally be almost entirely beneath low-water mark, but the weight of a large landslip from the cliffs forced the beds into an arch, and enabled me to examine the lower part of the section. Owing to this disturbance there is a little doubt as to the exact thickness of the lower beds :—

		Feet.
" Forest-bed "		
Weybourn Crag	Laminated green and blue micaceous and rather carbonaceous clay	4
	Green loamy sand full of marine shells, and containing teeth of *Arvicola intermedius*	3
	Laminated greenish clay as above	4

The section of the beds above the Weybourn Crag is shown in Fig. 4, p. 33. Here the Crag, which has been gradually changing in character south-east of Runton, consists of two masses of laminated clay between which the Weybourn Crag shells occur. The species found in place were —

Purpura lapillus, Linn.	*Astarte borealis,* Chem.
Trophon antiquus, Linn (reversed var.)	——— *compressa,* Mont
Littorina littorea, Linn.	*Cyprina Islandica,* Linn
Nucula Cobboldiæ, Sow	*Tellina Balthica,* Linn.
Leda oblongoides, S Wood.	——— *obliqua,* Sow
Lucina borealis, Linn.	*Mactra ovalis,* Sow.
Cardium edule, Linn.	*Mya arenaria,* Linn.
	Pholas crispata, Linn.

The other species mentioned in the table, p 18, as from Trimingham, were washed up on the shore after the bed had been scoured during continuous east winds, but there is no reason to doubt that they belong to the same horizon. The bed is exceptionally fossiliferous, but, owing to its inconvenient position at low-water mark, only a comparatively small number of species could be obtained *in situ.* The entire collection points to a more varied fauna than than that of Weybourn or even of East Runton; for the long list at p 18 was obtained from the examination of less than a twentieth of the material sifted at the latter place. Univalves and littoral shells have become, as we should expect, comparatively rare, but those from the laminarian zone have greatly increased in abundance.

Honing.—On the coast south east of this section no exposures of the Weybourn Crag are yet known; but since the district near Honing was mapped the new railway has been made, and Mr H B Woodward has collected the following shells from the cutting south-east of Black Mill. The bed is in all probability the Weybourn Crag, though it may possibly be rather newer :—

Turritella, sp.	*Tellina Balthica,* Linn.
Littorina littorea, Linn	*Tellina,* sp.
Nucula Cobboldiæ, Sow.	*Corbula striata,* W. & B.
Cardium edule, Linn.	*Mya arenaria,* Linn.
Astarte borealis, Chem.	*Balanus,* sp.
Cyprina Islandica, Linn.	*Foraminifera.*

A few sections in the Bure Valley, about the exact age of which there is considerable doubt, are described by Mr. Woodward in Chap VII ; but most of the fossiliferous sections are outside Sheet 68, and are referred to in the Memoir on the Geology of the Country around Norwich.

Age of the Weybourn Crag

From the details of the sections already described it is evident that while there can be no question that the Weybourn Crag lies beneath the Forest-bed, its relation to the Chillesford and Norwich Crags must, in this district, be proved by other than stratigraphical evidence, for no Pliocene beds are here seen between it and the Chalk. Failing vertical superposition we are obliged to fall back on the palæontological evidence, and on Lyell's test of the percentage of recent mollusca contained in the beds. The first point to be considered is whether the beds at all localities here included in the Weybourn Crag belong to one horizon For this purpose the annexed table has been drawn up to show the marine mollusca which occur at each locality (p 18)

On comparing the lists it is found that all the species which are at present only known at Runton, with the single exception of *Natica clausa,* are rare forms, the occurrence of which is probably almost entirely due to the more thorough search made at that place. Leaving out these rare forms the lists agree so closely as to leave no doubt that the beds are contemporaneous.

From the Weybourn Crag there have now been obtained 50 species and marked varieties of marine mollusca. Of these 4 are extinct, showing a per-centage of 8·0 compared with 15·5 and 16 0 from the Chillesford and Fluvio-marine Crags respectively But as the total number of species known from the Weybourn Crag is considerably smaller than from the older beds, and as forms dying out are likely to be represented by comparatively few individuals, the discrepancy is probably in reality much less

The proportion of Arctic to Mediterranean forms is —

	Total.	Arctic.	Mediterranean
Weybourn Crag	50	8	1
Chillesford Crag	90	7	2
Fluvio-marine Crag*	112	9	7

Two characteristic Arctic varieties appear for the first time in the Weybourn Crag, viz *A borealis,* oval var., and *Saxicava arctica,* gigantic var,—both, however, very rare The only other form unknown in older beds is *Tellina Balthica,* which occurs, as Messrs Wood and Harmer have pointed out, in great abundance at nearly every locality in the Bure Valley

The above analysis brings out very markedly the newer and more Arctic character of the Weybourn Crag marine mollusca as compared with those of the Chillesford Crag. On the other hand,

---

* Mr H B Woodward uses the term " Norwich Crag Series " for the entire group , and the term " Upper Crag " has been used by the Geological Survey for the Newer Pliocene division, including the Red Crag, as distinct from the Coralline or Lower Crag

TABLE OF MOLLUSCA FROM THE WEYBOURN CRAG.

—	Trimingham.	Sidestrand.	Overstrand.	Runton	Sherringham.	Weybourn.	—
Buccinum undatum, Linn -	r	r	vc	c			
Purpura lapillus, Linn. - -	c	c	c	vc	vc	vc	
Trophon antiquus, Linn - -				vr		vr	
——, reversed var.	r		r	vc		r	
Pleurotoma (Clavatula) linearis, Mont				2			
—— turricula, Mont -	vr			c			
Cancellaria viridula, Fabr				1			Arctic
Turritella terebra, Mont. (= communis, Risso.)	vr			r			
Scalaria Grœnlandica, Cham			c	vc	r	vr	Northern
—— Trevelyana, Leach -				2			
—— Turtonis, Turt. -				2			
Hydrobia (Paludestrina), subumbilicata, Mont.				1			
Littorina littorea, Linn -	vc	vc	vc	vc	vc	vc	
—— rudis, Maton -				r	r	r	
Natica catena, Da Costa -	2			vc	r	r	
—— clausa, Brod. and Sow				c			Northern.
—— helicoides, Johnst. -			1	c	r	r	Northern.
Velutina lævigata, Linn. -				1			
Trochus tumidus? Mont. -				3			
——, sp -				1			
Tectura virginea, Mull -				1			
Chiton, sp.				2			
Bulla alba, Brown -				4			
Melampus (Conovulus) pyramidalis, J Sow				r			Extinct
Pecten opercularis? Linn. -				2			
Mytilus edulis, Linn. -	r	c	c	vc	r	r	
Nucula Cobboldiæ, Sow. -	c	c	c	c		vc	Extinct.
Leda oblongoides, S. Wood -	c	c	c	vc	r	c	Arctic ?
Lucina borealis, Linn -	c	c	r	r.		2	
Cardium echinatum, Linn -				3			
—— edule, Linn. -	c	vc	vc	vc	vc	vc	
—— Grœnlandicum, Chem.				vr		?	Arctic.
Astarte borealis, Chem. -	vc	vc		vc	vc	vc	Arctic.
——, oval var -				1	1		Arctic.
—— compressa, Mont. -	vc	vc		vc	vc	c	Northern.
—— incrassata, Brocchi -	1			1			Mediterranean.
—— crebricostata, Forbes -				1			Arctic.
—— sulcata, Da Costa -	vc	vc		c	c	?	
Cyprina Islandica, Linn -	vc	vc	c	vc	vc	vc	
Donax vittatus, Da Costa -			c	r			
Tellina Balthica, Linn -	vc	vc	vc	vc	vc	vc	
—— obliqua, Sow -	vc	vc	vc	vc	vc	vc	
—— lata, Gmelin (T calcaria)	r			r		r	Extinct. Arctic
—— prætenuis, Leathes -				2			Extinct.
Scrobicularia plana, Da Costa -				3			
Mactra ovalis, J Sow -	c	c		c		vr	
—— stultorum, Linn -				1			
Corbula striata, W. and B -	c	c	1	c		r	
—— contracta? Say -	r			r			N. America
Saxicava arctica, Linn. -	r			c		r	
——, gigantic var. -				2			Arctic.
Mya arenaria, Linn. -	vc	c	c	vc	vc	vc	
—— truncata, Linn. - ▲ -	c	c		r		vr	
Pholas crispata, Linn -	c	c	r	c	vc	c	
Rhynchonella psittacea, Chem. -				2			Northern

c = common, vc = very common, r = rare, vr = very rare.
The figures 1, 2, &c denote the number of specimens found when four or less

the resemblance between the two faunas is equally marked, for a large majority of the species are the same in both, and there is scarcely so great a difference between the lists as is generally found on comparing the fauna of the most modern raised beaches and the recent fauna of the adjoining seas. It therefore appears that while the Weybourn Crag must be separated from the Chillesford Crag as a distinct horizon or zone, it cannot without violence be removed from the Newer Pliocene division and classed with the Glacial Deposits

The question whether the Weybourn Crag *as a whole* may not be the equivalent of the thick bed of clay at Chillesford and Aldeby, must for the present be left open. There is little palæontological evidence, and laminated clays of similar character occur on so many horizons that it is unsafe to attempt to identify them by lithological resemblance alone.

CHAPTER V —FOREST-BED.

Historical

For many years the deposit now generally known as the " Cromer Forest-bed " has been celebrated, and a mere list of the papers referring to it would occupy several pages * It will be best therefore simply to give an outline of the literature of the subject, noting all important papers, and mentioning the earliest discovery of any new fact

Though the teeth of elephants found near Cromer were known from an earlier period, the first published notice of the " Forest-bed " was in 1746 by W Arderon, in which he mentions " the roots and trunks of trees which are to be seen at low water in several places on this coast near Hasborough and Walket [Walcot]," and also mentions the fossil bones †

It is, however to Richard Cowling Taylor that we owe the first description of the beds   In a communication dated Aug 14, 1822,‡ he states that " from Happisburgh, to the North of Cromer, may be traced, at intervals, along the base of the clay cliffs, a remarkable stratum containing an abundance of fossil wood and the bones of large herbivorous animals mineralized with iron. The thickness of this singular bed does not exceed two feet, and frequently not more than one   It varies, in its material, from a red ferruginous sand to an ochreous coarse gravel cemented by iron "   [Taylor appears only to have seen sections of the hard ferruginous conglomerate often called the " Elephant Bed "]   " The stratified organic remains in the cliff of East Norfolk are buried beneath beds of blue clay, earth and sand, from 80 to 100 feet in thickness " He also alludes to a letter by Sir Thomas Browne, written in 1659, on the head and bones of a very large fish at Hasbro,§ apparently as referring to the same deposit ; but this is probably a mistake

In another paper, in 1824,‖ Taylor gives a still further description of the beds, mentions " stumps of trees rooted into the stratum," and considers the " Forest-bed " as " occupying the position usually assigned to the crag or upper marine formation ," but in this paper he also correlates the shelly gravels in the Glacial Beds with the Crag, and includes the Boulder Clay in the " upper marine formation "

Samuel Woodward, in his " Outline of the Geology of Norfolk," published in 1833, appears to have been the first distinctly to separate the " Forest-bed " from the Drift, but in his table of Strata he places it beneath the Norwich Crag

Sir C Lyell in 1840 gave a long description of the beds, but stated that he " was not so fortunate either here or elsewhere on this coast as to see the stools of trees erect in this stratum, but so many independent eye-witnesses have lately described them to me with such minuteness as to leave in my mind no doubt of the fact "¶

The Rev. Charles Green, in his " History, Antiquities, and Geology of Bacton," published in 1842, gave some valuable local notes ; but he divided

---

* For full list see Appendix to the Memoir on the " Geology of the Country around Norwich," pp 171 to 204 , those marked † referring to the neighbourhood of Cromer

Extract of a letter containing Observations on the Precipices or Cliffs on the N E Seacoast of the County of Norfolk —Phil Trans., vol. xliv, pt 1, No 481, p 275

‡ " Fossil Bones on the Coast of East Norfolk "—Phil. Mag , vol lx , p 132.

§ *See also* Excursions in Norfolk, 1818, vol 1, p 121

‖ " Remarks on the Position of the Upper Marine Formation exhibited in the Cliffs on the North-east Coast of Norfolk."—Phil. Mag., vol lxiii , p 81, 1824

¶ " On the Boulder Formation, or drift and associated Fresh Water Deposits, composing the Mud Cliffs of Eastern Norfolk "—Phil Mag , Ser. 3, vol xvi , p 345.

the "Forest-bed" into Eocene, Older Pliocene, and Newer Pliocene, and his statements are not always trustworthy   In 1845 Joshua Trimmer noticed the bed of *Mya truncata* over the Fresh-water Bed at West Runton * Prof. Owen, in his "History of British Fossil Mammals and Birds," published in 1846, described and figured many " Forest-bed " specimens

Prof Prestwich in 1861† cleared up a point which had lead to great confusion in most previous papers, by pointing out that at Mundesley there are two totally distinct Fresh-water Beds,—one beneath, the other above, the Boulder Clay This section had previously been taken as proving the interstratification of the Forest-bed and Drift

In the first edition of Lyell's "Antiquity of Man," published in 1863, a long description of the "Forest-bed " is given, and he says that "Thirty years ago when I first examined this bed I saw many trees with their roots in the old soil laid open at the base of the cliff near Happisburgh " But on comparing this with his paper of 1840 it is seen that the statement must be erroneous, for in the earlier account he distinctly says that he did *not* see them (*See* observations in Mr Norton's paper mentioned further on)

Mr John Gunn in 1864, in his "Geology of Norfolk," divided the beds on the coast into Norwich Crag, "Forest-bed," and Laminated Beds From 1865 to the present date a series of papers has been published by Mr S V Wood, jun , whose classification of the beds has already been referred to (p 9) The best general diagram of the coast between Happisburgh and Weybourn, was published by him in 1865, in a pamphlet privately printed A valuable account of the beds was given in 1868 by the Rev. O Fisher ‡ Prof Prestwich in 1871 gives a description of the coast section, and suggests the name " Westleton Beds " for the higher portion of the Pre-glacial Series.§

In the supplement to the Crag Mollusca by S V Wood, published in 1872, there is an Introductory Outline on the Geology by Messrs S. V. Wood, jun , and F W Harmer Sections are given to support their view that the " Bure Valley Beds " overlie the " Forest-bed,"—the Crag beneath it, mentioned by Lyell and other writers, not having been recognized by them

An important paper by Mr. Henry Norton, unfortunately only· to be had as a reprint from the Norwich Mercury of Nov 5th, 1877, questions, for the first time in print, the evidence on which the trees in the " Forest-bed," are stated to have been found rooted in the soil, and draws attention to the unsatisfactory nature of the evidence on which they are accepted as being in place In the same year the writer of this memoir published a paper in which the *Leda myalis* Bed was separated from the Forest-bed, while reasons were brought forward to show that the latter was not a land surface ; and in 1880 another short paper gave the classification adopted in his Memoir ‖ In 1880 Mr J. H. Blake read an address before the Norwich Geological Society, in which he maintained the importance of the " Rootlet Bed " as an horizon, and expressed his opinion that it was the only bed showing evidence of land-growth. (See also letter by C R in Geol. Mag., Decade II , vol viii , p 382)

General Description.

From the above outline it will be seen that our knowledge of the " Forest-bed " is of very gradual growth, and even now such a primary point as the relative order of it and the associated Crag beds is considered by many a debateable question. This difficulty is in great measure owing to the fact that the beds during the summer time, when geologists generally examine the coast, are almost entirely hidden by the beach, whereas it is only

---

* Proc Geol Soc , vol. iv , p 435, Journ Roy Agric Soc , vol vii , p 444, 1847
† "On some New Facts in Relation to the Section of the Cliff at Mundesley, Norfolk."—Geologist, vol iv , p. 68.
‡ On the Denudations of Norfolk.—Geol. Mag., vol v , p 544
§ " On the Structure of the Crag-Beds of Suffolk and Norfolk " Part III. The Norwich Crag and Westleton Beds —Quart Journ Geol. Soc., vol. xxvii p 452.
‖ Geol. Mag , Decade II , vol. iv , p. 300, and vol. vii , p 548

during the winter and equinoctial gales that clear exposures can usually be found. Having spent four winters on the coast studying the cliffs and adjoining country, and making detailed notes of every section directly it was laid bare, I think I may be exonerated from the charge of hastily forming the conclusions here given, though in some respects they do not agree with those of other observers.

Where most complete, the so-called "Forest-bed" consists of three divisions,—an Upper and a Lower Fresh-water Bed, and an intermediate Estuarine deposit. But the Lower Fresh-water Bed is very seldom preserved, though its flora is well known from the quantity of *Pholas*-bored cakes of peat and clay-ironstone found in the Estuarine Beds, and derived from the breaking up of the underlying deposit. The relation of the Lower Fresh-water Bed to the Estuarine "Forest-bed" seems to be somewhat similar to that of the recent "Submerged Forests" of estuaries to the deposits now forming in the same localities, in part from their destruction

The middle division, which is more particularly the "Forest-bed" of Norfolk geologists, least deserves the name; for wherever it can be studied, it is distinctly estuarine, though from containing large quantities of drift wood, and especially stumps of trees, many have accepted it without hesitation as a land-surface. It is from this division that most of the large mammalian remains have been obtained.

The upper surface of these Estuarine Beds is in many places weathered into a soil and penetrated by small roots (hence the name Rootlet Bed*), and here and there it is covered by, or eroded hollows in it are filled with, lacustrine deposits. These form the Upper Fresh-water Bed, in which most of the small bones and fresh-water shells are found.

It will be seen that though a land-surface does occur in the Pre-glacial deposits, it does not correspond with the horizon to which the name "Forest-bed" has been more especially applied. It is not improbable that there may be another land surface beneath the *Lower* Fresh-water Bed, for in one place the Weybourn Crag below the "Forest-bed" has a rather weathered appearance; but of this one cannot be certain. As the question whether the tree-stumps are or are not rooted in the "Forest-bed" has been much discussed, it will be advisable to give a brief outline of the reasons which have led me to the latter conclusion.

Though many of the published accounts of the "Forest-bed" appear at first sight very circumstantial, it is singular that no one appears to have compared the so-called soil with recent soils. If this had been done it is certain that the error which has arisen would in most cases have been avoided; for where the tree-stumps are imbedded in clay, the clay is well laminated,

* Attention was drawn to this bed in 1870 by Prof Prestwich (Quart. Journ Geol. Soc., vol. xxvii., p. 463); and subsequently by Mr. Gunn (*Ibid.*, vol. xxxii, p. 124), and Mr. Blake (Geol. Mag., Decade II., vol. iv, p 298)

undisturbed, and unweathered—which would not be the case had it been exposed to the air and to the burrowing of worms, and had thick roots forced their way into it. A second point is that in every case (and upwards of a hundred of the stools have been pulled up and examined at different localities) the roots do not end in small fibres, but are broken off, generally from one to three feet from the stem, and the ends are either rounded or frayed out. Taking as one of the typical instances the locality at Overstrand visited by many geologists on an excursion of the British Association in 1868, when a stool was dug up and placed in the Norwich Museum,* the writer found the bed to consist of a ferruginous quartzite-gravel mixed with some clay, and containing a large quantity of wood and many tree-stumps. None of the pieces of wood around or under the stumps were particularly rotten, as would be the case had they remained a short time in a soil on which vegetation was growing, and the bed was not weathered. Several stumps were dug out, and it was found that all the roots ended abruptly. Unfortunately the roots have been cut off the specimen in the Norwich Museum, to allow it to be placed in a case; the whole stump has, however, a battered look, unlike one that had been merely silted up in its natural position.

In a few instances, in cavities between the roots of stumps but little damaged, remains of a peaty loam, such as generally forms the soil in a fir forest, are seen, and yet the matrix in which these stools were imbedded was laminated clay. Some stools have the bark preserved in hollows, while it is worn off in exposed places. It is remarkable that a large proportion of lop-sided stumps (i e. stumps with all the roots growing from one side) are found. This would be inexplicable were the general description correct of the way the trees grew on the level surface of the pre-glacial soil; but when we consider them to have been drifted, it is just what might be expected, for many would have grown out of the steep river-bank, and been undermined and carried away by the current.

For a long while the statement that the roots had been found interlacing was puzzling, but a group near Trimingham showed that this observation might be accurate, and yet the trees be drifted. In Fig. 3 (p. 24) the stumps A and B have their roots interlacing, and have grown together so firmly that they cannot be parted without breaking. C is a third stump of fir entangled with the others, but nearly upside down; it appears to have grown out of a steep bank. The extremities of the roots and stem were in each case worn or broken off, and the stools were imbedded in a mass of clay pebbles and lignite, covered by laminated clay, which had to be cleared away before the trees could be properly examined. It therefore appears that all these stumps have probably been washed away by the wasting of the river bank, and settling, generally in an upright position, as we should expect from the

* *See* Norfolk News, Sept. 5, 1868

greater density of the roots and from the weight of the adhering soil, they have formed "snags" in the river, such as are constantly met with in streams flowing through a forest-clad country.

Fig 3

Plan of a Group of Trees in the Forest-bed at Trimingham
Scale, 2 feet to an inch.

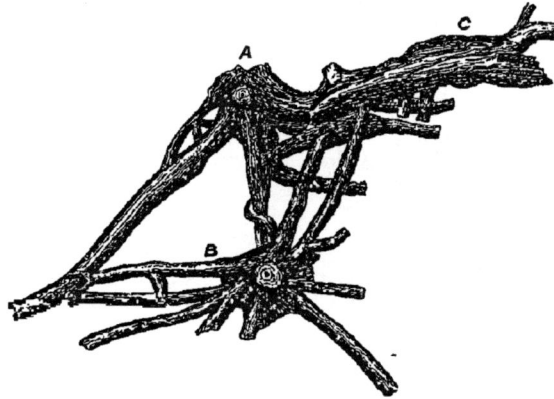

Details of the Sections

Weybourn.—In the neighbourhood of Weybourn the Lower Fresh-water Bed appears to have been overlapped; at any rate no trace of it can be found   The quartzite-gravels, belonging probably to the middle Estuarine division of the "Forest-bed," are almost unfossiliferous, nothing having been found in them at this locality except one or two fragments of bone and pieces of wood, their mode of occurrence is shown in Fig 2. Above them, for rather more than ¼ mile east of the Coastguard Station, there are fresh-water peaty loams belonging to the Upper Fresh-water Bed, lying in slightly eroded hollows cut off above by the Boulder Clay, so that we cannot say whether they are portions of a once continuous lacustrine deposit, or were formed in separate ponds   Beneath these, the beds are penetrated by small roots too much decayed for microscopic examination   At one spot only could any fossils be obtained   Just 500 yards E of the flagstaff a peaty seam yielded in abundance *Cypris Browniana* and opercula of *Bythinia*, but all purely calcareous fossils have disappeared, having been dissolved, as Mr Bristow suggests, by the peaty water   Shells must originally have been abundant, for a large quantity of the horny opercula were obtained by washing a little of the loam   A few yards further east the quartzite gravel rises and thins out against the Boulder Clay.

It is worthy of note that at Weybourn, under the Upper Fresh-water Bed, the surface of the Chalk is very irregular and much piped   In several places the Pliocene Beds have subsided into hollows, but the Boulder Clay continues across undisturbed, proving the piping to be pre-glacial   East of the point where the Fresh-water Beds disappear the surface of the Chalk becomes much more regular

Lower Sherringham.—No further exposures that can definitely be referred to the "Forest bed" occur till within ¼ mile of Lower Sherringham   Here we have the section given at p 14   The "Forest-bed" consists of 3 feet of stiff dark-blue clay and clay-pebbles, with drift wood, small cakes of peat and decayed leaves, teeth of elephant, and antlers of deer; but no shells could be found   This section is interesting, because, as the Rev O Fisher has pointed out,* it is the most westerly exposure of the typical "Forest-bed" The cakes of peat included in it also appear to point to the destroyed Lower Fresh-water Bed. The quartzite gravels, which seem nearly everywhere to form the upper part of the Estuarine division, and often overlap the clays, appear to have been at this point cut out by the *Leda myalis* Bed

From here to Sherringham the section is much obscured by talus, but one or two somewhat similar exposures can occasionally be examined, and in one place there seemed to be traces of a Pre-glacial soil At Lower Sherringham, opposite the village and immediately west of the Valley Gravel shown in the cliff, fossiliferous Fresh-water Beds are again seen Here the section is —

		Feet
Soil	- - - - - -	2
?	Sand with gravelly base - - -	6
?	Greyish loam and sand, well bedded - -	7
Upper Fresh water Bed	Dark-blue stony clay with decayed fragments of marine shells (derivative?) and opercula of *Bythinia* - - - - -	2
?	Gravel - - - - -	1½
Chalk with flints		

This exposure was noted several years ago, and has since been hidden by talus, so that one cannot re-examine the beds to discover to which divisions the upper portion belongs, but probably both the Arctic Fresh-water Bed and the *Leda myalis* Bed are represented A few yards west of this point what appeared to be a Pre-glacial soil was seen within 2 or 3 feet of the Chalk, but the section was too much obscured to enable me to be certain

Immediately E of Lower Sherringham sands and thin greyish loams containing occasional specimens of *Pisidium* and *Succinea* are found These may belong to the Upper Fresh-water Bed, but more probably they represent the higher Arctic one. At this point, and wherever all the Pre-glacial beds in the cliff happen to be sandy, it is almost impossible to trace definite lines of division, but the included fossils prove without doubt that very different conditions must have prevailed during the deposition of successive portions of the sand Where the beds are clayey, there is seldom much difficulty about the lines of junction, for the older bed generally shows more or less erosion. Below this Fresh-water Bed there are sands and quartzite gravels, here sometimes resting immediately on the Chalk without any intervening Weybourn Crag.

Beeston.—A short distance further S E, under Beeston Hills, we have the important exposure, shown in Sect. 3 of the folding plate Here the estuarine quartzite gravel is very thin, as is the Weybourn Crag, but it has yielded a few badly preserved bones Above it we find a bed of blue-black peaty loam, for the most part rather stony This bed is full of plant-remains, but, as at Weybourn, all purely calcareous fossils have disappeared It has yielded teeth and bones of pike, abundance of seeds, and opercula of *Bythinia*, but no shells. Among the common plants are several species of *Carex, Ceratophyllum demersum, Hippuris vulgaris, Rumex maritimus, Potamogeton heterophyllus, P trichoides, var tuberculata, P flabellatus, Chara,* &c Resting on this Upper Fresh-water Bed there is gravelly sand with occasional marine shells (the *Leda myalis* Bed); above which is found the Arctic Fresh-water Bed At a point mid-way between the Hill and the Stream (see folding plate) all the beds are fossiliferous, and the following section is shown; the beds continuing with the same character for a considerable distance both east and west, though the thicknesses vary slightly —

		Feet
Boulder Clay		
Arctic Fresh-water Bed	Sand and loam. Peaty laminated loam with *Salix polaris* and moss	7
Leda myalis Bed	False-bedded sand and sandy flint gravel with a few marine shells - - - -	4

		Feet
Upper Fresh-water Bed.	Peaty loam with opercula of *Bythinia tentaculata*, seeds, and fish bones - - -	5
"Forest-bed" (estuarine division).	Clay, quartzite-gravel, and sand, with occasional fragments of mammalian bone - -	6
Weybourn Crag.	Pan and stone bed, with clay, clay-pebbles, and marine shells. *Purpura lapillus, Littorina littorea, Cardium edule, Astarte compressa, Cyprina Islandica, Tellina Balthica, T. obliqua, Mactra ovalis, Mya arenaria* - - -	1

Chalk with flints

The exposure at Beeston is particularly important in showing clearly the succession, for all the beds between the Boulder Clay and the Chalk are represented, with the exception of the Lower Fresh-water Bed At the time this section was noted the cliff was exceptionally free from talus, for the erection of groynes at Sherringham had caused the beach to be thoroughly cleared away for some distance to the south-east

A few yards from the stream at Beeston the Pliocene Beds are cut out by Boulder Clay, and when they reappear half a mile further S E. the Fresh-water Bed is missing, and the estuarine division of the Forest-bed cannot definitely be recognized The section between East and West Runton Gap is shown in the folding plate, but a considerable portion of the estuarine beds could only be examined here and there, as they have for several years been almost entirely hidden under the beach.

Runton.—On the west side of West Runton Gap (sometimes called Woman Hithe), there is at the base of the cliff a bed of blue clay, belonging probably to the "Forest-bed," which, when traced towards the Gap, becomes whitish and weathered, and near the Gap is penetrated by small roots. Here it is immediately overlaid by marine sands with *Leda myalis* and *Mya truncata*, in the position of life; but in the centre of the roadway a thin seam of peaty sand full of fresh-water shells intervenes, and the clay is penetrated by small roots (Rootlet Bed). Within 50 yards the Fresh-water Bed is again cut out by the *Leda myalis* Bed ; nevertheless a continuous weathered soil can now be traced for at least half a mile. About 150 yards S.E. of the Gap the Fresh-water Bed re-appears, resting on an eroded surface of weathered laminated clay and sand with marine shells. It now continues without interruption for 350 yards, with a maximum thickness of about 6 feet.

The Upper Fresh-water Bed at Runton consists of peat or peaty loam with generally a sandy or clayey base, and from this locality most of the small vertebrate remains, and the fresh-water shells, in public and private collections, have been obtained. In the Appendix to the Pliocene section (pp 62–80) is a full list of fossils, but as the species vary according to the nature of the deposit, it is desirable to draw attention to the characteristics of each portion

Near West Runton Gap the bed is a loamy sand full of *Corbicula fluminalis* and *Paludina gibba*, but it does not exceed 8 inches in thickness Where it re-appears further eastward it is also sandy, especially at the base; and if this sand is carefully sifted it yields in abundance bones of small mammals, birds, reptiles, amphibia, and fishes, and numerous fresh-water shells Unfortunately this extraordinary abundance of small bones was only discovered when the bed was to a large extent hidden by talus, though for several months previously it had been well exposed. There is also a great variety of mollusca, including several species which are either extinct or not now living in England; the former are *Limax modioliformis, Paludina gibba,* and *Hydrobia Runtoniana ;* the latter include *Corbicula fluminalis, Hydrobia Steinii,* and *Valvata fluviatilis.* Still further east the base of the bed is clayey, with abundance of *Hydrobia Runtoniana,* and the upper part is peaty with large *Anodons,* elytra of beetles, and badly preserved seeds. Bones occur throughout, though, when found in the wet peaty portion, they are generally much decayed. Mixed with the perfect land and fresh-water shells a few worn and decayed fragments of *Tellina Balthica* and *Cardium edule* have been found, evidently derived from the underlying estuarine beds To the same cause we should refer the occurrence of a tooth of a seal, for there is not the slightest evidence of the irruption of the sea at this stage, for the other fossils are purely lacustrine and fluviatile. A single rolled fragment of an elephant's tooth has been found, but as none of the other bones are water-worn, and no other specimen of elephant is known from this horizon, this is also probably derivative

The roots which penetrate the underlying soil are here always too much decayed for microscopic examination, but from their shape and mode of growth they probably belong to pine or fir. When the pine grows on an alluvial soil saturated with water all the main roots spread horizontally to form a sort of platform, sending off a mass of small roots of nearly equal size vertically downwards. At Runton it seems that the stools have been washed away, leaving only the termination of the roots, but at the same horizon at Happisburgh one stool was found in the soil; and a root examined microscopically showed obscure traces of what appeared to he coniferous structure, but it was too much decayed for satisfactory determination

The clays and gravels which form the soil on which these trees grew, here belong to the estuarine division of the Forest-bed; but, unfortunately, the junction between it and the Weybourn Crag is for considerable distances hidden by the beach, and in many places it cannot definitely be said to which division an isolated exposure may belong

Beneath the Fresh-water bed there is laminated loam with *Tellina Balthica*, and pebbly quartzite gravel, weathered into a soil in the upper part, but well bedded two or three feet down These pebbly gravels, which are common all along the coast, are often cemented into a mass of ferruginous conglomerate, which, after the talus has been cleared away by storms, forms a conspicuous tabular mass at the base of the cliff, or on the foreshore This "pan" or "elephant-bed," as it is often called, is on no fixed horizon, but ranges throughout the "Forest-bed," sometimes at the base, but more commonly high up. It appears always to occur at the base of a mass of gravel or sand which rests on impervious clays.

Tracing the beds from West Runton Gap, the first characteristic section of the estuarine beds that has been observed, is a short distance west of the large Chalk boulders in the cliff. Here laminated clay full of lignite occupies a hollow eroded in the Weybourn Crag and nearly to the Chalk, but a few yards further it rises and is lost in the beach. Under the western end of the first Chalk boulder, the Fresh-water bed again appears in the cliff for about 10 yards, resting on weathered loamy gravel with estuarine shells

Near Wood Hill there is shown on the foreshore a bed of clay-pebbles resting apparently on an eroded surface of Weybourn Crag. This bed passes up into alternating laminated clays, sand, and gravel All the beds contain much drift wood and occasional derivative cakes of peat Bones, and marine, land, and fresh-water shells, occur abundantly near the base Owing to the peculiar nature of this deposit, which has been formed in part from the breaking up of the Weybourn Crag, it is very difficult to say to what extent the marine shells may be derivative, but most of the land and fresh-water species certainly belong to the bed; and so do many of the estuarine forms, for there are seams full of mussels in the position in life.

These beds of clay-pebbles maintain the same character for some distance S.E. of East Runton Gangway; they are extremely fossiliferous, and show better than any other portion of the deposit the curiously mixed or estuarine character of the typical "Forest-bed" fauna Mr. A C. Savin, of Cromer, has here obtained a number of mammalian remains Among those found in the Course of the Survey are—the scapula of elephant, jaw of *Trogontherium*, and antlers of several species of deer, now in the Museum of Practical Geology The quantity of bones seen here inclines one to think that at present this is the best locality for collecting from the estuarine division; it is also the only place where land shells are found in any abundance, *Helix* is particularly common, much more so than any fresh-water species In the list of species in the 8th chapter, those which may be derivative are marked as doubtful, but it is worth notice that some of the characteristic Crag forms undoubtedly belong to the bed Among these may be mentioned the well-known Norwich Crag fish, *Platax Woodwardi*, here very common, and occurring, though more rarely, in the Weybourn Crag *Melampus pyramidalis*, an extinct Crag shell, is also more abundant than in the older beds *Tellina obliqua, Nucula Cobboldiæ,* and the reversed *Trophon antiquus,* are plentiful, but may be derivative The whole of the marine species occur also in the Weybourn Crag, the more abundant forms are such as we find thrown up on sandy beaches at the mouths of estuaries (*Cardium edule, Mytilus edulis, Donax vittatus, Littorina littorea, L rudis, Purpura lapillus, Melampus*)

Mixed with the shells one or two stools of trees were observed, and in one place a trunk of fir over 18 feet long , but, as a general rule, the drift wood and shells occur in distinct beds, for heavy rains would wash trees into the estuary, at the same time damming back the tide, while storms would wash in marine shells from the open sea Thus the alternations of beds with lignite and marine sands do not necessitate any change of level during their formation Besides this little-altered drift-wood, derivative pebbles of lignite, jet, and very rarely of silicified wood, were found

On both sides of East Runton Gangway a mass of pan forms a conspicuous feature at the base of the cliff The beds immediately beneath could not be examined at this spot; but at the foot of the beach (which would be about 7 feet below the base of the pan) the bed of clay-pebbles is often well shown, and contains an unusual abundance of antlers of deer, belonging to at least three species. Several elephants' teeth were also found, but they were too much decayed for preservation A few yards east of the Gap a boulder of greyish granite, measuring $2 \times 1\frac{3}{4} \times 1$ feet, was to be seen among the clay-pebbles and bones. This is by far the largest boulder found in the "Forest-bed," and is also the only one of igneous origin yet noticed. A few bones occur in the pan, but they are usually much broken As a general rule, for all localities of the estuarine division of the "Forest-bed," the least damaged specimens have been obtained from clayey beds, but they usually need careful handling and gelatinizing , the bones from the pan or elephant-bed are harder, but more knocked about In the clays most of the bones occur in masses of rolled clay-pebbles, and very few in the laminated portion, though one or two found in the latter were unusually perfect

Between East Runton and Cromer the estuarine "Forest-bed" can only here and there be seen at the base of the cliff or on the foreshore: it appears gradually to become more carbonaceous, and contains few marine shells, except mussels About three-quarters of a mile N W of Cromer there is sometimes exposed at low water two or three feet of black mud representing the Lower Fresh-water Bed This mud can be traced for about 100 yards, cutting through the Weybourn Crag, and in one place for a few feet into the Chalk, so that it extends to extreme low-water mark Resting on and overlapping it there is greenish laminated sandy clay full of wood, and containing occasional marine shells and fir-cones This exposure of the Lower Fresh-water Bed is especially important, as being, with the exception of a similar bed at Trimingham, the only place where the horizon has been examined *in situ,* though from derivative boulders in the overlying estuarine beds, and from beach specimens at Happisburgh, its flora is fairly well known. The deposit is a tenacious and very carbonaceous river-mud with fish-bones, and abundance of seeds of water and marsh plants, a list of which is given at p 62

Opposite Cromer the "Forest-bed" is hidden under the sea-wall and by the beach retained by the groynes, but a few yards W of the wall, laminated clay with drift-wood and fir-cones is occasionally to be seen at the base of the cliff and on the foreshore Many tree-stumps are said to have been found when the sea-wall was being built, but now no clear sections are met with till the last groyne is passed. On the lower side of the groyne, when the beach has been scoured away by storms, clayey gravel is laid bare From this bed Mr. Savin has obtained many bones

Overstrand —Between the Lighthouse Hills and Overstrand village the "Forest-bed" changes very little In the upper part it consists of laminated blue clay with drift-wood, but (as far as the writer has seen) no bones Beneath there are generally alternations of clay and gravel with large drift-wood, bones, and mussels ; and at the base is found a bed of clay-pebbles with abundance of bones, resting on the fossiliferous clays of the Weybourn Crag The thickness of the "Forest-bed" near Overstrand appears to average about 15 feet , in one place it measured 24 feet

A large proportion of the mammalian remains in old collections were obtained from the Green Hill Rocks opposite the Lighthouse. Several hundred elephants' teeth must have been found, and yet probably the locality is not exceptionally fossiliferous. The reason why so many bones have been washed out is that the building of the jetty and groynes at Cromer stopped the travelling of the beach, and for many years the "Forest-bed" was continually bare. It has now been much denuded, and fewer fossils are obtained, but several teeth of elephant, a jaw of *Trogontherium*, and various other bones were found during the Survey. Mr A C Savin (of Cromer) has a large collection from this locality, and the majority of Miss Anna Gurney's specimens came from here.[*] Tree-stumps scattered throughout the beds are very common, but comparatively few trunks are seen. Most of the stools belong to fir or pine of moderate size; other trees, except willow, are very rare. There are also many derived cakes of peat, often bored by *Pholas*, with elytra of beetles and leaves. In isolated exposures the clays of the "Forest-bed" may be distinguished from those of the Weybourn Crag by their dark blue colour, the latter being greenish.

One or two sections will give an idea of the general character of the beds, the details of which vary slightly every few yards. The following was taken nearly under the Old Lighthouse :—

Feet

Boulder Clay		
Leda Myalis Bed (?)	Sand with a little loam, a few stones in the lower part - - - -	6
"Forest Bed" (estuarine).	Laminated clay and lignite - - -	12
	Alternating gravel and clay with a few seams of mussels and much lignite - -	7
	Clay-pebbles, with lignite, cakes of peat, and mammalian bones - - - -	3
Weybourn Crag	Greenish loam, clay, and clay-ironstone, full of casts of marine shells - -	(?)

A section at the eastern end of Kirby Hill shows —

Boulder Clay		
"Forest-bed" (estuarine).	False-bedded gravel full of small clay-pebbles -	1½
	False-bedded sand with a little loam and carbonaceous matter - - - -	2
	Laminated loam - - - -	1
	Lignite, clay-pebbles, and ferruginous gravel mixed - - - -	2
	(?) hidden by the beach - -	5
Weybourn Crag.	Green-bedded clay with decayed shells -	2

At this point the Boulder Clay has cut several feet into the "Forest-bed," and the mass of bedded blue clays shown further west has disappeared. On the foreshore, about mid-way between these exposures, there is this section —

Feet.

"Forest-bed" (estuarine)	Gravel of clay pebbles, with quartzite pebbles, bones, drift-wood, &c - -	about 4;
Weybourn Crag.	Laminated greenish clay with casts of marine shells	

Lying on and partly embedded in the clay-gravel is a stump of fir, 3 feet in diameter near the base, with the roots spreading over 11 feet in one direction, and 9 feet in another. In hollows there are here and there preserved portions of the bark, and also of a loamy peaty soil with seeds. This is by far the largest tree examined; for it has a spread of about 20 feet; no other is known to exceed 10 feet. By employing men to clear away the clay, one was

---

[*] Most of the specimens collected by Miss Gurney are in the Norwich Museum, and some of them were figured by Dr Falconer in his "Fauna Antiqua Sivalensis." Miss Gurney appears also to have distributed specimens of the teeth of *Elephas meridionalis* among various local collections, some being at Newcastle, others at Whitby, or in the South of England. These teeth, being occasionally unlabelled, have sometimes been considered to be of local origin, but in reality *E. meridionalis* appears, in the British Isles, to be entirely confined to the Newer Pliocene Beds of Norfolk, Suffolk, and Essex.

able to examine the termination of many of the roots; they were all worn, and one, which was traced for a long way among the clay-pebbles, measured about 3 inches at its broken and rounded extremity. It was cut off, and is now in the Museum of Practical Geology as an example of the ordinary worn state of the roots in the "Forest-bed" trees.

At Beck Hithe the Boulder Clay cuts deeply into the "Forest-bed" and the bones, though abundant, are much crushed and decayed. A few yards further, E., the line again rises above the beach, and at 150 yards from the old road to the shore the section is :—

		Feet.
Boulder Clay.		
(?)	Fine false-bedded sand - - - -	3
Upper Fresh-water Bed	{ Sand and carbonaceous blue clay, irregularly mixed - - - - -	2½
"Forest-bed" (estuarine)	{ Sand and laminated clay with fragments of *Mytilus* - - - -	5½
Beach.		

At this point no shells were noticed in the Fresh-water Bed.

About a quarter of a mile further, there is the following section, the exact position of which may be found by the Chalk boulders in the cliff above, and the old groyne on the shore opposite.

		Feet.
Boulder Clay.		
Upper Fresh-water Bed.	{ Sand irregularly mixed with carbonaceous blue clay : *Valvata piscinalis, Bythinia tentaculata, Pisidium amnicum, Unio or Anodon*	2
"Forest-bed," (estuarine)	{ False-bedded sand with clay-pebbles and fragments of *Mytilus*. (A perfect specimen of *Scalaria Grænlandica*) - - -	4½
	{ False-bedded sandy gravel, in places cemented into pan - - - - -	4
(?)	Hidden under the beach - - -	4
Weybourn Crag	} Sandy clay with decayed marine shells	

Beneath the Fresh-water Bed there are perhaps some small roots penetrating the estuarine sands, but they are very obscure and much decayed.

At 55 yards S.E. of the groyne we find :—

		Feet.
Boulder Clay		
Upper Fresh-water Bed.	} Peaty clay and sand with fresh-water shells -	4
"Forest-bed" (estuarine)	{ Laminated sandy blue clay - - -	2½
	{ (?) hidden - - - - -	3
	{ Dark blue pan with irregular ferruginous concretions like contorted beds - -	1+
Beach.		

At 80 yards :—

		Feet.
Boulder Clay.		
Upper Fresh-water Bed	} Sand and peaty loam with fresh-water shells -	7
"Forest-bed" (estuarine).	{ Sand - - - - -	1
	{ Bed of mussels in sandy clay - -	½
	{ Sandy gravel - - - -	3
	{ Pan - - - - -	1½
Beach.		

At 290 yards :—

		Feet.
Boulder Clay		
Upper Fresh-water Bed.	{ Stiff carbonaceous blue clay and a little sand, showing a contorted or concretionary structure. Fish bones, *Pisidium amnicum, Unio pictorum* - - - - -	3½
(?)	Laminated blue clay - - - -	2

Feet.

| "Forest-bed" (estuarine). | Pan, composed of unworn and worn flints, numerous quartzite-pebbles, clay-ironstone, quartz, silicious sandstone, black grit, soft micaceous sandstone, and containing bones and a little drift-wood | 2 |

Beach.

The Fresh-water Bed at this spot thins out rapidly in both directions, and appears merely to fill a small basin cut off above by the Boulder Clay

For some distance to the S E the cliff is usually obscured by talus, and no section of importance is seen till a point about 50 yards beyond the commencement of the highest cliffs at Sidestrand is reached Here the section is :—

Feet

Boulder Clay
Leda myalis Bed (?)	Fine light-coloured sand	7
	Gravelly sand	About 1
"Forest-bed" (estuarine).	Fine loamy sand with gravelly base, containing fragments of *Mytilus*	4
	Laminated clay and sand	2½

Beach.

For 190 yards to the S E no clear section has been seen, but at that point the "Sidestrand Unio-Bed," comes on The section is —

Feet.

Boulder Clay.
Leda myalis Bed (?)	Fine false-bedded loamy sand with thin gravel at the base	8
Upper Fresh-water Bed	Dark-blue thick-bedded sandy clay	7
	Bluish sand and gravel with much drift-wood	1

Beach.

About 18 yards further it has changed to —

Boulder Clay.
Leda myalis Bed (?)	Fine sand as above	9¼
Upper Fresh-water Bed.	Bedded blue clay	4½
	Stony blue clay	1

Beach.

Another section 90 yards further shows —

Boulder Clay.

Feet.

Leda myalis Bed (?)	Sand and a little gravel	5
Upper Fresh-water Bed.	Blue bedded clay	5
	Blue clay and gravel full of *Unios*	1½

Beach.

The next sections of importance are exactly under Sidestrand Church :—

Boulder Clay.

Feet.

| ? | Fine false-bedded sand and loam with a little small gravel at the base *Pisidium amnicum* (perhaps derivative) 6 inches beneath the Boulder Clay | 6½ |
| Upper Fresh-water Bed. | Sand, carbonaceous loam, and pebble gravel, with fragments of *Unio* | 3 |

Beach.

About 110 yards S.E. there is —

Boulder Clay, with uneven base.

?	False-bedded sand with thin blue clays and a little carbonaceous matter	3½ to 7
Upper Fresh-water Bed.	Blue-bedded clay. the lower part stony : *Pisidium amnicum*, *Unio* or *Anodon*	4 to 3
	Gravelly blue clay with *Unios*	0 to 1
"Forest-bed" (estuarine)	Ferruginous loamy gravel, with *Mya truncata* and *Tellina Balthica* in the position of life	1 to 0

Beach.

The two measurements were taken 15 yards apart; and a few feet in each direction the gravel with *Mya truncata* cannot be found, it is apparently cut out by the Fresh-water Bed   In one place the shell of the *Mya* has been entirely dissolved away, but the tough siphon-tubes are well preserved, looking much like portions of decayed roots of trees

The Fresh-water Bed can now be traced continuously for about 320 yards, when it is suddenly cut off by the Boulder Clay   It constantly shows slight variations, and one more detailed section must suffice   At 180 yards N W of the Boulder Clay scoop we have —

		Feet
Boulder Clay		
Leda myalis Bed ? } Sand and thin clays - - -		2
Upper Fresh-water Bed. ⎰ Laminated loam - - -		1
Blue carbonaceous clay, bedding obscure -		3½
Blue stony loam, with fresh-water shells, seeds, and drift-wood - -		1
"Forest-bed" (estuarine) ⎰ Clayey pan, with drift wood (*Mya* not observed, but may have entirely decayed) - -		1½
? (hidden by beach) - -		4
Laminated clay, clay-pebbles, lignite and a few bones - - - -		1 +

Within 50 yards the sand is cut out, and the Boulder Clay rests directly on laminated clays

The Sidestrand Unio-bed is very fossiliferous; but the gravelly portion, full of *Unio pictorum*, is generally obscured by talus.   The overlying clays (if dried and then washed in a sieve) yield abundance of seeds, small shells, and fish-bones, but mammalian remains and land shells are very scarce   This is probably the best place for collecting plants.   No leaves are found, except a few decayed fragments, though fruit or seeds of at least 40 species occur, and the clay is full of well-preserved moss   Among the shells a single specimen of *Hydrobia marginata* was obtained, unfortunately since mislaid, corresponding exactly with the variety found at Mundesley   A full list of the mollusca is given at the end of the chapter on the Natural History of these beds

For nearly half-a-mile no sections can be seen, for the Boulder Clay cuts through the beds to beneath the sea-level.   When the Pliocene beds reappear, the character of the upper portion of the section has a good deal altered.   A few yards from the S E end of the scoop we find —

	Feet
Boulder Clay.	
Sand with some blue clay in the lower part - -	15
Pan, full of quartzite pebbles - - - -	2
? (hidden under the beach) - -	4
Greenish laminated loam and beds of clay-pebbles -	2 +

About 90 yards further the Upper Fresh-water Bed seems to reappear, though no fossils could be found in it.   The section is —

		Feet
Boulder Clay		
Upper Fresh-water Bed ⎰ Gravelly sand irregularly mixed with a little carbonaceous blue loam - -		4
"Forest bed" (estuarine) ⎰ False-bedded gravelly sand - -		9
Quartzite gravel passing laterally into pan -		2
? (hidden by beach) -		7
Laminated blue clay and clay pebbles -		2

Probably the Chalk is about 15 feet below the base of this section, which would give a total thickness of 40 feet to the Pliocene beds here.

At 80 yards to the S E. we have —

	Feet
Boulder Clay	
Sand with irregular blue clays and thin lignite in the lower part -	8
False-bedded sand, gravel, thin loams, and lignite - - -	10
? (hidden by beach) - - - -	4
Laminated clay and clay-pebbles with a stump of fir - -	2

A few yards further, though not directly opposite, black carbonaceous stony silt, full of seeds, was seen on the foreshore, distinctly passing under the laminated clay. This silt belongs to the Lower Fresh-water Bed, and corresponds both in position and character with the exposure between Cromer and Runton. For 250 yards the base of the cliff is usually hidden by landslips, but the Lower Fresh-water Bed can be traced here and there on the foreshore.

At 100 yards S E of the old groyne at Trimingham (there is no other landmark visible by which to fix the spot) we have the sections shown in Fig 4

FIG 4

Section of the lower part of the Cliff near the old Groyne at Trimingham

Scale, 20 feet to an inch

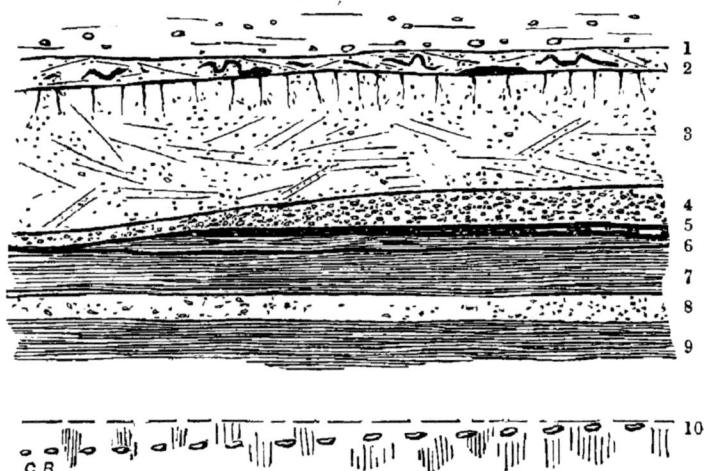

Contorted Drift?	}	1 Hard blue stony Boulder Clay (base only seen)
Upper Fresh-water Bed	{	2. False-bedded sand, irregularly mixed with carbonaceous blue clay
"Forest-bed" (estuarine)	{	3. Fine loamy bluish false-bedded sand, with very few stones, the upper part penetrated by roots (Rootlet Bed)
		4 Clay pebbles, gravel, sand, and lignite
Lower Fresh-water Bed	{	5. Carbonaceous green clayey silt
		6 Laminated lignite and loam.
Weybourn Crag	{	7. Green and blue laminated rather carbonaceous clay
		8 Sand with marine shells.
		9 Clay as above
Upper Chalk		10 Probable position of the Chalk

At the time the beds were examined the beach had been entirely swept away by a storm, and a continuous exposure could be traced to low-water mark All three divisions of the Forest-bed were well shown in vertical section, and the total thickness of the Pliocene beds will be about 40 feet A broken line has been put in to show the probable position of the Chalk, but it ought perhaps to be a few feet lower.

The Fresh-water Bed in the section just figured, and in numerous others which have been or will be described, shows a peculiar structure, the carbonaceous clay and sand being apparently contorted together At first sight, one might suppose this to be connected with the contortions in the Boulder Clay; but in numerous instances these small contortions in the Fresh-water Beds are cut off and overlaid by evenly-bedded fresh-water clays, proving

R 1195

C

that they originated contemporaneously with the deposit   A similar contorted structure is not uncommon in recent alluvium, and may originate in two ways :— An elephant, hippopotamus, or other large animal treading in the shallow water would easily squeeze the clays into these shapes   One may notice that the oxen and horses standing on the shores of the Broads often force up black mud through the gravel on each side of their footprints. Another mode of accounting for the contortion is that it is due to the lateral thrust caused by the alternate freezing and thawing of the beds in the winter.   But in either case it is noticeable that in the well-laminated fresh-water clays that are found at Sidestrand and a few other places, and which appear to have been formed in water too deep for freezing, or disturbance by the growth of water-plants, no contortions are found.   In the contorted beds the common mollusca are the almost amphibious *Succinea*, *Limnæa peregra* (*L limosa*), and *Pisidium pusillum*, while in the bedded clay of Sidestrand *Ancylus* (*Velletia*) *lacustris* is probably the most abundant species.

The Lower Fresh-water Bed is now cut out, but for a quarter of a mile to the S E , beyond slight variations in the relative thickness of the different beds, there is no other change, and the small roots can be seen about 8 feet above the beach wherever the section is free from talus   At about 3 furlongs from the groyne the three tree stumps shown in Fig 3 were found. The section is :—

			Feet
Boulder Clay.			
Upper Fresh-water Bed	{	False-bedded sand, with irregular seams of grey loam and a gravelly base - - -	2
"Forest-bed" (estuarine)	{	False-bedded sand, with a few seams of loam and scattered pebbles - - -	5½
		Laminated and false-bedded sand and clay -	1½
		? (hidden) - - - -	4
		Clay-pebbles and pan, with tree-stumps and lignite - - - - -	2
		Blue laminated carbonaceous clay, lignite, and clay pebbles - - - -	3 +

About 200 yards further, the bed of clay-pebbles which contains the tree-stumps yielded a jaw of cod,—the only marine fossil noticed in the "Forest-bed" in this neighbourhood.

The false-bedded sands now gradually change to laminated clay, and under Trimingham lime-kiln there is :—

			Feet
Boulder Clay.			
Upper Fresh-water Bed.	{	Sand with grey loam and a thin seam of gravel - - - - -	3
		Carbonaceous clay and sand, false-bedded together, a little gravel - - -	3
"Forest-bed" (estuarine)	}	Blue-bedded clay - - - - -	6

About 50 yards further the mass of laminated clay is cut out —

			Feet
Boulder Clay.			
Upper Fresh-water Bed	{	Sand and carbonaceous loam, with fresh-water shells - - - - -	6
"Forest-bed" (estuarine).	{	Laminated sand and loam - - -	5
		Blue clay, clay-pebbles, lignite, and cakes of peat, with plant remains and elytra of beetles	4 to 0
		Laminated blue clay - - -	0 to 4
		? (hidden) - - - -	3
		Small gravel, masses of clay pebbles, micaceous laminated clay and lignite, false-bedded together; the gravel contains many quite unworn flints A cone of Scotch fir and fragments of mammalian bone were also found -	3 +

The Boulder Clay gradually descends and cuts out the Fresh-water Bed, but the Estuarine division can be traced to near the western Chalk bluff at

Trimingham. There are continual variations, but it is unnecessary to give every change. The last section which could be seen was 80 yards from the Chalk :—

		Feet
Boulder Clay		
"Forest-bed" (estuarine). ⎰ Sand and loam - - - -		4
⎱ Laminated clay - - - - -		6

Unfortunately a persistent talus prevents us from tracing the beds till they disappear in the contortion, and it is at present rather doubtful how they end off. Not improbably Pliocene Beds will be found beneath the Chalk, which is here contorted into a loop and inverted. The Chalk cannot have been in its present position when the "Forest-bed" was deposited, for the laminated clays are seen close to it without their lithological character being in any way affected by the proximity. A small hill of this sort would also have entirely disappeared long before the whole of these Pliocene Beds could have been laid down, for the Chalk is exceptionally soft, and it would have been always exposed to atmospheric action and to the constant washing of peaty water. It has been stated that Crag occurs on the top of these Chalk bluffs; but this is a mistake; the shelly sand there seen is merely a patch of the ordinary Glacial sand.

On the S E side of the bluff the "Forest-bed" reappears within 140 yards, and as the base of the Boulder Clay is there a few feet higher than on the N W. side, the Upper Fresh-water Bed is again seen. At 180 yards from the Chalk the section is —

		Feet.
Boulder Clay.		
Upper Fresh-water Bed.	Sand and blue loam mixed - - -	1
	Sand irregularly mixed with blue clay. *Succinea* throughout - - - -	2½
	Blue bedded carbonaceous clay with seams of sand and a few small stones, twigs and shells throughout, *Succinea putris* very common, *Cylas cornea* one valve - - -	2½
	Contorted laminated clay and sand, with a little gravel and a carbonaceous seam at the base -	2
"Forest-bed" (estuarine).	Well-bedded blue clay with a few thin seams of gravel and sand - - - - -	4½
	Bedded sand and clay - - - -	1 +
Beach.		

A few yards further a small stool of fir was found lying horizontally in the well-bedded clay of the estuarine division. About 30 yards from this section the beds have changed to :—

		Feet.
Boulder Clay.		
Upper Fresh-water Bed.	Sand and grey loam - - -	6
	Carbonaceous loam and gravel - - -	½
"Forest-bed" (estuarine)	Sand with a few interrupted seams of loam, the upper part perhaps penetrated by roots	3
	Laminated clay and pan alternating, much lignite - - - -	2

The roots are rather doubtful at this point, for they have entirely decayed, and are only traceable as ferruginous lines in the sand. It is possible that in the last two sections we may have both the Arctic and the Upper Fresh-water Beds; but at the time these exposures were noted the writer was unaware of the distinction, and for the last two or three years this part of the cliff has been too obscure for detailed re-examination.

No more sections have been observed till the south-eastern Chalk bluff is passed. At 180 yards beyond it pan is seen at the top of the beach, but no clear exposure occurs for 130 yards further; here there is :—

	Feet.
Boulder Clay.	
Sand with a little loam and gravel - - - -	13
? (hidden) - - - - -	2½
Pan - - - - - - -	1
Dark blue stony silt mixed with ferruginous sand -	1

But the section is so isolated, that, in the absence of fossil evidence, it cannot
be said to which division the sand belongs   A few yards to the south-east the
Boulder Clay again ploughs through the beds, and for about three furlongs
no Pliocene beds are to be found

From the reappearance of the beds half-a-mile N.W of Mundesley Church
to Mundesley village, an almost continuous section has been examined,
though the whole of the cliff is never free from talus at one time, as landslips
occur immediately the buttresses are washed away   The first exposure
shows —

		Feet
Boulder Clay		
?	? (hidden) - - -	3
Upper Fresh-water Bed {	Fine false-bedded loam and lignite with fresh-water shells - - - - -	1½
	Gravel and sand - - - - -	½
Beach		

About 200 yards further there is the section shown in Fig. 5.

Fig 5

*Section of the lower part of the Cliff ¾ mile N W of the Coast Guard Station,
Mundesley.*

Scale, 20 feet to an inch

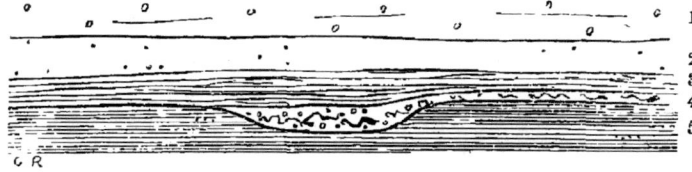

2nd Till -	1	Blue Boulder Clay, very chalky
Arctic Fresh-water Bed ? }	2	Sand
Upper Fresh-water bed {	3	Bedded blue loam, full of moss and seeds
	4	Blue loam mixed with gravelly sand, filling an eroded hollow , *Succinea.*
"Forest-bed" (estuarine) }	5	Laminated clay

The sand immediately under the Till is probably the Arctic Fresh-water
Bed, for it appears to be a continuation of the fossiliferous deposit at Mundesley, though at this point no plants were observed in it   The mosses in
the Upper Fresh-water Bed are here exceptionally well preserved, and fruit or
seeds of 12 or 13 species of water and marsh plants were found.

At 270 yards to the S.E is found —

			Feet
Boulder Clay			
Arctic Fresh-water Bed ? {	Bedded blue loam with fresh-water shells	-	2
	False-bedded gravelly sand with lignite	-	1
"Forest-bed" (estuarine) }	Laminated loam, sand, and lignite -	-	7

About 200 yards further :—

			Feet
Boulder Clay.			
Arctic Fresh-water Bed ? }	Laminated sand and loam with gravelly base	-	7
"Forest-bed" (estuarine) {	Gravel with clay pebbles, much lignite, a small tree-stump, and many derivative cakes of peat (one 5 feet long) containing cones of Scotch fir, reeds, seeds of bog-bean, and elytra of beetles - - - - -		1
	Laminated clay with a little gravel and sand; seam of mussels - - - -		4
	? (hidden by beach) -		9
	Bed of clay-pebbles - - -		1 +

The lithological character of the "Forest-bed" now changes continually, but as these variations are only such as occur in most estuarine beds, it is unnecessary to give all the details. Three furlongs N.W. of the Coast Guard Station, Mundesley, the base of the cliff is a mass of laminated clay with thin seams of sand; but within 70 yards it has entirely changed, by the gradual thinning out of the clays, to false-bedded sand. A quarter of a mile from the station the section is —

			Feet
2nd Till	-	Chalky Boulder Clay.	
Arctic Fresh-water Bed	{	Fine loamy sand with seams of grey loam: *Planorbis complanatus*	8
		False-bedded gravelly sand	2
"Forest-bed" (estuarine)	{	False-bedded sand and small pieces of lignite, clay-gravel, with *Littorina* and *Mytilus*, and laminated sand and loam with drift-wood	8
Beach			

This variable character in the beds continues to Mundesley, where on the foreshore, in beds rarely uncovered, many mammalian bones have been found, including three jaws of *Trogontherium*, now in Mr. Fitch's collection. The beds in the cliff yield comparatively few specimens.

The relations of the different beds at Mundesley will be best understood by reference to the folding plate at the end of this volume. It will be seen that there are here two marine or estuarine beds,—one above, the other below, the Upper Fresh-water Bed. The upper probably represents the *Leda myalis* Bed, but in this neighbourhood, where the Fresh-water Bed has thinned out, it is almost impossible to separate them, for the whole series is so full of lines of contemporaneous erosion that real breaks in the deposit are not easily traced, except by the fossils. Great care is also needed to prevent confusion of the fossils from the different fresh-water deposits, for at Mundesley there is a Post-glacial bed, which cuts into the "Forest-bed," and the Arctic, Upper, and (numerous derivative cakes of peat representing) the Lower Fresh-water Bed also occur. The general section is —

2nd Till	-	-	Boulder Clay, very chalky.
Arctic Fresh-water Bed	{	Sands with fresh-water shells, and clays with Arctic plants *Salix polaris*, &c
Leda myalis Bed	-	{	Marine sands and clays, with *Mytilus, Littorina, Cardium*, &c.
Upper Fresh-water Bed.	{	Blue peaty clay, full of *Unios*, seeds, and fish-bones (local patches only)
"Forest-bed" (estuarine)	-	{	Laminated clay and sand, with beds of mussels. Gravel, clay-pebbles, lignite, mammalian bones, and cakes of peat bored by *Pholas*, representing the destroyed Lower Fresh-water Bed

At this locality all the beds are fossiliferous, and can be seen in vertical succession after storms have cleared away the talus. The Upper Fresh-water Bed is very thin, and only preserved in small patches, which occur at about 2 feet above the beach on the S E side of the village, for about 60 yards beyond the broken sea-wall. The bed rests in slightly eroded hollows in the estuarine clays of the "Forest-bed," and does not exceed 6 or 8 inches in thickness, though it is very fossiliferous. At one spot the clay beneath it is weathered white, and shows obscure traces of roots. A derivative fragment of *Tellina Balthica* was washed out of the Fresh-water clay mixed with perfect specimens of *Valvata* and *Ancylus.*

For some distance there is no change of importance in the lithological character of the estuarine beds. At a quarter of a mile S E of the sea-wall, immediately above the beach, there were found a number of large derivative cakes of peat in the quartzite-gravel; these were all bored by *Pholas*, and contained large quantities of the peculiar fruit of the *Trapa natans*, a plant only known elsewhere in Britain by a few specimens from Bacton. From the similar contents of the different cakes at one locality, it is probable that they have not drifted very far, but at present the Lower Fresh-water Bed is unknown in place near Mundesley. N.W. of the village another collection was seen, but all the masses were composed of reeds, *Trapa natans* being absent.

When the beach between Mundesley and Bacton has been cleared away by N W gales, large quantities of bones are obtained, just below high-water mark, in alternating beds of clay-pebbles, laminated clay, and gravel with drift-wood and tree stumps These beds extend to the foot of the beach, and apparently to low-water mark, but sandbanks generally obscure the whole of the foreshore The fossils obtained are generally bones and teeth of *Elephas meridionalis* and *E antiquus*, and antlers of deer; but probably here, as elsewhere, the scarcity of small specimens is entirely owing to the little demand for them. An elephant's tooth has a definite price, but most collectors care little for the smaller things, and the long-shore men, when they notice them at all, find them so difficult to handle without breaking as not to be worth the trouble of preserving

About 500 yards from the sea-wall a perfect femur of elephant, 5 feet in length, was found partly imbedded in the upper surface of the estuarine division of the "Forest-bed" This specimen, now in the collection of Mr. Randall Johnson, at Waxham, is remarkable both for its perfect preservation and for the unusually high position, 4 feet above the beach, in which it occurred. The bones are here generally found in a bed about 5 feet lower, seen on the foreshore opposite

Half a mile from Mundesley the jaw of glutton, figured by Mr E T Newton,[*] was found about high-water mark About 250 yards further a rootstock of *Osmunda* was dug out of a bed of clay-pebbles near low-water mark. Nearly a mile from Mundesley there is the following section ·—

		Feet
2nd Till -	Boulder Clay, very chalky.	
Upper Fresh-water Bed.	Laminated sands and clays, with a little lignite in the upper part *Pinus sylvestris* - - -	5
"Forest-bed" (estuarine).	Laminated blue clay, with *Mytilus*	2
	Loamy gravelly sand, with *Mytilus*	1 +
Beach.		

Within a few yards in each direction the Till descends and rests immediately on the blue laminated clay

At a mile and a quarter from Mundesley the Till suddenly ploughs through the beds to beneath the sea-level, but just N W of the point where the Forest-bed disappears there is :—

		Feet
2nd Till -	Boulder Clay, very chalky.	
"Forest-bed" (estuarine)	Laminated clay and sand - - -	5
	Beds of clay-pebbles, with *Mytilus, Littorina, Balanus*, teeth of *Arvicola*, and limb-bone of *Trogontherium* - -	2
Beach.		

For nearly half a mile no sections are to be seen, but where the beds reappear the character is unaltered —

		Feet.
2nd Till -	Boulder Clay, very chalky.	
"Forest-bed" (estuarine).	Laminated sands and clays - -	6
	Laminated blue clay and sand, with a few pebbles and *Mytilus* - -	3
Beach.		

About 80 yards further it changes to :—

		Feet.
2nd Till -	Boulder Clay, very chalky	
?	Peaty matter, wood, and a little sand	$\frac{1}{2}$ to $1\frac{1}{2}$
?	Fine false-bedded sand and a little grey loam	6 to 5
"Forest-bed" (estuarine).	Clay-pebbles and lignite, alternating with false-bedded sand - - -	2
	Pan full of pebbles of quartzite, &c. -	
Beach		

---

* Geol. Mag , Decade II., vol. vii., p 424 , and Memoir on "The Vertebrata of the Forest Bed, p 17.

The pan here shows false-bedding with a northerly dip, and is composed of nearly unworn flints, flint quartz, quartzite, clay, and clay-ironstone pebbles, with rarely cherty sandstone (Neocomian ?), green-coated flints (Eocene), pyrites containing wood and jet; there is also a little drift wood, cakes of peat, and small selenite crystals. The only fossil found was a fragment of elephant's tusk about 5 inches in length.

At 350 yards N.W. of the first road to Bacton village there is :—

		Feet
Soil	- - - - - -	1½ to 2
Valley Gravel	⎧ Gravel and loam contorted together, and squeezing up the laminated clays of the "Forest-bed" - - -	7
"Forest-bed" (estuarine).	⎧ Laminated clay and sand, with a bed of wood at the base - - -	8
	Clay-pebbles and gravel, with large unworn flints, quartzite pebbles, &c -	3
	Laminated clay, clay-pebbles, and lignite - - - -	3
Beach		

Between this point and the road the beds are very sandy and gravelly The sand is principally quartz, and not flint, and the composition of the gravel is :—

Unworn and sub-angular flints	-	-	-	82
Quartzite pebbles (often large)	-	-	-	73
Flint pebbles	-	-	-	56
Quartz	- - - -	-	-	32
Hard sandstone (Neocomian ?)	-	-	-	6
Chert	- - -	-	-	2
Black grit	- -	-	-	2

In the neighbourhood of Bacton the Forest-bed shows extremely rapid changes in lithological character; and as the upper part rises 10 or 15 feet above the level of the beach, it can easily be examined, and may be described generally as a mass of false-bedded gravel and sand with lenticular beds of laminated clay, clay-pebbles, or lignite A few sections taken here and there will be sufficient to show the ordinary character.

At 150 yards S.E. of the road there is —

		Feet.
Soil	- - - - -	1½
1st Till	- - Hard stony loam - - -	3½
"Forest-bed" (estuarine).	⎧ Sand - - - -	6
	Pebble-gravel - - -	2½
	Laminated clay, disturbed, under-cut, and mixed with gravel -	3
	Laminated carbonaceous blue clay	
Beach.		

A few yards to the N W a mass of laminated clay comes on immediately under the Till. Within 60 yards to the S.E. three tree-stumps were seen on different horizons, and at a lower level a cake of *Pholas* bored peat was found

At 300 yards S E. of the road the section is —

		Feet
Soil	- - - -	2
1st Till	- - Stony loam - - -	4
"Forest-bed" (estuarine)	⎧ Gravelly sand and loam -	2½
	Stiff blue clay - - -	½
	Sand, gravel, and a little loam -	4
	False-bedded white sand, rather carbonaceous -	3½
	Laminated sand and clay - -	1
Beach.		

About 200 yards further it changes to —

		Feet.
Soil	- - - - - - -	2½
1st Till	- - Stony loam - - - -	6
P	{ Loam and blue clay, with a little sand and	
	gravel, contorted together - -	3
	Laminated clay and sand - - -	5
	Loamy sandy gravel, with *Mytilus edulis,*	
" Forest-bed "	*Lattorina littorea* - - -	½
(estuarine).	Gravel - - - -	1
	Laminated sand and blue loam - -	1
	P (hidden by beach) - -	5
	Laminated blue carbonaceous clay -	2

Close to the old site of the Coast Guard Station there is .—

		Feet
Soil	- - - - - - -	2
1st Till	- - Stony loam - - - -	4
Upper Fresh-water	{ Loamy sand - - - -	2
Bed	Sandy loam, bedding obscure -	
	Laminated sand and clay - -	1
" Forest-bed "	{ Laminated clay, with a few thin seams of	
(estuarine).	gravel and sand, full of *Mytilus edulis*	
	and *Lattorina littorea* - -	5½

These beds with marine shells were first described by Mr Green in 1842,[*] but at that time the exposures appear to have been much more fossiliferous than at present, the cliff has probably now been cut fully 100 yards further back, and the details of the section have quite altered   Mr Green mentions the following species as occurring here —

Lattorina littorea
Mytilus antiquorum. (=M. edulis, *Linn*)
Scalaria grœnlandica.
————— *minuta.*
Astarte plana (=*A borealis,* Chemn)
Fusus striatus (=*Trophon antiquus,* Mull)
——— *contrarius* (——— ———, reversed var)
Cardium, fragments.
Turbinolia.

" With these shells were vertebræ of fish . . scales of fish, bones and teeth of fish, and bones, teeth, and jaws of rodentia . .   In this deposit also occur the bones of larger mammalia, probably a species of deer, with the remains of birds "

" This bed of fossils seems to extend to some distance inland, for I have been informed that, when excavating a well near Bacton Green, about 300 yards from the beach, this same crag was met with."

To the above list Prof Prestwich adds *Lattorina rudis* and *Purpura lapillus* [†]

The next section of importance is seen near the Coast Guard Station, Bacton. At this point, and for several hundred yards on each side, the Fresh-water Beds again appear immediately under the Till .—

		Feet.
Soil	- - - - - - -	2
Intermediate Beds.	Laminated marl - -	1
1st Till	- - Stony Boulder Clay, with little chalk -	7
Upper Fresh-water	{ Mixed clay and sand, with fresh-water	
Bed.	shells . *Succinea putris, Bythinia tenta-*	
	culata, Cyclas cornea - -	2½
	Sand and loam - - -	2½
" Forest-bed "	{ Gravel, with thin clay seams -	3
(estuarine).	Laminated blue clay - -	5
	P (beach) - -	8
	Laminated greenish clay - -	1

---

[*] Geology of Bacton, p. 56.
[†] Quart. Journ. Geol. Soc., vol. **xxvii.**, p. 465.

Mr Green, who first discovered this Fresh-water deposit, adds :—

Limnæa palustris.	*Paludina.*
Bulimus (=*Zua* ?).	
Planorbis vortex.	*Cypris*
Valvata.	Fir cones

Near the next road to the shore the cliff becomes very low, and for a considerable distance it is nearly always hidden by blown sand, but nothing of importance was seen when the talus had been swept away by a storm. About 90 yards N W of Walcot Gap there is :—

		Feet
Blown Sand	- - - - -	6
Soil -	- - - - -	3
"Forest-bed" (estuarine)	⎧ Sand and a little gravel -	4
	⎨ ? (hidden by beach) -	8½
	⎩ Coarse green and ferruginous loamy sand and clay-pebbles - - -	1

At ¼ m S E of Walcot Gap, Fresh-water beds reappear, apparently forming the N.W. portion of the deposit, which extends to beyond Ostend Gap, filling an eroded hollow in the lower beds. Near the commencement the section is —

		Feet
Blown Sand	- - - - -	2
Soil	- - - - -	3½
1st Till	- Hard stony loam - - -	8
Upper Fresh-water Beds	⎧ Hard loam mixed with sand and a little gravel - - - -	2
	⎨ Hard-bedded blue clay, full of *Cyclas cornea* - - -	2
?	⎩ ? (hidden) - -	6
"Forest-bed" (estuarine)	⎧ Clay-pebbles, coarse red sand, carbonaceous clay, small gravel, and a little lignite and peat - - - -	1

The base of the Boulder Clay being here very low, and the beach high, no Pre-glacial beds can be seen, except after severe gales; in fact, one may often walk from Bacton to Eccles without being able to find a trace of any beds older than the Till

At Ostend* the Fresh-water Bed appears at the foot of the beach, where it was discovered by Mr. Green in 1841, but the section is now so altered that the very fossiliferous deposit he found is either entirely swept away or constantly hidden by the beach. There is now to be seen hard thick-bedded fresh-water loam, which appears to lie in alternating beds of laminated clay and lignite. In this could be found no mammalian remains, but teeth and scales of fish, *Spongilla fluviatilis*, and fruit or seeds of *Trapa natans, Ceratophyllum demersum, Hippuris vulgaris, Pinus sylves'ris, Pinus abies*, &c As Mr Green obtained a very important series of fossils from this place, it will be as well to quote his account, in case the bed should again be exposed

The bed "is composed of bluish mud, with occasional patches of brown clay, and extends several hundred yards along the beach" . . "I have obtained from this place the following shells :—

Cyclas cornea.
—— pusilla (*Pisidium*, sp)
Succinea intermedia (*S putris*).
Paludina.
Valvata.
Planorbis vortex.
Cypris.
Unio or Anodon
Ancylus lacustris.

---

* Pronounced Oastend (from oast = a kiln ?).

" Under this bed a greenish kind of mud occurs intermixed with sand, containing various mammalian and other remains   The following may be particularly named —

Elephas primogenus,—teeth and jaws.

Deer,—bones and horns of two kinds

Rodenta,—bones, jaws, and teeth of four species (probably arvicola, shrew, hedgehog,* and mole)

Sauria,—bones and jaws.

" I also here met with the remains of birds, fish, seed vessels, and fragments of wood "†

The bed of bluish mud is still to be seen, but no mollusca, except opercula of *Bythinia*, could be found   The "green mud intermixed with sand" probably includes portions of both the Fresh-water and Estuarine divisions   Mr Green figures, as having been found with the bones in their natural position, a skeleton of deer, and another of "saurian;" but the latter is composed of portions of two moles, and the former appears to be made up of several animals

This fresh-water deposit can be traced nearly continuously for a quarter of a mile S E of Ostend, gradually rising and allowing the underlying beds to be seen. Where good exposures can be examined, roots penetrate the weathered surface of the estuarine beds   Nearly a quarter of a mile from the Gap the section is :—

		Feet.
1st Till (base below high-water)		8
? (hidden)		
"Forest-bed" (estuarine)	Carbonaceous soil with a little lignite -	½
	Greenish unstratified loam, with small roots, bedding obscure -	1
	Passing into—	
	Laminated carbonaceous silt and green clay, with a little lignite, and calcareous concretions -	2
	Green clay, drift wood, and fir cones to low water -	1

South-east of Bacton the middle division of the "Forest-bed" appears to have become entirely fluviatile, and consequently it is difficult to separate it from the Upper Fresh-water Bed

About 100 yards S.E. of the last section, at half-tide, there is seen —

Lignite, with seeds of yew, and abundance of fir cones, resting on
Loam with small roots.

For about 100 yards further there is a very important section, only uncovered after exceptionally severe N.W. gales   The base of the Boulder Clay is several feet below high-water mark, and immediately under it we have greenish sandy clay, in places laminated in the upper part, alternating with beds of lignite full of fir cones and seeds. At one spot several trunks of fir lie close together and in the same direction, four of them being upwards of nine feet in length with neither end visible ; a few yards away there are two more trunks crossing one another.   Unfortunately there was so much water that it was impossible to ascertain whether these trunks were overthrown in place or formed a pine raft ;—they rest on a carbonaceous sandy and stony clay, probably a continuation of the soil already mentioned. The trunks are of moderate size, not exceeding a foot in diameter, and are compressed to about two or three inches ; the bark does not appear to be exceptionally thick.   Cones of Scotch and spruce fir are very abundant, one of the latter having been gnawed by a squirrel   Other seeds are common, including yew, sloe, and probably *Pyrus*

Just S. of the highest part of the cliff at Happisburgh the base of the Till again rises a few feet above the beach, and due N of the church another patch of the Fresh-water Bed is seen, consisting of lignite with many fir cones

---

* Afterwards described by Professor Owen as *Palæospalax magnus* (= *Myogale moschata*, Linn).

† *Op. cit.*, pp. 58, 59.

and seeds, resting on hard weathered green stony loam penetrated by roots. At this place there was imbedded the stump of a small tree with the roots penetrating the soil,—the only instance of a tree in its natural position that has been observed   The soil corresponds exactly in character with recent soils of the same neighbourhood, except that it is harder   The stones in it are all weathered; the bedding is obliterated, and so are all calcareous fossils, with the exception of a single much-decayed fragment of mammalian bone   Blue concretions of phosphate of iron occur here and at Ostend   The greatest thickness of the Fresh-water Bed in this patch does not exceed three feet, and it soon either thins out or entirely changes; for a few yards further, where the base of the Till has risen four or five feet, there is —

Till			Feet.
"Forest-bed"	Sand with a little clay and lignite	-	- 2 to 4
(estuarine)	Green laminated clay	- -	- 3
Beach.			

and from this point to Happisburgh Gangway we have the usual continual changes and false-bedding of the middle division of the "Forest-bed."

It is probable that from the two fresh-water deposits just described, the Rev. S W King obtained most of the plants determined by Professor Heer,* but as the Post-glacial alluvium S E of Happisburgh has till now been confounded with the "Forest-bed," it has been thought safer (in the absence of information as to the exact localities where the specimens were found) to omit from the lists one or two species for which we have no corroborative evidence   For the same reason, the reputed occurrence of the roe deer (*Cervus capreolus*), only known in the King Collection (in Mus , Jermyn Street), and from a second specimen of doubtful origin, is believed to be founded on Post-glacial specimens.

For 200 yards S E of the Gangway, the "Forest-bed" is traceable at the base of the cliff, and consists of laminated clay, sand, and clay-pebbles, full of drifted wood and tree-stumps   About 350 yards further, it is seen at the foot of the beach, and can be followed to within a quarter of a mile of the Low Lighthouse; but the character is peculiar, and it is uncertain to which division the exposure belongs.   It consists of carbonaceous silt, full of small pieces of wood, with occasional fir cones, passing laterally into hard blue-black carbonaceous clay with earthy ferruginous concretions containing scattered twigs

This is the last exposure of the "Forest-bed" visible north of Yarmouth , for a few yards further the base of the Boulder Clay sinks below low-water mark.   The "Forest-bed" mentioned by several authors as occurring at Eccles and Palling is undoubtedly a recent deposit, for it can be seen to rest on Boulder clay.

Though so little of the "Forest-bed" is above the sea level south of Happisburgh, there is evidently a considerable thickness below; for after the storm of January 30th, 1877, large slabs of fresh-water clay-ironstone, and pan were thrown up on the beach at Happisburgh and Eccles   These slabs are full of impressions of leaves of oak, elm, beech, birch, and willow; they contain seeds of the bog-bean and casts of *Unio pictorum, Paludina*, and a species of fish, probably the roach.   Fragments of this fossiliferous ironstone, which appears to represent the Lower Fresh-water Bed, occur at many places in the estuarine gravels of the "Forest-bed."

As, from the size and angularity of the slabs, the ironstone was evidently in place under the sea at Happisburgh, it was dragged for from a boat   At half a mile N.N E. of the Low Lighthouse we found a rocky bottom at 10 fathoms, and as the boat drifted further out the lead swung off what appeared to be a submarine cliff, and dropped into 15½ fathoms, the arming showing sand with black specks in this hollow.   We then tried to detach slabs of the rock with grappling irons, but after twice getting them fixed we had to abandon the attempt.   The teeth of the irons were bent by the strain, and had evidently played against a fine-grained tough ferruginous rock like the slabs found on the beach.   Six weeks later another attempt was made to examine this bed, but it was found that where previously there had been 10 or 15 fathoms, there was now only at most 6½   The presence of sandbanks near the shore causes

---

* *See* Lyell's " Antiquity of Man," 4th ed , p 256

the tide to flow in regular channels which, during gales, are scoured to a great depth, only to be again filled up. In this way submarine denudation proceeds at depths considerably greater than it is likely to do in the open sea.

There is no evidence of the full thickness of the "Forest-bed" at Happisburgh, but it extends from high-water to at least 10 fathoms below low-water (including the ironstone), which would make it over 70 feet From the occurrence of the submarine cliff mentioned above, it is clear that the ironstone rests not on chalk but on soft beds, which extend to a least 15½ fathoms These beds may be Eocene, but if belonging to the Crag, they raise the total thickness of the Pliocene Beds at this point to over 100 feet

About three-quarters of a mile from the shore opposite Happisburgh large quantities of bones and teeth of elephant, &c have been obtained by the oyster dredgers. The oysters are now all destroyed, and dredging is stopped, but fossils were already getting scarce. The Rev J Layton, who was living in the neighbourhood when the oyster-bank was discovered, made a large collection of the fossil bones * Mr Samuel Woodward, writing in 1833, observes that "The oyster-bed off Hashro' was discovered in the year 1820, and during the first 12 months many hundred specimens of the molar teeth of the elephant were destroyed by the fishermen, who amused themselves by breaking them, their wonder being excited by the grinders separating into laminæ"† The "Forest-bed" specimens dredged from the Happisburgh oyster-ground must not be confounded with the Pleistocene mammalia obtained abundantly by trawlers on the Dogger Bank As the Yarmouth trawlers pass Happisburgh on the way to the Bank, and also trawl in that neighbourhood, some of the dredged fossils in collections have probably been put down to the wrong locality ‡

Age of the "Forest-bed."

From the details already given it is clear that the Cromer Forest-bed lies above the Weybourn Crag, but from the correspondence of the fossils, as far as they are comparable, the two deposits appear to be closely allied. In the Estuarine division of the "Forest-bed" we find numerous characteristic Crag species, and the marine mollusca agree so exactly with those of the Weybourn Crag that evidently there was not a sufficient lapse of time between them to allow of any noticeable change in the fauna. Unfortunately too few land and fresh-water shells are known from the older Crags, and too few marine shells from the "Forest-bed," to admit of a numerical comparison; but no marine forms are yet known to occur in the "Forest-bed" that have not been found in the Weybourn Crag. Of the mammals several species are common to the "Forest-bed" and Norwich Crag, but these are more fully referred to in Chap. VIII, and in Mr. Newton's Memoir.

The "Forest-bed" bones are generally broken, but not rolled; and the only instance in which several have been found in their natural position is a collection of the foot-bones of an elephant, now in the Norwich Museum. It is, therefore, possible that some of the mammalian remains in the estuarine beds may have been washed out of the destroyed Lower Fresh-water Bed, but there is not a trace of any derivative fossil from Pliocene beds older than the Weybourn Crag. From the abundance of uninjured

* Layton, "Account of the Fossil Remains in the Neighbourhood of Hasborough," Edin. Journ of Sci, vol. vi , p. 199, 1827.
† S. Woodward, Geology of Norfolk, p 23.
‡ See papers by W. Davies, Geol. Mag., vol v., pp. 97, 443.

delicate land and fresh-water shells in the estuarine clay at East Runton, there can be no doubt that they are contemporaneous with the deposit, while it is probable that in the bones associated with them, we have the corresponding vertebrate fauna of the period. The scattering of the skeletons and breaking of the bones, may be sufficiently accounted for by the evidence of strong currents in the false-bedded masses of clay-pebbles and gravel in which the mammalia occur.

The mammals of the Upper Fresh-water Bed evidently belong to the deposit; and it is noticeable that several Pliocene forms are found, including *Rhinoceros Etruscus* and *Arvicola intermedius*; but there is at present no trace of the elephant, though in the underlying beds its teeth are amongst the most common fossils. The general character of the fauna and flora will be again alluded to in the chapter on Climate.

CHAPTER VI.—LEDA-MYALIS BED.

General Description.

The marine deposit overlying the "Forest-bed" at West Runton has been known for many years, but its exact relation to the Crag and to the Glacial Beds is still an open question The name "*Leda-myalis* Clay" was first used as a local term for this particular section by Prof. W. King in 1863[*], and has since been adopted by me, wherever seen, for the horizon between the Upper Fresh-water Bed of the Forest Bed Series and the Arctic Fresh-water Bed. At present very little is known about its fauna, for the bed is very sparingly fossiliferous ; but the fossils that do occur are generally found in colonies in the position of life. It is this bed that has often, though erroneously, been correlated with the Bure Valley Beds, and has led some to place the Norwich Crag over the "Forest-bed."

The general character of the *Leda-myalis* Bed is a fine false-bedded loamy sand with grains of Chalk, thin seams of loam or clay, and a little gravel. The whole deposit, which nowhere exceeds 20 feet in thickness, is much more constant in lithological character than any of the associated beds.

Details.

In the immediate neighbourhood of Weybourn no trace of this horizon has yet been found, and the first fossiliferous section occurs about 700 yards west of Old Hithe. Here, above the shelly Weybourn Crag, may be seen a bed of stiff blue clay with fragments of oysters, but as there is much talus on each side of the section, and a glacial disturbance also affects the beds, it is impossible to trace the clay more than a few yards.

Though unfossiliferous sections under Skelding Hill have in previous chapters been doubtfully referred to this horizon, no exposure showing either fossils or satisfactory stratigraphical relations, occurs in this direction till we arrive at a point a quarter of a mile west of Lower Sherringham, and nearly under the style at the edge of the cliff. Unfortunately at this point there are constant landslips, and all that can definitely be made out is, that, resting directly on the Weybourn Crag, and lying in a basin eroded through the "Forest-bed," there is a mass of sand and small gravel, the lower 5 feet of which is full of oysters with the valves united. The character of this deposit shows a depth of water of at least 5 fathoms, probably of about 10, while the underlying Weybourn Crag is a shallow-water bed formed at or just below low-water mark. This oyster bed thins out very suddenly both east and west; for though so thick in the centre, and full of fossils, no shells are seen in it 20 yards away in either direction. Owing to the mud streams and constant slips, it has not been possible properly to examine the section, but it is likely to yield an important fauna. The shells are difficult to extract, being saturated

---

[*] Geologist, vol. vi , p. 160. When I first used the name (Geol Mag , Decade II., vol iv , p. 304,) I was unaware that it had been previously given.—C R.

with water and very tender, but when dried they harden, and will bear handling. The species obtained were :—

Littorina littorea, Linn.	*Mytilus edulis*, Linn.
Natica, sp.	× *Ostrea edulis*, Linn.
Purpura lapillus, Linn.	*Tellina Balthica*, Linn.
Cardium edule, Linn	——— *obliqua*, Sow.
× *Cyprina Islandica*, Linn. (young only).	*Balanus*, sp.

Those marked × had the valves united   A few yards both to the right and to the left the clays of the " Forest-bed " come on between the Weybourn Crag and the *Leda-myalis* Bed.

The next fossiliferous exposure is at Beeston, where gravelly sand with occasional scattered marine shells, can be seen in vertical section definitely between the Upper and the Arctic Fresh-water Beds (see folding plate), all the beds being fossiliferous. The only shells that could be found here were *Tellina Balthica* and *Cyprina Islandica*

From Beeston to Cromer the bed appears to be continuous, except where cut out by the Boulder Clay, but the only fossiliferous sections are at West Runton, and between that place and Wood Hill   At West Runton on each side of the Gap is found the bed with *Mya truncata*, so often alluded to by different authors, and first mentioned by Trimmer in 1845.* The section on the east side of the Gap is :—

		Feet.
Soil -	- - - - - -	1
Contorted Drift -	- Contorted stony loam, marl, and sand -	30
Leda-myalis Bed	⎰ Fine false-bedded sand with thin seams ⎱ of loam, and gravelly base full of ⎰ shells - - -	15
Upper Fresh-water Bed	Fresh-water sand and peaty loam -	1
" Forest Bed " (estuarine).	⎰ Weathered loam with roots and frag- ⎱ ments of marine shells (Rootlet Bed)	?

The following species of mollusca were found in the *Leda-myalis* Bed, but here, as at Sheringham, the exposure has been very obscure for several years —

Buccinum undatum, Linn.	*Cardium edule*, Linn
Littorina littorea, Linn.	*Cyprina Islandica*, Linn
——— *rudis*, Maton.	× *Leda myalis*, Couth.
Purpura lapillus, Linn.	× *Mya truncata*, Linn.
Trophon antiquus, Linn	*Mytilus edulis*, Linn.
——— ——— reversed var	*Ostrea edulis*, Linn
Natica catena ? Da Costa.	*Tellina Balthica*, Linn
× *Astarte borealis*, Chem.	

The shells marked × were found in the position of life with the valves united. Trimmer also mentions *Tellina obliqua*, *Mya arenaria*, and *Natica helicoides* from this spot. Besides these marine species, the bed contains a good many fresh-water forms, evidently washed out of the sands two or three yards away.

Under Wood Hill a few scattered shells have also been found, including a single valve of *Tellina obliqua*, though the bed is generally from 10 to 15 feet thick, fossils are very rare and confined to the base.

To the south-east of Wood Hill, the *Leda-myalis* Bed can be traced as far as Cromer with the same lithological character, but no fossils have yet been found in it. During some alterations to the cellar of a house on Cromer sea-wall the sands were well shown, though neither the top nor bottom was exposed. Between Cromer and Kirby Hill, unfossiliferous sections can be seen whenever the cliff is free from talus ; but the bed is becoming attenuated, and towards Beck Hithe it appears to thin out altogether against the Boulder Clay.

---

* "On the Cliffs of the Northern Drift on the Coast of Norfolk, between Weybourne and Happisburgh."—Quart. Journ. Geol. Soc., vol. 1, p 218. Proc Geol. Soc, vol. iv., p. 435.

Though the horizon may be represented by unfossiliferous beds in several places, it has not been again recognized till we reach Mundesley At that place the mass of clay-pebbles, with *Littorina* and *Mytilus* cutting through the Upper Fresh-water Bed, has, from its stratigraphical position, been referred to the *Leda-myalis* Bed   It is clear that this littoral deposit can scarcely be the exact equivalent of the deeper water sands of Sherringham and West Runton , but a submergence of about 50 feet would not in any probability occur suddenly, though the marine and fresh-water beds of West Runton are in contact, without intervening estuarine beds   The Mundesley clay may, therefore, represent a slightly earlier or later stage of the same deposit, intermediate between the period of greatest submergence and the earlier or later period of elevation.

The marine bed at Mundesley probably extends for some distance in either direction, but when the underlying *Unio* Bed dies out, it is nearly impossible to separate the *Leda-myalis* Bed from the very similar estuarine clays of the "Forest-bed " The horizon has not yet been recognized further south-east or inland.

Relation to the Crag.

From its unconformity with the under- and over-lying Fresh-water Beds, and the small fauna yet obtained, it is impossible at present to say definitely whether the *Leda-myalis* Bed is more allied to the Crag or to the Glacial Deposits. As far as known, the shells correspond with those of the Crag, including two well-known forms,—the reversed *Trophon antiquus* and *Tellina obliqua ;* not one of the 19 species yet collected being a new arrival. Therefore, as the most marked line of distinction is where the definite Glacial Deposits come on above, till further evidence is obtained the bed will be included in the Newer Pliocene.

CHAPTER VII.—INLAND SECTIONS OF THE PLIOCENE BEDS.

Owing to isolation and the absence of fossils, it is in many cases difficult to say to which division of the Pliocene Beds the inland sections in the district here described may belong. The whole of the beds are therefore taken together, attention being drawn to the probable age of the different exposures, where it can be inferred with safety.

Details

West of Weybourn the only sections known are at Letheringsett, in Quarter-Sheet 68 S W. From the position and lithological character of the beds there is little doubt that they represent the beach deposit of the Weybourn Crag sea. No fossils were found, but the absence of shells is a common character in shingle beaches.* The largest pit, marked *Kiln* on the map, is half a mile north-west of Letheringsett; it shows —

			Feet.
Soil			
Contorted Drift	{	Boulder Clay, very chalky	5
		Streaky brick-earth and marl	0 to 1
Weybourn Crag	{	Shingle, almost entirely flint	3
		Loamy sand and large worn flints	1
Chalk, probably 20 feet above the level of the stream.			

Another part of the same pit shows 3 or 4 feet of alternating laminated clay and lines of pebbles. A pit by the R. of Rock Hill, now disused and much obscured, shows similar though more sandy beds resting on the Chalk, which at that point is nearly 50 feet above high-water mark.

Bacton being the only place where Pre-glacial Beds appear at the surface near the coast, and can be followed inland to the Ant and Bure Valleys, the description will be commenced at that place, and the sections traced southward to Dilham, and thence in a westerly direction to Aylsham.

Bacton and the Ant Valley

The beds immediately under the Boulder Clay at Bacton are generally the quartzite-gravels, quartzose sands, and laminated loams of the "Forest-bed," and it is probably to this division of the Newer Pliocene that all the sections between Bacton and Honing belong.

The soil in the valley between Bacton and Ridlington shows an abundance of quartz and quartzite pebbles. In a pit at the east corner of Ridlington Common the following section is seen :—

			Feet.
Soil	Stony loam		2
"Forest-bed"	{ Laminated sandy loam		2
	Pebbly and sandy quartzose gravel		3

Another pit, 170 yards further west, shows coarse sand and quartzose gravel.

At Crostwight the exposure in the valley widens to about a mile, and the Pliocene Beds rise to a considerable height. A pit on the highest part of Crostwight Heath shows in one place angular gravel, probably Post-glacial, resting on quartzite gravel; at another point at the same height the pebble-

---

* Mr. Woodward has recognized similar representatives of the Pliocene Beds at Broom Green and Guist, some distance south-west of Letheringsett.

gravel is at the surface. On Fox Common fine quartzose sand is seen, but there is no clear section. A pit half a mile south of Crostwight Hall shows 10 feet of sand and gravel made up of worn and unworn flints, quartzite pebbles, &c with box stones. Similar beds apparently continue to the water-level and to the top of the hill.

At Honing, light-coloured sand with quartzite pebbles has been dug at Furze Close; and on the Common east of Newbridge there are several pits in coarse sand, or false-bedded sandy gravel, composed of quartz pebbles, sub-angular flints, &c. The fossiliferous Weybourn Crag found in the railway cutting at Black Mill has been already mentioned in Chapter IV. On the Common north of Dee Bridge light-coloured pebbly sand with much quartz is seen about 8 feet above the Alluvium. A pit north of the Dairy House Farm shows strongly false-bedded orange sandy gravel with ironstone nodules.

"North-east of Bengate, Worstead, a pit showed 10 feet of greenish-grey sand and pebbly gravel; and by the Almshouses, further north, pebbly gravel and grey laminated clay were to be seen beneath a peaty deposit (Alluvium)"*

At Brumstead, a well half a mile west of the church, and close to the Alluvium, showed :—

	Feet.
Soil and loam - - - - - - -	2½
Fine whitish sand (2 feet of water) - - - -	5

At Stalham, a well at the Board School showed ·—

		Feet.
Glacial -	Brick-earth - - - -	9 or 10
? -	Sand, clay, and gravel -	10
"Forest Bed" ?	Clean sand - -	3

The bottom of this well is probably 8 feet below the water-level in the canal.

Two brick-yards west of Smallburgh Poorhouse appear to be in weathered pre-glacial laminated loams, but the sections are not good enough to decide the question.

In a pit at Sloley Upper Street there is 13 feet of false-bedded rather loamy sand, with a little quartz-gravel, thin clays, and a lenticular mass of clay-pebbles. About 40 per cent of the stones are foreign. The pit has been dug to the water-level.

"A shed-horn of a species of deer was found in sinking a well at Sloley; the specimen is now in the Gunn Collection, Norwich Museum."†

Bure Valley.

The following notes are by Mr Woodward ·—

In the Bure Valley the beds comprise pebbly gravel and sand, with here and there "jambs" of laminated clay and occasional patches of shells. In thickness they probably do not exceed 30 feet. The sections in the lower part of the valley (in Quarter-Sheet 66 N E) are described in the Memoir on the Geology of the Country around Norwich, where also the relations of the beds to other portions of the Norwich Crag Series are discussed.

In the area now under consideration the beds that underlie the Lower Glacial Brickearth (Contorted Drift) have been divided thus —

Norwich ⎰ Pebbly sands and pebble beds. [Bure Valley Beds.]
Crag ⎱ Laminated Clay. [Chillesford Clay.]
Series. Sand and pebbly gravel. [Chillesford Crag]

Messrs Wood and Harmer have made these subdivisions in the beds at Burgh Kiln, near Aylsham,‡ but they are far from persistent anywhere in the district, and the beds which these geologists separate from the Norwich Crag, and term "Bure Valley Beds" (Lower Glacial Sands of Wood and Harmer) cannot, in my opinion, be so distinguished. The occurrence in them of *Tellina Balthica*, regarded by Messrs. Wood and Harmer as a test for Glacial

---

* From Mr Woodward's Notes   † Ibid
‡ *See* their Map of the Crag District (Palæontograph Soc.), Section No. IX

and Post-glacial beds, has been shown to have no weight, from its abundance at the base of the " Pre-glacial Forest-bed Series "* (See also Mr. Reid's remarks, pp 9, 17)

Laminated clay too occurs at various horizons in the series, hence lithological characters cannot be depended on for the identification of local and minute divisions. Looked at in a large way, the beds maintain a general character of false-bedded sand and pebbly gravel, often streaked with laminated clay, which renders the determination of the series easy at a glance In the Bure Valley, below Buxton and Lammas, the upper portions of the series, consisting generally of pebbly sands and pebble beds, contain shell-patches with *Tellina Balthica*, and although these beds have not proved to be fossiliferous in the area now under consideration, there can be little doubt that, like the so-called typical " Bure Valley Beds," they contain no representatives of a higher horizon than the Weybourn Crag.

Tuttington —By the wood, west of Blackwater Beck, a gravel-pit showed 6 feet of coarse flint-gravel and sand, with quartzite, &c.

At Stow Heath, Felmingham, the gravel rests on brickearth, possibly one of the laminated clays in the Crag Series.

Oxnead.—Several pits in this parish show the pebbly gravel resting on the Chalk, with here and there traces of the Contorted Drift above. The Crag Series is in places disturbed, partly perhaps by subsidence of the beds, caused by " pipes " in the Chalk. About 20 feet of false-bedded sand and gravel was to be seen in this neighbourhood; and in one pit about 4 feet of laminated clay was seen resting on false-bedded sand, and capped by about 9 feet of pebbly sand.

Brampton —West of Oxnead Bridge a pit showed 8 feet of pebbly sand, with seams of laminated clay, resting on an irregular " piped " surface of Chalk

East of Field Barn a pit showed about 15 feet of pebbly gravel resting on the Chalk South-east of Hudson's Bay the Chalk is capped by a bed of unworn and rounded flints, called the Stone-bed, and in one part of the pit there is a bed of brown brickearth, either a clay bed in the Crag Series or a mass of Contorted Drift

West of Brampton Hall a pit showed 5 feet of brown brickearth, resting on the same thickness of sand and pebbly gravel.

Marsham —R. C. Taylor first observed the Crag in this neighbourhood. He has remarked that " At Marsham, and in the adjacent vales, it is again discoverable, accompanied with many bones of animals, large vertebræ, and horns of deer."[†]

Since then, a section opened in gravelly beds at this locality displayed a layer of iron-pan, from which Mr T. G Bayfield obtained casts of *Mytilus, Cardium*, and *Donax* [‡]

Burgh-next-Aylsham.—South-east of Burgh Hall the following section was exposed :—

Norwich Crag Series.	Pebbly sand and gravel, - 12 to 15 feet.	
	Laminated clay and sand - } 1 foot.	
	Stone bed - - - }	
	Chalk.	

At Burgh Kiln the best section in the area is to be seen, though unfortunately the pit is not now worked (1879). It is as follows :—

Norwich Crag Series.	Sand and gravel - - - 6 feet.	
	Laminated clay with gravelly and } 6 or 7 feet.	
	sandy seams - - - }	
	Gravel and sand, with clay-pebbles } 1 foot to 1 foot 6 ins.	
	Stone bed - - - }	
	Chalk with flints - - - 6 to 8 feet shown.	

---

* *See* Proc Norwich Geol. Soc, vol. i., pp 50, 141.
† Geology of East Norfolk, p 17.
‡ Norfolk News, Sept. 9, 1871.

FIG 6

Section at Burgh, near Aylsham.

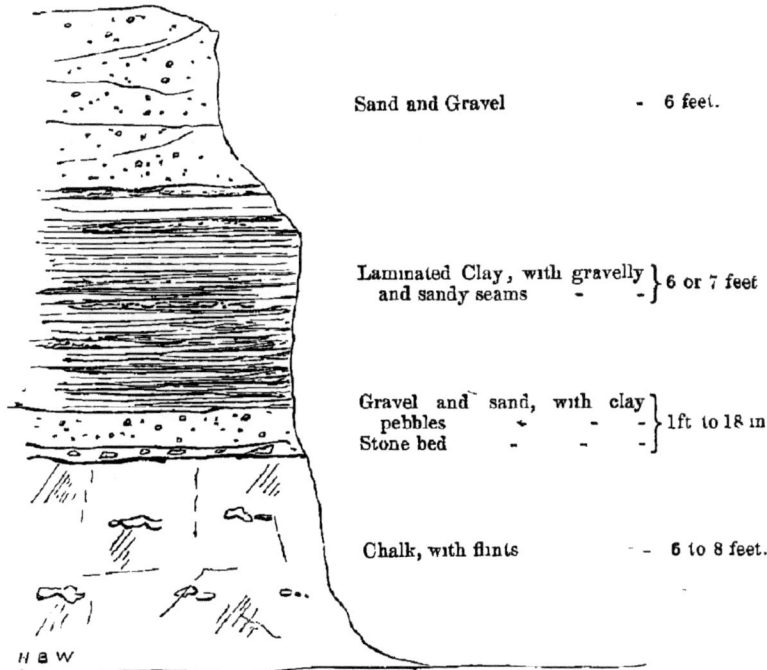

Sand and Gravel - 6 feet.

Laminated Clay, with gravelly } 6 or 7 feet
and sandy seams - -

Gravel and sand, with clay }
   pebbles - - - } 1ft to 18 in
Stone bed - - -

Chalk, with flints - - 6 to 8 feet.

H B W

Shells of the Norwich Crag were noticed here by Mr Gunn and Professor Prestwich,* and I obtained a few fragmentary specimens.

The following list includes all the species recorded from this locality :—

†Littorina littorea, *Linn*
 Scalaria Grœnlandica, *Chemn*
 Trophon antiquus, *Linn*, var. striatum
  „ „ „ var contrarium.
 Turritella terebra, *Linn*
†Astarte borealis, *Chemn.*
† „ compressa, *Mont.*
†Cardium edule, *Linn*
†Cyprina Islandica, *Linn*
†Corbula striata, *Walker* and *Boys*
†Cyclas cornea, *Linn*
†Corbicula fluminalis, *Mull.*
†Leda oblongoides, *S. Wood.*
†Lucina borealis, *Linn*
 Mactra ovalis, *J. Sow*
†Mya arenaria, *Linn.*
 Tellina lata, *Gmel*
† „ obliqua, *G Sow*

Aylsham.—The occurrence of the Crag at this locality was noticed by R. C. Taylor   He observed that " at Aylsham, on sinking a well in 1824, at " the depth of 60 feet, a bed 4 feet thick of crag shells was met with. They

---

* Quart Journ. Geol. Soc., vol. xxvii , pp. 459, 468.
† On the authority of Mr. F. W. Harmer.

" consisted of the genera *Murex* [=*Trophon antiquus?*], *Turbo* [=*Littorina*
" *littorea?*], *Natica, Mactra, Venus* [=*Astarte* or *Lucina*], and *Tellina.*"*

While resident at Aylsham a well was sunk for the cottage at the siding by
the lane between Mucklands and The Greens, and the following beds were
proved —

Glacial -	Loam	-	-	-	- 4 feet.
Crag Series - {	Sand and gravel	-	-	-	- } 35 feet.
	Stone-bed at base	-	-	-	
Chalk					

From the Stone-bed I obtained *Astarte borealis, Cyprina Islandica,* and *Mya
arenaria*

At the Lime-kiln west of Hudson's Bay a section showed pebbly gravel and
sand with much ironstone, resting on the Chalk   East of Millgate a pit
showed brown loam (Contorted Drift) resting irregularly on disturbed sands of
the Crag Series   East of Bushey Place sand and pebbly gravel have been
dug , and at one point (above the letters *ce* of Place on the map) Chalk was
reached   Between Aylsham and Spratt's Green, and west of Burgh Church,
several pits have been opened through the Crag Series to the Chalk.

North of Drabblegate 15 feet of pebbly gravel and sand, with much ironstone, was exposed.

North of the Rookery, by Aylsham Wood House, a gravel-pit showed among
the stones, abundant flint-pebbles, quartz, quartzite, and a large block of
Basalt, about 18 inches square.

Ingworth —North of the letters *Ing* of Ingworth Bridge (on the map) gravel
and sand have been dug.

Blickling.—By the river east of the Tanning Office, 20 feet of sand and fine
gravel have been exposed

                                                 H B WOODWARD.

---

* Geology of East Norfolk, p. 17.

CHAPTER VIII.—CLIMATE, PHYSICAL GEOGRAPHY, AND NATURAL HISTORY OF THE NEWER PLIOCENE PERIOD.

Discrepancies in the evidence as to Climate.

In Chapter IV. attention was drawn to the very arctic character of the marine fauna of the Weybourn Crag; a character which, as the late Mr. S. V. Wood so ably showed with regard to the mollusca, became steadily more and more prominent during the whole of the Pliocene Period, from the Coralline Crag upwards, through the gradual dying out of the southern forms, and multiplication of the northern.

But when we turn to the land and fresh-water mollusca the result is diametrically opposite; for of the 61 species now determined, 50 are at present living in Norfolk, 6 are extinct, 2 are continental forms living in the same latitudes as Norfolk (*Hydrobia Steinii*, Sweden and near Berlin, and *Valvata fluviatilis*, Belgium and Germany); and the other 3 are all southern forms not now living in northern Europe (*Hydrobia marginata*, South of France, *Lithoglyphus fuscus*, Danube, and *Corbicula fluminalis*, Nile). There is not a single species having an especially arctic range. It may be objected that the "Forest-bed" fauna and that of the Weybourn Crag are not exactly contemporaneous, and that a change of climate may account for the discrepancy. But, in reply to this, it is enough to point out that the most typically southern of the fresh-water mollusca occur mixed with the arctic marine shells in the Weybourn Crag; and therefore we may fairly conclude that the two faunas lived in adjoining districts during the same period. I have laid special stress on the comparison of the mollusca, for we have long lists of the species inhabiting the land, the sea, and the lakes; nevertheless, as far as known, the same discordance affects other classes. The land mammals have a decidedly southern facies, while the few marine forms seem rather northern.

For evidence of climate, the first place must be given to the plants, as the same slow variation which renders plants so very unsatisfactory in questions of classification, gives them the highest value when we inquire into climate; besides which, plants, as a rule, are more directly affected by changes of temperature than animals. The "Forest-bed" has yielded oak, beech, elm, pine, fir, and yew. It is, therefore, clear that the conditions cannot have differed greatly from those of Norfolk at the present day, or these trees could not have flourished. To explain the apparent contradictions in the evidence as to the climate of the period, it will be necessary to give an outline of the physical geography, and show its bearing on the character of the fauna and flora.

Physical Geography.

In the following outline the rule has been followed of not assuming any tilting or disturbance in beds of so recent a date unless such can be clearly proved. In this instance the facts tell strongly against any tilting, and we are not merely confined to negative evidence; for if the various sections of the Upper Fresh-water Beds are examined, we find that all appear to have been formed in large shallow lakes, like the present Broads of Norfolk, or in sluggish streams connected with them Moreover, where the streams cut into the underlying estuarine beds, they all scoop to about the same depth, probably having eroded their channels till they reached the sea-level. If Mr. Gunn[*] and Mr. Blake[†] are correct in correlating the fresh-water bed at Kessingland with that at West Runton, and there is very little doubt of the accuracy of this view, the bed can be traced for 40 miles at the same level, and showing the same shallow water conditions, so that a tilting of not more than 10 feet would have left clear traces of its influence. The line along which this bed can be followed lies not merely in one direction, for the coast curves, and we can trace the horizon both southward and westward.

Further evidence of the regularity of the rise and fall of the land, is the way in which the different deposits thin out as they are traced westward. In that direction the Chalk rises, and the marine appear to overlap the fresh-water beds against the rising land. The lower portion of the " Forest-bed," which contains most of the large mammals and a very littoral marine fauna, is also overlapped; and the Rev. O. Fisher is probably correct in stating that it only extends a short distance west of Lower Sherringham. This view accounts without difficulty for the absence of the fresh-water and estuarine beds in the neighbourhood of Norwich, for that district was probably above water and covered by fir forests during the formation of the Cromer "Forest-bed."

The most important feature in the physical geography of the period was undoubtedly the large "Forest-bed" river; and if the direction of the flow of this river can be traced, we have the key by which the general structure of the country can be made out. With a view to decide this question, the old river gravels have been carefully examined, for they must have been derived from the land over which the river flowed These gravels commonly contain fully 40 per cent. of stones other than flint; and after a study of the Glacial gravels and Boulder Clay stones, it is at once clear that they must have come from quite different districts. The proportions of the different rocks in 500 stones over an inch in diameter[‡] obtained at Bacton was:—

Little-worn flints - - - -	141
Pebbles of light-coloured fine-grained quartzite	125
„ flint - - -	101
„ vein quartz -	54

---

[*] Quart Journ, Geol. Soc, vol xxxii, p 125
[†] Proc. Norwich Geol Soc, vol. i., p 137.
[‡] If smaller stones had been chosen the proportion of quartz would have been larger. The sand is mainly composed of grains of quartz, not flint.

Pebbles of hard sandstone -   -   -   -   6
   ,,   fine-grained grit   -   -   5
Angular Greensand chert   -   -   4
   ,,   green or bluish slaty rock   -   -   3
Clay-ironstone (very variable)   61

Various other rocks have been obtained in smaller numbers; and in the following list an attempt has been made to show the probable age of the deposits from which the whole have been derived. Jurassic rocks are entirely unrepresented in the river gravels, though Professor Prestwich has recorded their occurrence in the marine Crag at Weybourn and other localities:—

Clay-ironstone with plant remains Cakes of peat, often bored by *Pholas*	Lower Fresh-water Bed.
Jet, amber, and brown coal -	Upper Eocene?
Green-coated flints (common) - Hertfordshire pudding-stone - Silicified wood - - -	Eocene.
Unworn Chalk flints -	Chalk.
Greenish chert - - Cherty sandstone with fossils -	Greensand or Neocomian.
Well-worn pebbles of white or cream-coloured fine-grained quartzite, vein-quartz, black or purple grit, hard coarse sandstone, &c. - - -	Pebble-beds of Cretaceous or Neocomian age?
Angular fragments of a fine-grained green or bluish slaty rock - - - Carboniferous Limestone chert Fragments of *Hyalonema* -	Carboniferous.

In these Pre-glacial beds no igneous rocks occur, with the exception of the single large granite boulder already mentioned (p. 28).* The liver coloured quartzites so characteristic of the Trias and Permian in the Midland Counties are also missing; so that, even if the pebble-bed is of Triassic or Permian age, it cannot have been derived from those rocks in the Midland Counties. In fact, if the river had flowed from the south, west, or north, it must have brought a quite different collection of stones. From the north-east it would probably flow entirely over Chalk. It therefore seems that only from the south-east and east could the stones be derived. The evidence appears to point to a river flowing (tracing it towards its source) first over the Lower Tertiary basin which we know exists east of Yarmouth, then over Chalk, Greensand, and a conglomerate probably of Cretaceous or Neocomian age, which overlapped against the Palæozoic rocks, as beds of that age are known to do near Harwich.† The Palæozoic rocks probably came to the surface as part of the old ridge which

---

* Mr Woodward mentions basalt at Aylsham. *See ante,* p. 53.

† The pebble-beds may, however, be of Eocene age, for similar quartzite pebbles occur in the Bagshot Sands near London.

Mr. Godwin-Austen has described. From them the angular pieces of slate and carboniferous-limestone chert were probably derived.

If this be the correct reading, the river can be no other than the Rhine,—a view held by various writers ever since the Forest-bed was first known.[*] That the river must have been very large is shown by the uniformity of the composition of the gravels at considerable distances apart;—the gravel of a small stream will generally be of local origin. From the size and angularity of many of the stones it is evident that they must have been brought down by river-ice. But this would not necessarily point to a more arctic climate than that of Norfolk at the present day, for during severe winters the ice-floes on the Thames are quite capable of transporting the largest of the boulders. Professor Prestwich remarks[†] that on the table-land above the Meuse, in Belgium, there is a gravel of a very similar character, and suggests that the stones may have been brought to Norfolk by some old river traversing the Ardennes. The plateau gravels above the Meuse are, however, full of veined quartzites of a character unknown in the "Forest-bed." The Forest-bed river appears certainly to have flowed from that direction; but it seems unnecessary to bring the materials such a long distance, though a large stream with floating ice could probably do so.

Acting on the hypothesis just brought forward, a sketch map of the physical geography of the country during the deposition of the "Forest-bed" has been constructed, and by reference to it the peculiar character of the fauna and flora can be explained.

FIG 7.

Sketch Map of the Rhine Estuary during the formation of the Cromer "Forest-bed."

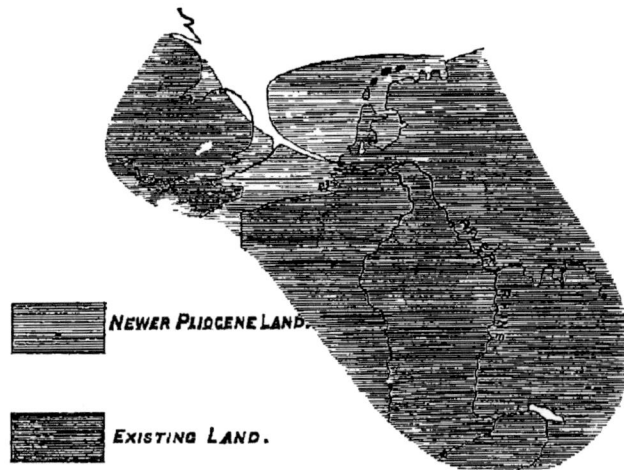

NEWER PLIOCENE LAND.

EXISTING LAND.

Note.—In this map the estuary alone has been reconstructed, no attempt has been made to show the different course of the Rhine and Thames during the deposition of the "Forest-bed."

[*] *See* especially J. Gunn, "The Anglo-Belgian Basin," Geol. Mag., vol iv, p. 158, 1867.
[†] Quart Journ. Geol. Soc., vol xxvii, p 477, 1871.

During the formation of the Coralline Crag there was a considerable submergence of the land, and free connection between the German Ocean and more southern seas. Afterwards the land rose, and the connection with all seas, except the Arctic, was cut off.* A further rise caused the Weybourn Crag to be deposited in a channel scoured through the older beds to the Chalk; this scouring probably taking place without the beds rising above the sea-level. At this period the whole of the southern part of the North Sea appears to have been land, except the large estuary; a change from its present state of less magnitude than at first sight appears, for the sea is extremely shallow. A rise of a few feet caused the Lower Fresh-water Bed to be formed, and then a slight subsidence allowed the peat to be bored by *Pholas*, broken up, and re-deposited in the estuarine division of the "Forest-bed." The relation of the Lower Fresh-water Bed to the "Forest-bed" appears, as already mentioned, to have corresponded with that of the "submerged forests" at the mouths of our present rivers to the estuarine deposits now forming. Another rise of a few feet, and the estuarine "Forest-bed" was turned into land, forming the "Rootlet-bed" of Messrs. Gunn and Blake. This land was flooded, and the shallow lakes, of which the Upper Fresh-water Bed is the evidence, spread over the greater part of the area. As the rise of the tide in estuaries is very variable and sometimes great, it may be to such variations that some of the smaller changes are due

After the deposition of the Fresh-water Beds, a submergence of about 50 feet apparently caused the *Leda-myalis Bed* to overlap most of these shallow water deposits, and in places to cut out the older Crags, and abut against a cliff in the Chalk, for it is full of Chalk grains.

Changes in the Fauna and Flora.

If the marine fauna of the different Crag beds is examined, it is seen that there is a gradual dying out of southern forms and increase of northern, till at last in the Chillesford and Weybourn Crags the mollusca have a thoroughly arctic facies. This change has generally been referred to the greater intensity of the cold; but in working out the physical geography of the Pliocene Period, I have been led to agree with Prof. Prestwich, that it is only to a small extent due to general climatic changes. When the connection with southern seas was cut off, the direct cooling action of northern currents, without any from the south, must have had some effect on the temperature of the water.† But, I believe, the change in the fauna was principally due to the sea being fully exposed to the north, so that there was a constant

---

* *See* Godwin-Austen "On the Kainozoic Formations of Belgium," Quart Journ. Geol Soc, vol. xxii, p 238, 1866, and Prestwich "On the Structure of the Crag Beds," *ibid.*, vol xxvii., p. 475, 1871.

† *See* Prestwich, op cit, p 478.

supply of arctic species brought by every tide or storm, while at the same time the southern forms had to hold their own without any aid from without; and if one was exterminated, it could not be replaced In this way, of two species, a southern and a northern, equally fitted for any station, the northern would have the best chance of surviving, and would probably exterminate the southern. The fact that not a single southern species appears for the first time in the Fluvio-marine, Chillesford, or Weybourn Crags seems clearly to show that they could not migrate into the district, owing to some barrier.

Taking now the land fauna and flora, it is seen that the same elevation which would raise a barrier to the migration of marine species, would form a highway for the land and fresh-water, and we can apply to them the same reasoning as is used above, merely changing *north* for *south.*

Thus in the "Forest-bed" we find a distinctly southern land fauna contemporaneous with an equally marked arctic marine fauna; the plants at the same time showing that the average climate was much the same as that of Norfolk at the present day, though perhaps more continental, *i.e*, hotter in summer and colder in winter.

Analysis of the Fauna and Flora of the Weybourn Crag and "Forest-bed."

In analyzing the fauna and flora of the Weybourn Crag and "Forest-bed" the first thing that strikes one is the marked contrast, long since pointed out by Lyell, between the familiar character of the plants, most of which are now living in Norfolk, and the strange appearance of the mammals. We can point to no part of the world where a similar assemblage is now living, for though South Africa shows an equally varied fauna of large species, the deer of the Forest-bed are there replaced by antelopes. Of 25 large land mammals found in the Forest-bed, only three are now living in Britain, or have been living there within the historic period, and only five still exist in any part of the world. The small inconspicuous mammals, which are also the lowest types, are mostly recent forms; but as the smaller species are practically unknown from beds beneath the Forest-bed, any comparison between the different Pliocene Beds must deal exclusively with the larger species, for the large forms are fairly well known from each horizon. Mr. E. T. Newton has drawn up the following table for the comparison of the Forest-bed vertebrate fauna with that of the older and newer beds; but any definite conclusions are at present rendered unsafe through the deficiency of our knowledge of the Norwich Crag mammals. It is interesting, however, to notice the persistence of the lower types through long periods; the fish of the Coralline Crag being, like those of the Weybourn Crag, principally existing forms.*

* *See also* E. T Newton, Memoir on " The Vertebrata of the Forest Bed," p 136

Distribution of the Mammals.

	Total Species	Living	Extinct
Coralline and Red Crag	45	0	45
Norwich Crag - -	17	about 5	12
Forest-bed -	39	17	22
Pleistocene	49	41	8

The numbers from the Coralline and Red Crag are taken from a paper by Messrs. A. and R. Bell,* those of the Norwich Crag from Mr. Woodward's Memoir; the Pleistocene species are given on the authority of Prof. W. Boyd Dawkins.†

At first it does not seem clear why the Glacial Period should have exterminated so many large mammals and left the smaller species; but a more minute examination of the fauna shows that most of the forms which did not survive till Pleistocene times were highly specialized herbivora which would die out through the gradual change in the vegetation as the climate became colder. The surviving forms, on the other hand, are principally the omnivorous voles, mice, and shrews, and the carnivora. All these can accommodate themselves without difficulty to a change of diet, and would probably be able to exist through the Glacial Period north of the Alps, or if locally exterminated could pass that barrier, and return when the climate ameliorated.

The occurrence of the glutton, now an exclusively northern species, might be thought to imply greater cold during the formation of the Forest-bed than is now felt in Norfolk, but the great climatic range of many living carnivora, which seems limited more by want of food, competition, or human agency than by temperature, renders the occurrence of a single species now confined to northern latitudes of very little value in evidence, when counterbalanced by the numerous ungulata.

The large number of mammals already known from the Forest-bed, seems clearly to point to a connection with the continent; for no island could support so large a fauna, including as it does about 15 species of deer, three of elephant, and numerous other large forms. A study of the lists of fossils shows clearly that we may expect not merely a fauna and flora equal to that now living in this country, but one as varied in character as that of central Europe, with the addition of numerous large mammals which have since been exterminated by the cold of the Glacial Period or by human agency.

It is instructive to compare the entire fauna and flora of the Forest-bed with the recent fauna and flora of Britain, classed according to the conditions under which the species live. For this mode of analysis brings out the fact that while of the Forest-bed aquatic and marsh-loving forms we have a fair knowledge, of the others, except the land mammals of the plains, at present very little is known. For this purpose the following table, which includes only the more important classes, has been drawn up.

* Proc. Geol. Assoc., vol. ii., pp. 185, 270, 1872
† Quart. Journ. Geol. Soc., vol. xxxvi., p. 395, 1880.

In the first column the approximate number of existing British forms, with the addition of a few mammals exterminated within the historic period, is shown; in the second is given the total number of species known from the Forest-bed and Weybourn Crag.

	British	Forest-bed.
Bats - - -	14	0
Land mammals - -	29	38
Amphibious mammals (fresh-water)	4	5
Marine mammals - - -	28	6
Birds - - -	354	2
Reptiles - - -	5	2
Amphibia - - -	7	4
Fresh-water fish	52	10
Marine fish - -	210	9
Land shells - -	77	17
Fresh-water shells -	48	43
Marine shells - -	465	53

The land shells of the Forest-bed are exclusively forms found on alluvium or in wet moss; there is not a single representative of the numerous species confined to calcareous soils. No fresh-water shell needing swiftly running water has yet been found

Both the fauna and flora, leaving out the large mammals and other extinct forms, are curiously like that of the " Broad District " of Norfolk at the present day; and this, like the rest of the evidence, points to a wide alluvial plain with lakes and sluggish streams, bounded on the west by a slightly higher sandy country covered with fir-forests and distant from any hills. A careful examination of the deposits now forming, and of the natural history of the neighbouring country, will, more than anything else, assist in the study of these Newer Pliocene Beds; for, notwithstanding the great changes which have taken place since the Forest-bed was formed, conditions almost exactly similar to those which held at the time of the Upper Fresh-water Bed, reappear at the present day in the Broad District

Geologists often speak of the Forest-bed fauna as practically worked out; but from the large number of species added to the lists in the course of the Geological Survey, and from the numerous forms only known from single specimens, it is evident that even of the land mammals, though so many species are known, probably only about a third of the total fauna is represented. For many years the large mammals have been collected, but until lately little has been done with the smaller vertebrata; about 30 species are known only in the collections of the Museum of Practical Geology, and of Mr. A C. Savin, of Cromer. In the invertebrata the lists have been more than doubled; but no exhaustive collecting was attempted, for in most cases only a few pounds' weight of material was taken from each bed, sifted, and the fossils examined, so as to give a general idea of the conditions under which the bed was formed, and of its fauna. The only class which approaches completeness is the fresh-water mollusca, of which we may have about two thirds of the species then living in Britain.

TABLE OF THE FLORA OF THE PLIOCENE BEDS NEAR CROMER *

(Determined by W. Carruthers, F.R.S.),

SHOWING ALSO THE RANGE OF THE SPECIES INTO OLDER AND NEWER BEDS.

W. = Weybourn.   Sh. = Sherringham.   Bees. = Beeston   W.R = West Runton   E.R. = East Runton
C = Cromer   Ov. = Overstrand.   Sid. = Sidestrand   Trim. = Trimingham.   M. or Mun. = Mundesley
Bac. = Bacton   Ost = Ostend.   Hap = Happisburgh

	Coralline Crag	Red Crag	Fluvio-marine Crag	Weybourn Crag	Lower Fresh-water Bed.	"Forest-bed" (estuarine).	Upper Fresh-water Bed.	Pleistocene (British)	Living (British)	
CRYPTOGAMIA.										
Chara, sp.			.	..	Cr.	.	Bees., Sid	?	?	
― sp		.		.			. Sid.		?	
Equisetum, sp.	.	.		..	Mun	Ov	Sid	?	?	Horse-tail.
Osmunda regalis, Linn			..	.	.	Ov., Bac	. .		×	Fern-royal.
GYMNOSPERMÆ.										
Taxus baccata, Linn				..	Mun. Trim., Mun.	Cr., Trim.	Mun., Ost., Hap.	×	×	Yew.
Pinus sylvestris, Linn		.		.	Trim., Hap.	Hap.	Mun., Hap	×	×	Scotch Fir.
― *abies*, Linn	.			..				...	×	{ Spruce Fir Extinct in Britain.

* There are also a large number of undetermined forms, and it is not improbable that some of these may be extinct, or at least extinct in Britain Of most of the plants we have only the seed or fruit The two species already recognized as locally extinct (*Trapa natans* and *Pinus abies*) are both conspicuous and well-marked forms about which there can be no doubt.

Table of the Flora of the Pliocene Beds near Cromer—*continued.*

	Coralline Crag	Red Crag	Fluvio-marine Crag	Weybourn Crag	Lower Fresh-water Bed	"Forest-bed" (estuarine)	Upper Fresh-water Bed	Pleistocene (British)	Living (Brush)	
MONOCOTYLEDONS.										
Phragmites communis, Trin					Mun, Bac	.	Bees, Sid, Mun	x	x	Reed
Carex, several sp.			.				Sid.	?	?	Sedge.
Juncus, sp.					...		Sid, Mun.	?	?	Rush
Zannichellia palustris, Linn.							Bees, Sid, Mun	...	x	Horned Pond-weed.
Potamogeton heterophyllus, Schreb					Cr, Trim.	...	Bees, Sid, Mun		x	Pond-weed.
Potamogeton trichoides, Cham, var tuberculata, Bab							Bees, Sid, Mun		x	Pond-weed.
Potamogeton flabellatus, Bab					Trim	.	Bees, Mun	.	x	Pond-weed.
Potamogeton crispus, Linn.								.	x	Pond-weed
DICOTYLEDONS.†										
Alnus glutinosa, Linn	.	.	..	..	Cr, Hap	.	W R, Ost	x	x	Alder.
Betula alba, Linn			..	.	Hap	Ov.	Hap ?	x	x	Birch
Fagus sylvatica, Linn	..				Hap.			x	x	Beech.
Quercus robur, Linn				..		Ov.	..	x	x	Oak
Corylus Avellana, Linn.				..		.	Ost.	x	x	Hazel

† *Nuphar luteum* and *Nymphæa alba* have been recorded from the "Forest-bed" at Happisburgh (Lyell, Antiq. Man, Ed 4, p. 256). The specimens may have been obtained from a recent deposit in that neighbourhood, till lately confused with the much older "Cromer Forest-bed." Therefore, until the horizon is definitely fixed, the species must be omitted from the Forest-bed flora.

Table of the Flora of the Pliocene Beds near Cromer—*continued.*

	Coralline Crag	Red Crag	Fluvio-marine Crag	Weybourn Crag	Lower Fresh-water Bed	"Forest-bed" (estuarine).	Upper Fresh-water Bed	Pleistocene (British)	Living (British)	
Salix, sp.					Hap			?	?	Willow
——, sp					Hap			?	?	Willow
——, sp					Hap			?	?	Willow
Ulmus, sp.					Hap			×	,	Elm
Ceratophyllum demersum, Linn					Mun		passim	×	× ?	Hornwort
Euphorbia?					Cr				×	Spurge
Rumex maritimus, Linn							Bees, W R, Sid, Ost	×	×	Golden Dock
——, sp.							Sid		?	Dock
Menyanthes trifoliata, Linn					Cr, Mun, Hap		Mun	×	×	Bog-bean
Myriophyllum, sp							Sid.		?	Water Milfoil
Hippuris vulgaris, Linn					Cr		Bees, Sid, Mun, Ost	×	×	Mare's-tail
Trapa natans, Linn †					Mun		Ost	×		Extinct in Britain
Pyrus, sp					Mun		W R, Hap	?	?	Apple ?
Prunus communis, Huds							Bees, W R, Sid		×	Sloe
Trifolium?					Cr, Trim		Bees, Sid, Mun, Ost		?	Clover ?
Ranunculus aquatilis, Linn							W.R		×	Water Crowfoot
——, sp									?	Buttercup.
Thalictrum flexuosum? Bernh.							Sid, Ost.		×	Meadow-rue

† The same variety is found in a sub-fossil state in the peat mosses of Scania　　(*See* Areschoug, Journ. of Botany, new set., vol ii, p 239.)

TABLE OF THE FAUNA OF THE PLIOCENE BEDS NEAR CROMER.

	Coralline Crag	Red Crag	Fluvio-marine Crag	Weybourn Crag	Lower Fresh-water Bed	"Forest-bed" (estuarine).	Upper Fresh-water Bed	Pleistocene (British)	Living (British)	
SPONGIA										
Cliona, sp.								×	×	Boring sponge
Spongilla fluviatilis, Johnston				E R			Sud., Ost.		×	Fresh-water sponge.
FORAMINIFERA (Determined by H. B. Brady, F.R.S.†)										
Miliolina pulchella? D'Orb	×	×	×	E R				×	×	
Lagena sulcata? W & J		×		E.R.				×	×	
— squamosa? D'Orb	×	×	×	E.R.				×	×	
Polymorphina lactea, W & J	×	×	×	E.R.				×	×	
— compressa, D'Orb	×	×	×	E.R.				×	×	
Truncatulina lobatula, W & J	×	×	×	E.R.				×	×	
Rotalia Beccarii, Linn	×	×	×	E R				×	×	
Polystomella crispa, Linn		×	×	E.R.					×	
— arctica, P. & J.								×	×	Northern

† With regard to the Foraminifera, Mr Brady writes "The list appears to me to suggest a sub-arctic fauna of 50 fathoms or thereabouts The furthest point south at which good specimens of *Polystomella arctica* have been found, is a little north of Shetland, the rest might have come from comparatively shallow water from any part of our own coast"

Table of the Fauna of the Pliocene Beds near Cromer—*continued*

	Coralline Crag.	Red Crag	Fluvio-marine Crag	Weybourn Crag.	Lower Fresh-water Bed.	"Forest-bed" (estuarine)	Upper Fresh-water Bed	Pleistocene (British)	Living (British)	
ECHINODERMATA.										
Echinus, sp.	×	.	?	F R				?	?	Indeterminable spines
CIRRIPEDIA.										
Balanus crenatus, Brug.		×	×	E R				×	×	
—— *Hameri*, Ase		×	×	E R				×	×	
—— *porcatus*, Da C		×	×	E R				×	×	
ENTOMOSTRACA.										
(Determined by G S Brady, M D, F R S)										
Cypris Browniana? Jones ...										
Cythere angulata, Sars. ...	:	.	.	E R.			W	×	×	
—— *tuberculata*, Sars. ...	:	.	:	E R.				×	×	Extinct.
—— *villosa*, Sars.		:	:	E R.				×	×	
—— *concinna*, Jones ...	:	:	:	E R.				×	×	
—— *pellucida*, Baird	:	.	:	E R.				×	×	

Table of the Fauna of the Pliocene Beds near Cromer—*continued.*

	Coralline Crag	Red Crag.	Fluvio-marine Crag	Weybourn Crag	Lower Fresh-water Bed	"Forest-bed" (estuarine)	Upper Fresh-water Bed	Pleistocene (British).	Living (British)	
Cytheridea elongata, Brady			.	E.R.			..	×	×	
—— *punctillata,* Brady			..	E R	.	..	..	×	×	
sp.				B R		..	.	×	×	
Cytherura clathrata, Sars			..	E R	..	..	.			
COLEOPTERA					.	..				
(Determined by C. O Water-house)					.	.				
Donacia sericea, Linn.				..	Ov, Trim., M., Bac Trim. Trim.	.	W.R.	×	×	
Pterostichus madidus? Fab			..		..	..	..		× ?	
Timarcha? sp				..	.	..	.			
POLYZOA					..	.	.		?	
Lepralia? fragment		.	. .		E R.	..	..	. :	?	
Undetermined casts					Ov	.	.	:		
BRACHIOPODA					..	.	.			
Rhynchonella psittacea, Chemn.		×	×	E R	..	..	...	×	×	Northern *

* Living British species which are also marked "Northern" do not range as far south as Norfolk, those marked "Arctic" are only rarely found as far south as Scotland.

E 2

Table of the Fauna of the Pliocene Beds near Cromer—continued.

LAMELLIBRANCHIATA (Marine).	Coralline Crag	Red Crag	Fluvio-marine Crag	Weybourn Crag.	Lower Fresh-water Bed.	"Forest-bed" (estuarine).	Upper Fresh-water Bed	Pleistocene (British)	Living (British)	
Pholas crispata, Linn	⋮	×	×	passim.	⋮	R, M.	⋮	×	×	
Mya arenaria, Linn	×	×	×	passim	⋮	R.?	⋮	×	×	
—— truncata, Linn	×	⋎	⋮	W, E.R, Sid, Trim.	⋮	Sid	⋮	×	⋎	
Saxicava arctica, Linn.	×	×	×	W, E.R, Trim		⋮	⋮	×	×	Arctic.
——, gigantic var	⋮	⋮	⋮	E.R,	⋮		⋮	×	⋎	N. America.
Corbula striata, Walker and Boys.	⋮×	⋮×	⋮×	W, E.R, Ov., Sid, Trim	⋮		⋮	×		
Mactra ovalis, Sow	⋮	×	×	E.R, Trim	⋮		⋮	×	×	
—— contracta? Say.	⋮	×	×	W, E.R, Sid, Trim	⋮		⋮	×	×	
—— stultorum, Linn				E.R		⋮	⋮		⋎	
Scrobicularia plana, Da C	⋮	×	×	E.R.	⋮	⋮	⋮	×	×	Arctic.
Tellina Balthica, Linn				passim.	⋮	R.	⋮	×	×	
—— lata, Gmel.	×	×	×	W, E.R, Trim	⋮		⋮	×	⋮	Extinct
—— obliqua, Sow				passim	⋮	R?	⋮	×	⋮	Extinct
—— praetenuis, Leathes.		?	?	E.R, Ov	⋮	R.	⋮		⋮	
Donax vittatus, Da C		×	×	passim.	⋮	R.?	⋮	×	×	
Cyprina Islandica, Linn.	⋮×	⋮×	⋮×	W, Sh, E.R, Sid, Trim.	⋮	R.?	⋮	×	×	Arctic.
Astarte borealis, Chemn.	⋮	⋅	×		⋮		⋮	×	×	

Table of the Fauna of the Pliocene Beds near Cromer—*continued*

	Coralline Crag	Red Crag	Fluvio-marine Crag	Weybourn Crag	Lower Fresh-water Bed	"Forest-bed" (estuarine)	Upper Fresh-water Bed	Pleistocene (British)	Living (British)	
Astarte borealis, oval var ⋮	⋮	×	·	Sh, E R	⋮	⋮	⋮	?	?	Arctic.
— *compressa*, Mont ·		×	×	W, Sh, E R, Sid, Trim	⋮			×	×	Northern.
— *crebricostata*, Forbes	·	×	?	E R	·	·	·	×	×	Mediterranean.
— *incrassata*, Broc ⋮		×	×	E R, Trim	⋮	·		?	⋮	
— *sulcata*, Da C.	:	×	×	W?, Sh, E R, Sid, Trim.	⋮	⋮		×	×	
Cardium echinatum, Linn. ⋮		×	×	E R	⋮	R, Sid, M		×	×	
— *edule*, Linn ·		×	×	passim,	⋮	,		×	×	Arctic
— *Grœnlandicum*, Cheinn.	: ×	×	×	W?, E.R.	·	·	·	×	×	
Lucina borealis, Linn. ⋮	×	×	×	W, E B, Ov, Sid, Trim.	⋮			×	?	Arctic ?
Leda oblongoides, S Wood ·		×	×	passim	⋮	R ?		×		Extinct
Nucula Cobboldiae, Sow	×	×	×	W, E R, Ov, Sid, Trim.	⋮	R, Ov, M. Bac.	·	×	×	
Mytilus edulis, Linn. ⋮		×	×	Passim.	·	⋮		×	×	
Pecten opercularis? Linn.				E.R.						
GASTEROPODA (Marine)										
Melampus pyramidalis, Sow ⋮	·	×	×	E R	⋮	E. R.	⋮	×	⋮	Extinct
Bulla alba, Brown ·		:	×	E R.	⋮	⋮	⋮	×	×	Northern
Chiton, sp				E R	·				?	

Table of the Fauna of the Pliocene Beds near Cromer—*continued*

	Coralline Crag	Red Crag	Fluvio-marine Crag	Weybourn Crag	Lower Fresh-water Bed	"Forest-bed" (estuarine)	Upper Fresh-water Bed	Pleistocene (British)	Living (British)	
Tectura virginea, Muller	×	×	×	E.R				×	×	
Trochus, sp (T tumidus?)		?	×	E.R.				×	×	Fragment of a large species
——, sp.				E						
Velutina lævigata, Pennant.		×	×	E R		R ?		×	×	
Natica catena, Da C.		×	×	W, Sh, E R, Trim				×	×	
—— *clausa*, Brod and Sow.		×	×	W, Sh, E R, Ov ER		R , Bac, R , M		×	×	Northern
—— *helicoedes*, Johnston		×	×	passim				×	×	Northern
Littorina littorea, Linn.		×	×	W, Sh, E R				×	×	
—— *rudis*, Maton		×	×	E R		R , Ov , M , Bac.?		×	×	Northern.
Hydrobia subumbilicata Mont			×	W, Sh, Er, Ov						
Scalaria Grœnlandica, Chemn		×	×	E R.				×	×	
—— *Trevelyana*, Leach.		×	×					×	×	
—— *Turtonis*, Turton		?	×	E R., Trim				×	×	
Turritella terebra, Linn		×	×	E R				×	×	
Cancellaria viridula, Fab	×	×	×	E R, Trim				×	×	Arctic
Pleurotoma linearis, Mont		×	×	E R				×	×	
—— *turricula*, Mont		×	×	W, E R		R ?		×	×	
Trophon antiquus, Linn		×	×	W, E R, Ov, Trim.		R ?		×	×	
——, reversed var.		×	×	passim				×	×	
Purpura lapillus, Linn		×	×			R , M , Bac ?		×	×	
Buccinum undatum, Linn.	×	×	×	E R, Ov, Sid, Trim.				×	×	

Table of the Faúna of the Pliocene Beds near Cromer—continued

	Coralline Crag	Red Crag	Fluvio-marine Crag	Weybourn Crag	Lower Fresh-water Bed	"Forest-bed" (estuarine)	Upper Fresh-water Bed	Pleistocene (British)	Living (British)	
LAMELLIBRANCHIATA. (Fresh-water.)										
Anodonta cygnea, Linn.			· x		·	⋮	W.R, M	x	x	
———, var Anatina.							W R		x	
Unio pictorum, Linn				E R	Hap	R	W R, Sid, M	x	x	
*Pisidium amnicum, Muller							W R, Sid, M	x	x	
** —— astartoides, Sandb					·	·	W R	?	x	Extinct
—— pusilum, Gmel							W.R	x	x	Perhaps three varieties of one species (P. fontinale, Drap)
—— nitidum, Jenyns						·	W.R		x	
—— roseum, Scholtz							W R	x	x	
—— Henslowanum, Shep					·	·	Sh., W R, Sid, Trim		x	
—— pulchellum, Jenyns				·		·	W R	x	x	
—— Casertanum, Poli.			x				W R	x	x	
Sphærium corneum, Linn					⋮		Sid, M, W R, Ost	x	x	
—— rivicola, Leach							W R, M	x	x	
—— ovalis, Fér.							W.R		x	
Corbicula fluminalis, Muller		x	x	E R		R	W.R	x	x	Southern Living in the Nile

* Pisidium astartoides has generally been considered a variety of P. amnicum, though at West Runton the two species are found side by side with the valves united. Among several hundred specimens of each, no intermediate forms could be found. At present there is no agreement among conchologists as to the limits of the different species in the genus Pisidium, but nearly all the British forms seem to occur in the sandy portion of the bed at West Runton.

Table of the Fauna of the Pliocene Beds near Cromer—*continued*

GASTEROPODA (Land and Fresh-water)	Coralline Crag	Red Crag	Fluvio-marine Crag	Weybourn Crag	Lower Fresh-water Bed	"Forest-bed" (estuarine)	Upper Fresh-water Bed	Pleistocene (British)	Living (British)	
Limax Sowerbyi, Fér	.	.	. ×	.	.	...	W R.	×	×	
—— *modioliformis*, Sandb.							W R		.	Extinct.
Vitrina pellucida, Muller	..	..	× ×	.	..	..	W.R, Sid. Sh, W R.	×	. × ×	Very large at West Runton.
Succinea putris, Linn.	.	..	×	.	..	R				
—— *oblonga*, Drap			×		..	..	W R, Trm	×	× × ×	A single specimen with three coloured bands.
Helix arbustorum, Linn.			×	E R.	..	R	W R	×	× × ×	
—— *nemoralis*, Linn.					..	..	W R	?		
—— *hispida*, Linn.			×		..	R	W.R.	×	× × × × × × ×	
—— var *concinna*			.		.		W.R.	×		
—— *fulva*, Muller	.	..	×		..		W R	×		
—— *pulchella*, Muller				.	..	..	W.R	×		*H tenuilimbata*, Sandb.
—— *pygmæa*, Drap					..	..	W.R	×		
Zua subcylindrica, Linn (*Z. lubrica*)	.	.	.	.	..	.	W.R.	× ×	× ×	
Clausilia, sp (*C. perversa*?)		×	×		..	..	W R		×	Fragments only.
Pupa muscorum, Linn (*P. marginata*).										
Vertigo antivertigo, Drap.	..	..	×	..	..	..	W R	×	×	

Table of the Fauna of the Pliocene Beds near Cromer—*continued.*

	Coralline Crag	Red Crag	Fluvio-marine Crag	Weybourn Crag	Lower Fresh-water Bed	"Forest-bed" (estuarine)	Upper Fresh-water Bed	Pleistocene (British)	Living (British)	
Carychium minimum, Muller	·	:	×	·	·	·	W.R.	×	×	
Planorbis corneus, Linn		:	×	·	·	R	W R, Std.	×	×	C. ovatum, Sandb.
——— albus, Muller	:	·	:	:	:	:	W R	×	×	Pl clathratus, Sandb
——— crista, Linn (Pl. nautileus).		×	×	·	:	:	W.R.	×	×	
——— carinatus, Muller		·	:	:	:	.	W R	×	×	
——— complanatus, Linn	·	×	×	:	:	R	W.R.	×	×	
——— vortex, Linn		·	·	·	:	:	W.R.	×	×	
——— spirorbis, Linn	:	·	:	:	M	:	Std., W R, Ost	×	×	
——— contortus, Linn		×	×	:	:	:	W.R	×	×	
——— nitidus, Muller	·	·	·	·	·	·	W.R, Std.	×	·	
Physa fontinalis, Linn		·	×	·	:	·	. W R	×	×	
Limnaea limosa, Linn (L. peregra)	:	·	×	E R	:	R	W R	×	×	
——— stagnalis, Linn		×	×	·	:	R	W R, Std.	×	×	L. labo, Sandb
——— palustris, Müller	:	×	×	:	:	.	W R	×	×	Velletia lingulata of Sandb
——— truncatula, Muller		·	×	·	·		W B, Std.	×	×	
Ancylus lacustris, Linn	:	·	×	E R	Bac.			·	:	Southern. Now confined to the Danube
Lithoglyphus fuscus, Pfr		×	×	·	M					
Bythinia tentaculata, Linn.	:	:	:	:	Hap.?		passim	×	×	
——— Leachii, Shep		·	×	:	:		W R	×	×	
Paludina gibba, Sandb.	·		×	·	:	R	W R, M.?	×	:	Extinct. P. contecta of Crag Moll.
——— vivipara, Linn.		:	×	·	:			×	×	

Table of the Fauna of the Pliocene Beds near Cromer—*continued*.

	Coralline Crag	Red Crag	Fluvio-marine Crag	Weybourn Crag	Lower Fresh-water Bed	"Forest-bed" (estuarine)	Upper Fresh-water Bed	Pleistocene (British)	Living (British)	
Paludina media, S. Woodw	.	×	×			R		:		Extinct
—— ? *glacialis*, S V Wood.			×	F.R.	:	R		×	.	Extinct
—— sp						R.				Extinct
Hydrobia marginata, Mich				:	:		Sid	×		Southern *Belgrandia nana*, Sandb
—— *Steini*, v. Martens							W.R			Extinct in England Living in Sweden and near Berlin
—— *Runtoniana*, Sandb					:	:	W R		:	Extinct
Valvata fluviatilis, Colb. ...						:	Sid	×	× ?	Extinct in England. Living in Belgium and Germany
—— *piscinalis*, Muller						R	Sh, W.R. Sid, M.	×	×	
——, var *antiqua*			×				W R	×	×	
——, depressed var							W R			
—— *cristata*, Muller	:		×	:	.	.	W R	×	×	

The following species of mollusca have also been recorded :—

Venus fasciata from Weybourn (Prof. Prestwich)

Leda lanceolata from Weybourn (Prof. Prestwich); probably a mistake for *Leda oblongoides*, which is common, but not included in Prof Prestwich's list.

Unio margaritifer from West Runton (Prof Prestwich) Mr. A. Bell subsequently stated that the species is in reality *U littoralis*. I have been unable to find either, but the thick-shelled *Anodonta cygnea*, var *anatina*, may have been mistaken for a *Unio*

Limax agrestis (Mr. A. Bell) is probably *L modioliformis*, Sandb

Ancylus fluviatilis (Mr A Bell) I have not seen

Table of the Fauna of the Pliocene Beds near Cromer—*continued.*

VERTEBRATA (Determined by E T Newton) PISCES	Coralline Crag	Red Crag	Fluvio-marine Crag	Weybourn Crag	Lower Fresh-water Bed	"Forest-bed" (estuarine)	Upper Fresh-water Bed	Pleistocene (British)	Living (British)	
Raja batis, Montagu									×	Common skate.
—— *clavata,* Belon				E.R.					×	Thornback
Acanthias vulgaris, Risso				E R					×	Piked dog-fish
Galeus canis, Linn				E R					×	Tope
Acipenser, sp							Sid ?		×	Sturgeon
Platessa, sp.				E R.					×	Plaice ?
Gadus pollachus ? Linn				E.R.					×	Pollack
—— *morrhua* Linn.				E R						Cod
Fish otolitis ? species						Tr , M , Bac				Undetermined
—— *? species*									˙	Undetermined.
Tinca vulgaris, Cuv							W.R		×	Tench
Abramis brama, Linn							W R		∧	Bream
Leuciscus erythrophthalmus, Linn					Hap ?		W R		∧	Rudd
—— *rutilus,* Linn							W R		×	Roach
—— *cephalus ?* Linn							Ost ?		×	Chub
Barbus vulgaris ? Flem.							W.R		×	Barbel
Esox lucius, Linn						E R.	W B , B , Sid , Ost ?		×	Pike
Platax Woodward, Ag	×	×	×	E R , W				×		Extinct

Table of the Fauna of the Pliocene Beds near Cromer—*continued.*

	Coralline Crag	Red Crag	Fluvio-marine Crag	Weybourn Crag	Lower Fresh-water Bed	"Forest-bed" (estuarine).	Upper Fresh-water Bed.	Pleistocene (British)	Living (British)	
Acerina vulgaris? Cuv.							W R.		×	Ruff
Perca fluviatilis, Linn							W R., Ost. ?	×	×	Perch.
AMPHIBIA										
Triton cristatus, Laur							W R		× ?	Common warty newt
Bufo, sp							W R		×	Toad
Rana esculenta? Linn							W R., Sid ?		×	Edible frog.
—— *temporaria?* Linn									×	Common frog
REPTILIA										
Pelias berus, Linn							W.R.		×	Viper
Tropidonotus natrix, Linn.							W R., Ost ?		×	Common snake
AVES.										
Anser, sp						E R.	W.R.		?	Goose.
Anas?							W R.			Duck.
Several species undetermined										

Table of the Fauna of the Pliocene Beds near Cromer—continued.

MAMMALIA	Coralline Crag	Red Crag	Fluvio-marine Crag	Weybourn Crag	Lower Fresh-water Bed	"Forest-bed" (estuarine).	Upper Fresh-water Bed	Pleistocene (British).	Living (British).	
Delphinus, sp. (= D. tursio?)	·		×	·	·	Ov	·	?	?	Dolphin
——— delphis? Linn				·	·	Ov	·	×	×	Narwhal
Monodon monoceros, Linn.			? · ×	·	·	M ?	·	×	×	Whales
Balænoptera?			×	·	·	Cr, M , Bac	:		·	Mammoth Extinct
Elephas primigenius, Blumb †				:	:	Ov. passum	:	⌣		Extinct.
——— meridionalis, Nesti ‡						passum		×	×	Extinct.
——— antiquus, Falc ‡				·	·		W.R, Ost			Living near Moscow
Myogale moschata, Linn. ..				·	·		W R, Ost		×	Common shrew.
Sorex vulgaris, Linn				·	·		W R, Ost		×	Lesser shrew.
——— pygmæus? Pallas						·	W R, Ost		×	Mole
Talpa Europæa, Linn.						·	W R		×	Long-tailed field mouse
Mus sylvaticus, Linn.	:		:	:	:				⌐	Squirrel.
Sciurus vulgaris, Linn				·	·		Ost ? Hap ?			Extinct in Britain; living in eastern Siberia
Arvicola gregalis, Pallas				·	·		W R			Extinct in Britain; living in Central Europe
——— arvalis, Pallas	:	·	·	:	:	·	W R	×	·	

† Represented by a somewhat extreme form, which may eventually have to be regarded as distinct
and Memoir on "The Vertebrata of the Forest Bed," p. 107
‡ Also found in the Pliocene Beds of the Val d'Arno.

See E. T Newton, Geol Mag, Dec II, vol. viii., p. 316,

Table of the Fauna of the Pliocene Beds near Cromer—*continued*

	Coralline Crag	Red Crag	Fluvio-marine Crag	Weybourn Crag	Lower Fresh-water Bed	"Forest-bed" (estuarine).	Upper Fresh-water Bed	Pleistocene (British).	Living (British).	
Arvicola arvalis, var. (*A. nivalis?* Martins)			×				W.R	×		Extinct in Britain, living in the Alps and Pyrenees above 4,000 feet
—— *amphibius?* Linn.			? ×	E.R.		E.R	W.R., Ost?	×	×	Water vole
—— *intermedius*, Newton			×				W.R., Ost			Extinct. Very abundant; probably an amphibious species.
—— *glareolus*, Schreb. ...							W.R.	×	×	Bank vole
Castor Europæus, Owen. ...						R., Ov., M., Bac	W.R.	×		Beaver
Trogontherium Cuvieri, Owen.						Ov., R.	W.R., Ost	×		Extinct
Cervus verticornis, Dawkins						Bac, &c.	W R			Extinct.
—— *Sedgwicki*, Falc. (*C. dicranios?* Nesti)†						M. Hap.?				Extinct.
—— *Polignacus*, Robert.†						Hap.		×		Extinct.
—— *megaceros*, Hart						M				A dredged specimen only.
—— *latifrons*, Johnson.						Bac				Extinct.
—— *Guettar*, Dawkins, MS										Extinct
—— *Fitchi*, Gunn, MS.						Cr				Extinct.
—— *Etuerrarum?* C & J†						Cr, &c.		×		
—— *elaphus?* Linn.								×	×	Red deer. A very doubtful determination

† Also found in the Pliocene Beds of the Val d'Arno

Table of the Fauna of the Pliocene Beds near Cromer—continued

	Coralline Crag	Red Crag	Fluvio-marine Crag	Weybourn Crag	Lower Fresh-water Bed	"Forest-bed" (estuarine).	Upper Fresh-water Bed	Pleistocene (British).	Living (British).	
Cervus Dawkinsi, Newton.	.	.	×	.	.	?	.	.	.	Locality unknown
—— Carnutorum, Laugel †	.	.	.	.	.	Hap.	.	×	×	Extinct. A dredged specimen only.
—— capreolus, Linn.	.	.	.	.	.	Hap.? Cr.?	.	.	?	Roe deer. Specimens of doubtful origin
—— bovdes, Gunn, MS	.	.	.	.	.	Cr	..	.	.	Extinct Exact locality unknown
Capreus Savini, Newton.	.	..	.	..	..	Ov	..	..	.	Extinct
Bos primigenius? Cuvier	.	.	.	.	.	Cr., M , Hap.?	.	×	?	Ox
Sus scrofa, Linn	.	.	.	.	.	Std , Hap.?	.	×	×	Pig.
Hippopotamus major, Owen †	.	.	.	.	.	Cr , M., Bac., Hap.	.	×	..	Hippopotamus
Rhinoceros megarhinus? Christ †	.	.	×	.	.	Cr	.	×	.	Extinct
—— Etruscus, Falconer †	.	.	.	.	.	Ov , M , Bac., Hap	W.R.	×	.	Extinct.
Equus Stenonis, Cocchi †	.	.	.	.	.	Cr , Std.	W.R	..	.	Extinct.
—— caballus-fossilis, Rutimeyer	.	..	..	.	,.	Cr , M.	W R	..	?	Horse.
Phoca, sp.	.	.	.	.	.	R	W R	×	.	The West Runton specimen is probably derivative.
Trichechus Huxleyi, Lankester.	.	×	..	..	.	Cr.	.	..	×	Extinct.
Martes sylvatica, Nilsson.	.	.	×	.	.	Std.?	W.R.	?	×	Marten.
Machærodus, sp.	.	.	.	.	..	..	..	.	.	Extinct Exact locality doubtful
Felis ?	.	.	.	..	.	?	.	.	.	Locality unknown.

* Also found in the Pliocene Beds of the Val d'Arno † Also found in the Pliocene Beds of Saint Prest

Table of the Fauna of the Pliocene Beds near Cromer—*continued*

	Coralline Crag	Red Crag	Fluvio-marine Crag	Weybourn Crag.	Lower Fresh-water Bed	"Forest-bed" (estuarine)	Upper Fresh-water Bed.	Pleistocene (British)	Living (British)	
Canis vulpes? Linn.	.	...	.	.		.		×	×	Fox
— *lupus?* Linn.								×	:	Wolf Locality un-known
Gulo luscus, Linn.	...			:	:	M	Ost.?	×		Glutton Living in northern Europe, &c.
Ursus spelæus, Blumb.								×		Extinct.
— *ferox-fossilis?* Busk.	:	:	:	:	:	Ov., Hap? M.?	W R, Ost	×	:	Bear

Several other species of mammalia have been recorded, but the evidence being unsatisfactory they are omitted from the above table   A full list of these rejected forms will be found in Mr. Newton's Memoir on "The Vertebrata of the Forest Bed"

CHAPTER IX.—PLEISTOCENE.

GLACIAL DRIFT.

Introductory.

Nearly the whole of the surface-area of the district described in this Memoir is taken up by Boulder Clays and the associated Gravels, and it is only in the cliff sections, and in a few of the valleys, that the Chalk or the Pliocene Beds can be seen. The Glacial Deposits on the coast have of late years been generally known as the "Cromer Till" and the "Contorted Drift," with overlying "Middle Glacial" sands and gravels; but there is much uncertainty in the use of these terms, and still greater uncertainty as to the mode of formation of the contortions, and the correlation of the Boulder Clays with similar beds in other districts.

The following is the succession of the glacial beds now to be described:—

Boulder Gravels and Sands.
Sands and Loams ("Middle Glacial"?)
Contorted Drift.
Sands.
Second Till. ⎫
Intermediate Beds. ⎬ Cromer Till.
First Till. ⎭
Arctic Fresh-water Bed

Literature.

The first description of the contorted beds near Cromer was given in 1824 by R. C. Taylor,* and in 1827 he published three papers "On the Geology of East Norfolk," &c.,† with a section of the cliffs. Samuel Woodward in 1833, in his Geology of Norfolk, also gave a long description and sections of the cliffs; but, as far as can be made out, the divisions shown are purely lithological, and not intended to represent a definite succession. The next account was contained in the first edition of Lyell's "Principles of Geology," published in the same year, and in 1840 he gave a still fuller one.‡ No description, perhaps, has equalled this for the clearness and accuracy with which the facts are noted. The various subsequent editions of Lyell's works all contain essentially the same account. By Lyell the transportation of the materials in this district was first referred to the agency of floating ice, and by him the beds were separated into unstratified till, and contorted beds, though these were considered to alternate and to have been formed contemporaneously. In 1845 §

---

* "Remarks on the Position of the Upper Marine Formation in the Cliffs on the North-east Coast of Norfolk." Phil. Mag., vol. lxiii., p. 81.
† *Ibid.*, ser. 2, vol. i., pp. 277, 327, 346, 426. [Also reprinted together, with additions.]
‡ *Ibid.*, ser. 3, vol. xvi., p. 345.
§ "On the Cliffs of Northern Drift on the Coast of Norfolk." Quart. Journ. Geol. Soc., vol. i., p. 218.

and 1851 * Trimmer described the Cromer cliffs, suggesting that the contortions had been formed by the melting of included masses of ice   He divided the Drift on the coast into " Upper " and " Lower Erratics,"—the Lower being the Boulder Clay, and the Upper the Gravel which generally covers the higher lands   In 1864 Mr Gunn, in his " Sketch of the Geology of Norfolk," divided the Drift near Cromer into Lower Boulder-Clay or Till, Stratified Clays, with Sands and Gravel, and Upper Boulder-clay. In 1868 the Rev O. Fisher described the contortions in a paper on the " Denudations of Norfolk "†   In the same year Messrs S V Wood, jun., and F W. Harmer published an abstract of a paper in which the Weybourn Sand is made to pass by alternation into the Cromer Till ‡   The succession given is —

Sands and Gravels (Middle Glacial)

Lower Glacial ⎧ Contorted Drift
             ⎨ Sand on an eroded surface of Cromer Till
              Cromer Till.
             ⎩ Weybourn Sand, passing, by interbedding, into the Cromer Till.

"Forest-bed"

Messrs Wood and Harmer in 1872 gave a fuller account of these beds in the Supplement to the Crag Mollusca, publishing with it a map of the district and a series of cliff sections §   In 1877 they brought forward the theory that extensive valley erosion had taken place after the formation of the Contorted Drift, and previous to the deposition of the Middle Glacial Sands and the Chalky Boulder Clay.‖   In the same year Mr Belt published a paper in which (apparently) he considers the "Contorted Drift" to be older than the first Boulder Clay, and to be a later stage of the Pre-glacial laminated loams.¶   In a paper on the Newer Pliocene Beds near Cromer I showed that, as Lyell originally pointed out, the Weybourn Crag comes below, and not above, the "Forest-bed," and that the Till is quite unconnected with these deposits*,** and in another paper, in 1880, on the " Glacial Deposits of Cromer," I divided the Drifts as in this Memoir, and attempted to account for the contortions by the agency of land-ice.††

In this summary only the leading papers and those bringing forward new views are alluded to, but a full list of the literature of the subject will be found in the Memoir on the country around Norwich, those marked (†) referring to Cromer and the neighbourhood

The classification adopted in this Memoir for the Pleistocene Deposits has already been given, but it has been found impossible to correlate the beds described by previous writers with those adopted by others or with the horizons traced by the Survey   Most observers apparently describe as " Cromer Till " the blue base of the Drift, whether it is the true unstratified Till of Happisburgh or merely the unweathered lower part of the Contorted Drift   In many papers the Pre-glacial blue clays have also been confused with the Till

* " Generalizations respecting the Erratic Tertiaries   ' *Ibid*, vol vii., pp.
19–81
  † Geol Mag , vol. v , p 544
  ‡ Ibid , vol v , p 452
  § Palæontographical Society, vol xxv (issued for 1871)
  ‖ Quart. Journ Geol Soc , vol xxxiii , p. 74
  ¶ Geol Mag., Dec II , vol iv., p. 156
  ** Ibid , p. 300.
  †† Ibid., Dec II , vol vii , p 55.

CHAPTER X.—ARCTIC FRESH-WATER BED.

During a visit to England in the year 1872, Mr Alfred Nathorst, of the Geological Survey of Sweden, discovered, immediately under the Till at Mundesley, a bed of clay and loam containing *Hypnum turgescens* and leaves of *Salix polaris.** No further account of this bed appears to have been published till 1880, when, in a short paper in the Geological Magazine†, I showed that it is separated from the "Forest-bed" by the marine *Leda-myalis* Bed, and placed it, on account of the very arctic character of the climate it showed, at the base of the Pleistocene Deposits under the name "Arctic Fresh-water Bed."

During the progress of the Geological Survey, the Arctic Fresh-water Bed has been discovered at two new localities about 14 miles apart,—at Beeston, and at Ostend, near Bacton. From the character of the deposit, and from the way it appears to be cut out by the Boulder Clay, there is very little doubt that the three exposures known only represent isolated patches of a once continuous and important horizon.

Details.

No sections of the bed have been seen near Weybourn, but at Lower Sherringham, on each side of the village, directly under the Boulder Clay, there are sands and thin loams with *Succinea* and occasional *Pisidia*, which probably represent this bed

At Beeston there is the section shown in the folding plate Here, for a considerable distance, in fact till the Boulder Clay cuts through the beds to near the beach line, sands and loams with occasional fresh-water shells occur about 10 or 15 feet above high-water mark, immediately under the Boulder Clay At one point, midway between Beeston Hill and the small stream, there is a lenticular mass of laminated peaty loam, which has yielded well-preserved plant remains, including moss and numerous leaves of *Salix polaris*. No other locality for the arctic plants is at present known west of Cromer Several of the loams at Beeston and Sherringham have a rather weathered appearance, and seem to have been penetrated by small roots; this is in keeping with the amphibious character of the mollusca, which remind one much of those of the loess of the Rhine, the land forms being only such as ordinarily live on Alluvium, and can survive submergence for a limited time, while the fresh-water species can live in damp mud The species found were *Succinea putris, S. oblonga, Helix hispida? Valvata piscinalis,* and *Pisidium Henslowianum.*

Though it is probable that further search may lead to the discovery of localities for the Arctic Fresh-water Bed near Cromer, at present there is an interval of about 10 miles to the next exposure A short distance north-west of Mundesley there is the original section discovered by Mr Nathorst. The details of the section vary continually, but at one of the most fossiliferous spots, immediately under the rain-water spout between the Coast Guard Station and the road to the Manor House, there is —

* *See* Lyell, "Antiquity of Man," 1873, pp 261, 262, and Journal of Botany, N S., vol. ii, p 225
† Geol Mag, Dec. II., vol. vii, p 548

		Feet
2nd Till -	Chalky Boulder Clay.	
	Hard blue loam and a little sand - - -	3
Arctic Fresh-water Bed	Stiff blue clay with moss, *Hippuris vulgaris, Salix polaris,* elytra of beetles, *Succinea putris, S oblonga,* and bones of *Spermophilus* - -	1½
	Sand and blue loam, contorted together . fresh-water shells	

The *Spermophilus,* at present the only vertebrate known from this horizon, was found a few inches under the Boulder Clay in digging out a lump of the fresh-water clay to wash for plant-remains * The specimen was much crushed , in fact, though it was probably nearly a whole skeleton, the only recognizable parts were a few teeth, tail-vertebræ, and foot-bones; and the thin seam of sand in which it occurred was flattened to about an eighth of an inch By drying and washing the clay through a sieve the leaves can be obtained uninjured, and so well preserved that the twigs of *Salix polaris* retain their original glossy chocolate-brown color The leaves and moss may be dried in ordinary botanical paper.

Unfortunately the continuation of this deposit both eastward and westward, is much obscured by talus, and where plants are absent the shells alone are not sufficient to show whether the bed belongs to the Arctic Fresh-water Bed or to the upper part of the " Forest-bed "

About 80 yards north-west of the Gap near Ostend Brick-kiln, Bacton, when the beach is very low, and the base of the Boulder Clay can be examined, the Arctic Fresh-water Bed is again seen The section is —

		Feet
Soil	- - - - - - - -	3
1st Till -	Bedded marl, much piped - - -	2
	Laminated sand and loam - - -	3
	Hard Boulder Clay with little Chalk - -	5
Arctic Fresh-water Bed.	Hard bedded blue loam, sand, and gravel · Arctic plants in the loam, *Salix polaris, Betula nana,* &c - - - - -	2 +

This bed was only once seen After a severe gale the beach was exceptionally low, and a good exposure of the loam was laid bare at the foot of the cliff From this several species of plants were obtained, but a few days later it was entirely hidden, and has not since been uncovered The base of the Till is very low at Ostend, and the beach exceptionally high, so that the beds immediately under the Boulder Clay are as a rule, entirely hidden, and there is also a considerable thickness of beds always obscured by the slope of the beach The connection of the Arctic Fresh-water Bed with the Upper Fresh-water Bed seen near low-water mark, has not yet been made out, and it is doubtful whether the *Leda-myalis* Bed is represented For about 300 yards N W of the Gap, fresh-water beds have been seen here and there at the base of the cliff ; but further observations are needed before they can be definitely referred to this horizon , they may belong to the " Forest-bed "

Though the term " Fresh-water Bed " has been used, the deposit may perhaps be more accurately described as a flood-loam or sand, for the greater part of it does not appear to have been permanently under water, the most abundant shells being *Succineæ,* and not fresh-water species. No sections of the Arctic Fresh-water Bed are yet known except the three already described

The similarity of lithological character in all the beds beneath the Boulder Clay has necessitated the inclusion of the Arctic Fresh-water Bed in the Pre-glacial Series in the separate Sheet of cliff sections† , but in this Memoir it has been placed at

---

* *Vide* Geol. Mag., Dec II , vol iv., p. 51, 1882.
† Horizontal Section, Sheet 127.

the base of the Pleistocene Beds, because the change from the climate of the "Forest-bed," shown by the plants, is so great that it seems a misnomer to speak of the bed as "Pre-glacial." Trees have entirely disappeared, and the plants include the dwarf arctic birch and arctic willow. The fauna and flora show the first incoming of arctic *land* species*, and indicate a lowering of the temperature by about 20 degrees,—a difference as great as that between the South of England and the North Cape at the present day, and sufficient to allow the seas to be blocked with ice during the winter, and glaciers to form in the hilly districts

It appears to be commonly felt that Lyell's classification, in which the Pliocene division extends into the middle of the Glacial deposits, is very inconvenient; and in talking with geologists one finds that most of them insensibly speak of Pleistocene as equivalent to the whole of the Glacial and Palæolithic periods. Others separate the "Forest-bed" from the Crag, and class it with the Pleistocene, but it certainly is much more naturally connected with the older deposits

For these reasons the classification adopted in this Memoir appears to be the simplest, though it necessitates a slight alteration in Lyell's test, founded on the per-centage of extinct mollusca.

---

* The Glutton is the only arctic land species yet known from the Forest-bed (*see ante*, p. 60).

CHAPTER XI.—CROMER TILL.

Introductory.

Fiom the manner in which beds of different ages have been contorted together in the neighbourhood of Cromer, it is impossible to make out any succession whatever in the Glacial Deposits, from the study of the cliffs near, or on the west of that town, it will, therefore, be necessary to reverse the order adopted in treating of the Pliocene Beds, and to commence the description at Happisburgh. In that neighbourhood there is a singularly regular and definite succession in the Drifts, and each bed can be traced for several miles to the north-west till it is either overlapped or lost among the contortions.

Near Happisburgh the Till consists of three members,—an upper and a lower unstratified Boulder Clay, and an intervening bed of well-laminated loam or marl. As there is not the slightest change in the lithological character of the two Tills over the whole distance through which they have been traced, a single description of each will suffice

First Till.

Resting on a planed and nearly horizontal surface of any of the older deposits, there is a perfectly unstratified hard and very tough Boulder Clay. This "First Till" consists of a mixture of about equal parts of shelly sand and clay, with the addition of numerous striated pieces of hard Chalk, Oolites, and a smaller quantity of various Palæozoic rocks, granite, and trap of different kinds. Boulders over a foot in diameter are very scarce. The shells, though abundant, are certainly derivative; for, as a rule, they are sharply fractured, sometimes striated, and in the interior of one or two the remains of a quite different matrix from that in which they are imbedded has been found. The common species are all now living in Norfolk; and the large thick-shelled varieties that occur are such as need a sandy bottom, and would not live in the clay with which they are now mixed. The materials contained in the Till, arranged according to the probable age of the beds from which they are derived, are as follows:—

?
{ *Tellina Balthica*, thick variety (common)
——— *lata* (1 valve).
Mya arenaria (common).
——— *truncata* (1 valve).
Cardium edule (common).
Cypriaa Islandica (common).
Littorina littorea (1 fragment)).

Forest-bed
{ Lignite
Fragments of bone } (very rare)
Green-coated flints

Upper Chalk	Soft Chalk (not much). *Belemnitella mucronata* (common) Black unworn flints Porous flint, like that of Trimingham.
Yorkshire ? Chalk	Pebbles and boulders of hard Chalk bored by annelids and subsequently striated. Grey flint.
Red Chalk	Red marly Chalk
Kimeridge Clay	Septaria bored and subsequently striated Fossiliferous shale. Belemnites
Lias	*Gryphæa incurva*
New Red ?	Soft red sandstone
Carboniferous	Fossiliferous limestone. Chert Sandstone.
Old Red Sandstone ?	Hard red sandstone
?	Gneiss, Basalt, Mica Schist, Grey Granite, pebbles of red Jasper, &c. &c

At Eccles the First Till occurs on the foreshore beneath recent alluvium, but a quarter of a mile south of the Lighthouse it is cut out or forced beneath the sea-level by a disturbance in the Contorted Drift North-west of the Lighthouse it reappears at the foot of the cliff, and as it is traced northward the base gradually rises and allows the Pliocene Beds to be seen beneath it, the thickness at this point is about 10 feet North of the Station House it increases in thickness, from 15 or 20 feet near Happisburgh, to a maximum development of 25 feet under the highest part of the cliff Beyond this point it gradually thins out, seldom exceeding 10 feet near Ostend Gap About 260 yards south-east of Walcot Gap the valley has cut through the Drifts, and exposes Pliocene Beds at the surface. Half a mile further the Till reappears in the cliff, but though it has not suffered from recent denudation its greatest thickness near the Coast Guard Station is only 10 feet, and a short distance beyond, where the valley again cuts through the beds, it has thinned to about three feet East of Bacton Green it reappears for a short distance with a thickness of from two to four feet, but is soon cut out by Valley Gravel, and when Boulder Clay is again seen the First Till has been entirely overlapped, and the Second Till rests directly on Pliocene Beds.

Intermediate Beds.

The Intermediate Beds consist of well-laminated ripple-marked clays and marls with seams of fine false-bedded sand, deposited on the hummocky surface of the First Till. When the face of the cliff is clean, they contrast very markedly with the over- and under-lying unstratified Boulder Clays, being quite free from stones, and even more finely laminated than the Pre-glacial clays.*

Between Eccles and Happisburgh these beds are nearly continuous, though in places the sands which here immediately overlie them cut through to the First Till. About 180 yards north-west of Happisburgh Gap the Second Till comes on, and the thickness of the Intermediate Beds is from 15 to 20 feet. At this point the relations of the various beds are well shown, though the top of the First Till is not so hummocky as usual. There are several slight unconformities in the laminated loams, pointing to contemporaneous erosion and filling up, and about the middle of the section there is also a small contortion overlaid by undisturbed beds From this point the beds continue with the same character and average thickness till they are cut

---

* On this account Mr Gunn's term "Laminated Beds" applied to the Pre-glacial deposits, is liable to mislead the student

FIG. 8.

Cliff section near Happisburgh.

Scale, 20 feet to an inch.

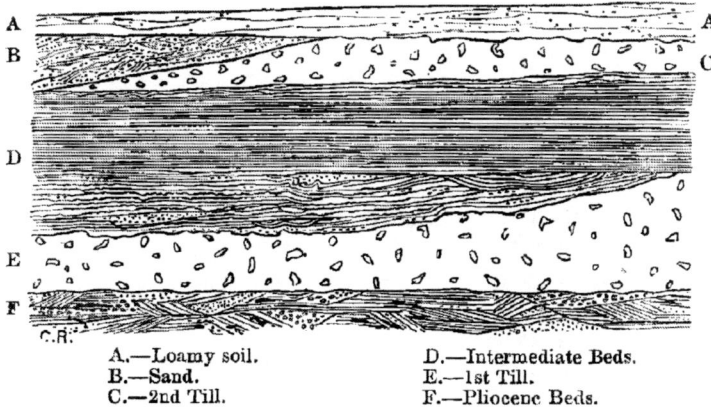

A.—Loamy soil.   D.—Intermediate Beds.
B.—Sand.   E.—1st Till.
C.—2nd Till.   F.—Pliocene Beds.

through by the valley a short distance north-west of Ostend. This is the only place where they come to the surface inland, and being the only good brick-earth free from stones to be had in the district, they are a good deal worked. Near Bacton Coast Guard Station they reappear with a thickness of only four or five feet, but being near the surface, they are so much weathered and disturbed by vegetation that the structure is generally obliterated. For nearly a mile no Glacial Beds newer than the First Till are seen, and at the north-west side of the old valley the Second Till, as already mentioned, rests directly on Pre-glacial Deposits, having overlapped both the First Till and the Intermediate Beds. Beyond this point no sections are known, though in the description of the Contorted Drift (Chapter XII.) one or two localities will be noticed where these beds perhaps reappear for a short distance.

Though the Intermediate Beds have been carefully searched, they have as yet yielded no trace of fossils, except that here and there at the base they contain shell fragments derived from the underlying Boulder Clay. If the bed were a marine deposit it would most probably contain foraminifera and entomostraca, even if mollusca were not found, for the material is quite suitable for their preservation. The occurrence of derivative fragments of shell shows that the apparent absence of a contemporaneous fauna is not due to the dissolution of the fossils by percolating water. The absence of all sign of life appears to point to a fresh-water origin for these beds, and for the similar unfossiliferous laminated clays which are so common in glacial deposits in other parts of England. Modern Glacier-lakes commonly show a similar barren character. The relation of the Intermediate Beds to the underlying Till is very peculiar; for the junction, though so irregular, does not generally appear to be an eroded line, and stones derived from the Boulder Clay are very rare.

Second Till.

Above the Intermediate Beds there is a second mass of un-stratified Boulder Clay, clearly distinguishable from the First Till by the abundance of soft Upper Chalk that it contains. This

"Second Till" is so like the Great Chalky Boulder Clay, that near Happisburgh, where it caps the cliff, it has been mistaken for that deposit, and it is quite possible that some of the Boulder Clays further south, commonly referred to the Chalky Boulder Clay, belong in reality to the Second Till. Though the Second Till seems so different from the First, closer examination shows that this difference is more apparent than real, consisting only in a change in the relative proportion of the ingredients. The First Till was described as a mixture of about equal parts of shelly sand and clay; the Second Till is nearly half soft Chalk and half clay, with a little shelly sand, the other materials being the same as in the older deposit. Arranged as before, they are:—

?	{ Tellina Balthica Cardium edule Cyprina Islandica
Forest-bed -	{ Splinter of wood Green-coated flint Flint, quartz, and quartzite pebbles
Upper Chalk -	{ Much soft Chalk. Unworn black flints Belemnitella mucronata. Inoceramus
Lower Chalk -	Soft grey Chalk
Yorkshire Chalk	{ Hard Chalk, always striated and often bored (about as much as in the First Till) Grey flints
Kimeridge Clay	{ Septaria Belemnites
Lias - -	{ Earthy limestone and mud stones Gryphæa incurva
Trias - -	Quartzite and other pebbles
Carboniferous -	{ Coal Measure sandstone Carboniferous Limestone.
Old Red Sand-stone or Silurian }	Hard red Sandstone
?	{ Chert Purple Basalt ? Gneiss. Red Granite

Between Eccles and Happisburgh the Second Till is missing, and the first section seen is 180 yards north-west of Happisburgh Gap (see Fig 8). Here it rests, with a sharply defined but slightly undulating junction, on the Intermediate Beds, just as the First Till rests on the Pre-glacial laminated clays From this point it is continuous to near Ostend, though its average thickness is only about 7 feet, and its greatest never exceeds 10 feet. From Ostend to Bacton Coast Guard Station the cliff is very low, and the Second Till is not seen; but at the latter place it comes on for a short distance in the highest part of the cliff, much weathered, and with a thickness of only a foot or two The cliffs then become lower, and the next section is near Paston, a mile from the Coast Guard Station, on the north-west side of the old valley Here, as already mentioned, the Second Till has overlapped the Intermediate Beds and the First Till, and rests directly on Pre-glacial Beds From this point to Mundesley the bed is continuous, though it seldom exceeds 10 feet, north-west of Mundesley it is rather thicker, averaging about 13 feet for nearly a mile At this point the Trimingham disturbance commences, and the Till is contorted into the newer beds Over the more easterly of the Chalk bluffs there is a patch, probably a boulder, of this Till, but beyond this it has not been traced, or, if it occurs, the disturbance is so great that the different Boulder Clays cannot be separated The total distance over which this horizon has been followed is about seven miles

Origin of the Till.

From the thoroughly unstratified character of the Till it cannot be a sedimentary deposit, for a fall of even a few inches through water would be sufficient to arrange the materials. Nevertheless, though the Till is quite unstratified, it here and there shows obscure horizontal streaks, which at first sight might be taken for lines of bedding, but which on closer examination appear to be formed of crushed lumps of different materials, in some cases Chalk, in others clay, or sand, while in a few instances they are formed of crushed boulders of sandstone or rotten granite. This structure is still better seen in the Boulder Clays of Holderness, where boulders are more abundant, and the crushing and flattening out, even of such hard rocks as Carboniferous Limestone and Coal-Measure Sandstone, is of common occurrence. In that district shells also are found crushed, and the pieces scattered over an area of several inches. The bedding in the Till is therefore such as would be caused by the sliding pressure of an ice-sheet, and may be exactly imitated in dough or putty mixed with lumps of ochre; a similar streaky structure is often seen in badly made cake.

One of the principal difficulties to be overcome before the sub-glacial origin of the Boulder Clays in the East of England can be accepted, is the very miscellaneous character of the boulders contained in them,—a collection such as no ice-sheet would be likely to pick up unless it followed a very zigzag course. But when the boulders are examined more closely they show that their transportation has been a very complicated process; for the limestones, including hard Yorkshire Chalk, Carboniferous Limestone, and Septaria from the Kimeridge Clay, have often been bored by annelids and *subsequently striated*. This apparently points to the agency of floating ice, probably only coast ice, which would bring stones from all parts and scatter them on the sea-bottom, where they would be bored by the annelids, and be subsequently ploughed up and striated by the advance of the ice-sheet into the shallow water. Though the First Till is the earliest known bed which has been to any great extent accumulated by ice, the period immediately previous, when the arctic birch and willow flourished in Norfolk near the sea-level, must have been quite cold enough for the formation of coast-ice capable of bringing abundance of stones from Scotland and Scandinavia.

When we attempt to discover the direction of the ice-flow, the absence of hard rocks under the Till precludes any hope of finding striæ. But another test is available; for where the ice has flowed over laminated clays, the beds have been slightly crumpled. Unfortunately, at present, owing to the tendency of the clays to slip, no satisfactory exposure showing the direction of the folds has been obtained. The one mentioned in my paper on the Glacial Deposits of Cromer,* turned out afterwards to be too near a contortion of subsequent date to be trustworthy.

---

* Geol Mag , Dec 11, vol vii, p 57

After the deposition of the First Till, the ice appears to have retreated, perhaps only for a few miles, leaving the Boulder Clay with a curious hummocky surface, over which was deposited ripple-marked clay and marl in thin beds. This deposit seems to be glacier-mud, such as would flow from beneath the ice, and be spread over the surface lately abandoned. Such an evenly-bedded loam cannot be taken as sufficient evidence of an inter-glacial warm climate, though it is traceable nearly continuously for at least four miles; for at the present day the glaciers of the Alps and the ice of Greenland advance and retreat short distances without any very marked cause. The Second Till only differs from the First in the shelly sand being replaced by Chalk,—a change which may be accounted for on the supposition that the first advance of the ice ploughed out most of the sand-banks, leaving the second only bare Chalk to grind up.

CHAPTER XII—CONTORTED DRIFT AND ASSOCIATED DEPOSITS

Order of Succession.

Though near Mundesley there is a distinct succession in the beds above the Till, in most places the subsequent disturbances have been so great as to affect the whole series of deposits. The order, where least disturbed, appears to be —

Unfossiliferous Boulder Gravels and Sands.
Sands and loams with *Nassa reticosa*, &c.
Boulder Clay.
Fine sands.
Till.

While this seems to have been the original succession everywhere in the cliffs, the beds are now often contorted together, and in some places inverted. It will be best, therefore, to give a general outline of the character and extent of each horizon; and then the contorted beds, taken together, will be described in detail, commencing at Happisburgh. To obtain a clear understanding of the nature of the disturbances, reference to the separate Sheet of cliff-sections is, however, absolutely necessary, for it is impossible in words to give a correct idea of the complicated foldings. (*See* Horizontal Section, Sheet 127.)

Sands

Resting on an eroded surface of the Second Till, or, in one or two places, directly on Pliocene beds, there are fine false-bedded loamy sands, always chalky and carbonaceous, and of a peculiar pale tint, easily recognizable. These beds can be traced from Happisburgh to Trimingham, a distance of nearly nine miles, but at the latter place they are lost in the contortions in the same manner as the Till. At Mundesley the sands have a thickness of about 40 feet, and form a conspicuous feature in the cliff, but they have nowhere yielded fossils. It has not been thought necessary to give a name to this unfossiliferous horizon.

Boulder Clay or Stony Loam.

The next division is the bed to which the term "Contorted Drift" more properly applies. This Boulder Clay rests on an eroded surface of any of the older beds, and often ploughs deeply into them. Though in general composition much like the underlying Till, it has a peculiar structure, such as might have resulted if the materials had been deposited in heaps, and afterwards

flattened out into lenticular masses. No clear evidence of a
sedimentary origin has, however, yet been seen: for the included
masses of sand, where bedded, have often the lines of bedding
vertical. The fossils, as in the Till, are only fragments of marine
shells, and the included nests of sand, often full of the same
species, probably represent the deposit from which the shells were
derived. This Boulder Clay is traceable as a tolerably regular bed
about 30 feet thick, between two masses of bedded sand and gravel,
from the cliff-end near Happisburgh to Trimingham. North-west
of Trimingham, though continuous to Weybourn, it is inseparable
from the other beds, and will be described in the general account
of the coast section.

Sands and Loams.

Above this Boulder Clay there are apparently two masses of
sand and gravel of different ages; the lower fossiliferous and probably equivalent to the "Middle Glacial" Sands of Yarmouth, the
other unfossiliferous, and generally much coarser, capping the hills,
perhaps forming a continuation of the "Cannon-shot Gravels" of
Norwich. These deposits, where contorted, are inseparable, and
all that can be done is to point out the general character and
distribution of each

Between Mundesley and Sidestrand the "Middle Glacial" may
be represented by bedded sands and marls which overlie the
Boulder Clay, and are often cut out by the coarser gravel.
These appear to be distinctly marine, though, except shell fragments (which may be derivative), the only fossil there obtained was
a perfect valve of *Balanus.* West of Cromer, though the stratigraphical relations cannot be made out, several contorted masses
of this sand are visible, and it is principally from the character of
the fossils found in them that this horizon has been correlated
with the interglacial sands of Yarmouth. The shells include
among others, the extinct Crag forms *Nucula Cobboldiæ* and *Nassa
reticosa*

There has been much discussion as to the contemporaneous or
derivative origin of the "Middle Glacial" fauna, and it is interesting to trace in a new district the same peculiarities in the
fossils which led Mr. S V Wood to consider the fauna to be
contemporaneous with the deposit.[*] It is not improbable that a
large proportion of the fragments of the common shells may be
derivative; but near Cromer, as at Yarmouth, the peculiar and
characteristic types are the most perfect Though the commonest
forms are *Tellina Balthica, Cardium edule, Cyprina Islandica,*
and *Mya arenaria,* of the last three nothing but small fragments were seen, and of *Tellina Balthica* only a few nearly perfect
valves, but the single specimens of *Nassa reticosa, Anomia,* and
Dentalium were nearly perfect, as were two or three of *Scalaria
Grænlandica* and *Natica Grænlandica* ? The reappearance of

---

[*] Rep Brit. Assoc for 1870, Trans. of Sections, p 90, "Supplement to the Crag
Mollusca," p. xxii , and Quart. Journ. Geol. Soc., vol, xxxvi , p 484.

Crag forms may be explained by the submergence of the land to a greater extent than had occurred since the time of the Coralline Crag, thus re-opening the connection with the southern seas, and allowing species long exterminated in this area to again migrate into it *

Boulder Gravels and Sands

These Gravels, capping most of the hills near Cromer, form the heathy table-land which adds so greatly to the beauty of the district. To this division Trimmer gave the name "Upper Erratics;" his "Lower Erratics" including all the underlying Boulder Clays, which he correlated with the Great Chalky Boulder Clay of Suffolk † Messrs. Wood and Harmer identify these Gravels and Sands with the "Middle Glacial Sands" of Yarmouth, and consider that they fill old valleys excavated in the Contorted Drift.‡ But an examination of the cliffs or of the published section will at once dispel this idea, for it is seen that the basin-shaped hollows in which the Gravels lie are in every case the result of contortion, and not of erosion.§

• These Gravels, like the similar deposits near Norwich, are characterized by the large well-worn flints which they contain; and, as far as can be judged by the mapping and inland sections, the two deposits are continuous. The relation to the Contorted Drift is peculiar, and will be again referred to. There is a more or less eroded line at the junction, and the Gravels often do not seem so much disturbed as the underlying beds , yet all the large contortions clearly affect both deposits, and in no instance has a contortion been found cut off above by the Gravel. The general structure perhaps indicates that the formation of the contortions and the deposition of the Gravels were proceeding simultaneously. No fossils whatever have yet been seen in this bed, except a few derivative fragments from the Boulder Clay, and a broken molar of Elephant.

Description of the Cliff Section.

Happisburgh.—At the cliff end near Happisburgh the stony Boulder Clay of the Contorted Drift rests directly on the Intermediate Beds, but a few yards north, near the Cart Gap, the fine sands appear between. A quarter of a mile further, the first large contortion appears, forcing the whole of the lower beds beneath the beach line, and allowing a mass of sand to occupy the whole of the cliff for about 400 yards. The manner in which some of the beds have been nipped out by the contortion is not easy to account for. Near the Low Lighthouse the section, taking the thickness of the beds at the points where they successively rise above the beach, is —

		Feet.
Soil - - - - - - - -		2
Boulder Gravel - {	False-bedded sand with thin seams of gravel, and a line of unworn flints, marking the horizon of a dissolved bed of re-constructed chalk shown further south in the middle of the sand -	30

---

* See also p. 58
† Quart. Journ. Geol Soc., vol. vii, pp. 19-31.
‡ Ibid , vol xxxiii., p. 74
§ See Geol. Mag , Dec. II, vol. vii , p 59

			Feet
Contorted Drift		Sand and stony loam, irregularly mixed -	8
		Shelly Boulder Clay - - -	6
		Blue loam with seams of sand, much contorted - - - -	7
Sands - -		False-bedded fine loamy sand -	20
Intermediate Beds -		Bedded blue loam - -	3
First Till -		Hard stony Boulder Clay -	10+

The total height of the cliffs nowhere exceeds 45 feet, and it is probable that the lower beds are not continuous all the way under the Boulder Gravel, though just north of the Lighthouse they can be seen in vertical succession, only a portion, however, of the highest and lowest beds being visible

The Sands continue, but a short distance to the north-west the Contorted Drift thins out and does not come on again till Hasbro' Gap is passed. The highest part of the cliff north of Happisburgh shows well the erosion at the base of the Contorted Drift, but the irregularity is not usually so great

Paston —As the height of the cliff becomes less, the Stony Loam and the Sands successively thin out, and do not reappear for three miles, till Paston Cliff is reached. At this place the Stony Loam has thickened to about 40 feet, and a contortion brings in a mass of gravelly sand, as at Happisburgh It is noticeable that here again there is a thin bed of reconstructed Chalk in the middle of the sand. Between Paston and Mundesley numerous small contortions and included nests of gravel are seen in the Contorted Drift, but otherwise the beds call for no remark.

Mundesley to Trimingham —North-west of Mundesley the beds undulate a good deal, the disturbance gradually extending into the lower deposits, and becoming more violent, till at last, at Gimingham and Trimingham, it affects the solid Chalk At Gimingham the Contorted Drift has cut through or " eaten up " all the beds between, and rests directly on the Chalk, with which it can be seen to be mixed on the foreshore The normal position of the Chalk would be below low-water mark ; but it has been thrown into a series of undulations, which have the effect of raising it above the sea-level, and allow it to be examined on the foreshore for nearly three-quarters of a mile These undulations, which at very low tides may be seen to form definite anticlinal and synclinal folds, have their axes parallel with the coast line, though minor flexures often obscure the structure when only a small exposure can be seen. The bending has been so violent as to squeeze up a ridge of Chalk ; of which, judging from the dips on the foreshore, the two Chalk bluffs seen in the cliff appear to be the last remnants In all probability, about 200 years ago there was a continuous cliff of disturbed Chalk, at least half a mile long, though the greater part of this must have been denuded long before the first scientific account of the coast was written Though no record can be found of a continuous Chalk cliff at Trimingham, the older writers on the geology of this coast all mention *three* pinnacles, while at the present day there are only *two* The destroyed mass was a short distance south of the remaining ones , and Lyell describes it as extending a few yards only into the cliff, so that before long it would be entirely destroyed. The two remaining bluffs also extend only a short distance, and are rapidly getting smaller , in a few years the sea will have surrounded them, and probably in 50 years the last remnant of this interesting contortion will have entirely disappeared from the cliff The northern Chalk bluff was 106 yards in length when Lyell measured it, but is now less than 40 yards, and the part where he saw Boulder Clay extending for 7 feet under the Chalk has been destroyed This mass has been forced up till its surface is 40 feet above high-water, and probably about 60 feet above its original level. It forms an inverted anticlinal bent inwards, or to the south-west, over the Boulder Clay, which can be seen behind and under it when the cliff is free from talus (see Fig. 13, p 116).

That this contortion is of Pleistocene date is proved by the similar disturbance of the overlying beds, and by the intrusion of tongues of Boulder Clay into the Chalk. Lyell was fully aware of this conformity, and gave illustrations of it, he mentioned the mixture of Chalk and Boulder Clay on the foreshore, and considered that the contortion must clearly have been formed subsequently to the deposition of the Drift Many later writers, however, have

FIG 9

Cliff Section north of Happisburgh.

Scale, 150 feet to an inch

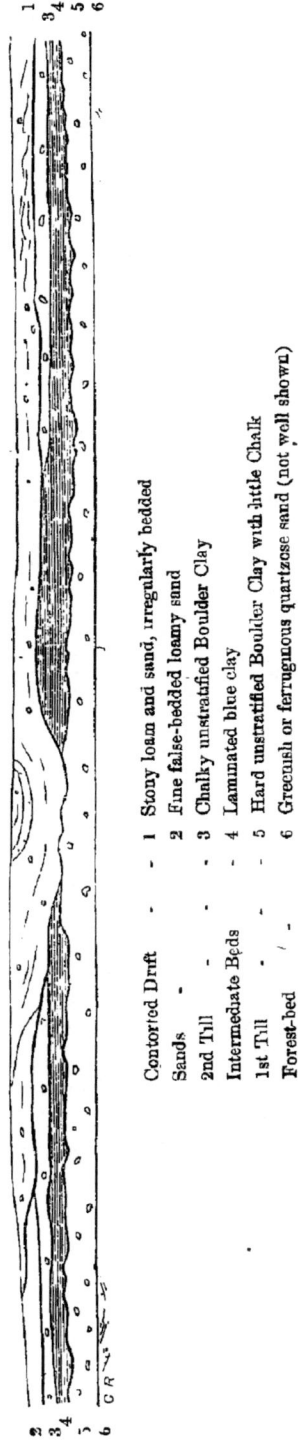

Contorted Drift　-　-　- 1　Stony loam and sand, irregularly bedded
Sands　-　-　-　- 2　Fine false-bedded loamy sand
2nd Till　-　-　- 3　Chalky unstratified Boulder Clay
Intermediate Beds　-　- 4　Laminated blue clay
1st Till　-　-　- 5　Hard unstratified Boulder Clay with little Chalk
Forest-bed　-　-　- 6　Greenish or ferruginous quartzose sand (not well shown)

adopted the view that these Chalk bluffs are the remains of pre-glacial isolated stacks or pinnacles, and in a recent paper Mr. A J Jukes-Browne supports this theory *

The principal difficulty in the way of the acceptance of this view, is the great improbability that a small hill of Chalk could exist all through the time of the deposition of the beds from the Weybourn Crag to the Contorted Drift; for this would necessitate its exposure at three distinct periods to the action of the atmosphere, rain, and frost, and at three other periods to marine denudation, its height causing it to be exposed during the whole of this time The Boulder Clay under the folded Chalk, which Mr. Jukes-Browne considers to be evidence of undermining (apparently not having been able to see it on account of the talus), is certainly connected with the contortion, as is also the case with the alternations and intrusive tongues of Boulder Clay seen on the foreshore The origin of the contortion will be discussed further on (see p 115).

The Rev O Fisher has described and figured some cavities in these Chalk bluffs, which, as they are only exposed through the removal of the Drift, he considers "must have been formed and filled in the interval between the formation of the bluff and its envelopment in Boulder Clay." Mr Jukes-Browne considers these to be old sea-caves, and, taken in connection with the undercutting, he thinks they prove old marine action on the Chalk cliff

For a long time these caves were a great difficulty, and though, in reply to Mr Fisher's question as to their origin, I suggested that those seen by me were formed by the sharp folding of the Chalk, which opened cracks, it was not until the winter of 1880–81 that a large one could be examined.†

On the north side of the southern bluff of Chalk there was a small opening, which on clearing away the talus proved to be the entrance to a long but very narrow cave This cave was about three feet high, and the width perhaps sufficient to have allowed me to creep into it as far as could be seen,'though, as it would have been impossible to turn, I only went a yard. At about 20 feet from the entrance, the cavity bent sharply to the left, and might continue some distance further The deposits in this cave were merely a little sand and clay, only extending a foot or two from the entrance, washed in from the Boulder Clay; beyond, there was nothing but fallen lumps of Chalk and unworn flints, mixed with oxide of manganese, which also filled all the minor cracks. Similar unworn flints projected from every part of the sides and roof, half exposed by the dissolution of the Chalk

Some of the smaller fissures and caves in both bluffs were filled with beds of sand and loam, mixed with oxide of manganese, to near the roof, but none of them contained anything like the materials of the Pre-glacial beds seen only a few yards away. As the Rev O Fisher has seen a better section of these stratified beds than any exposed of late years, his section will be quoted The cave in which the deposits occurred was seen in the eastern face of the northern Chalk bluff, which, projecting beyond the general coast line, can be examined on three sides The height of the cavity (of which a figure is given in the Geological Magazine, Dec II, vol. vii, p. 149,) was 6 feet, and the width about 3 feet The following is Mr Fisher's section —

a. Sea sand with rolled and subangular pebbles - 4 in
   On this rest fragments of chalk and flint, and flints fallen from the roof.
b. Laminated calcareous sand with specks of carbonaceous matter. The material is apparently derived from partially dissolved chalk - - - - - 10 in.
c. Black carbonaceous layer - - - 2½ in
d. Calcareous sand without carbonaceous matter - - 1 ft
e Disintegrated chalk
f. Fine sand
g Disintegrated chalk.

Mr. Fisher informs me that the "carbonaceous layer" may be oxide of manganese, which is common in all the cavities now to be seen.

---

* Ann Nat Hist, ser v, vol vi, p 305
† Mr. H B Woodward has noticed similar sandy pockets in the disturbed Chalk at Trowse —" Memoir on the Geology of the Country around Norwich," p. 136

These deposits are very like ordinary "cave-earth" formed from the dissolution of the Chalk, alternating near the mouth of the fissure with sand and gravel washed in from the Boulder Clay   The cavities were probably formed, like most caves, by the slow percolation of surface water, and their gradual formation has probably taken place without the Chalk being exposed at the surface.   The sharp bending of the Chalk caused incipient fissures, which have been slowly enlarged during the whole period between the formation of the contortions and the present day.   This explanation seems to be supported by the number of unworn flints which the cavities contain, and also by the amount of water which, percolating through the Drifts, is given out by the gravel patches in the neighbourhood.

Several authors mention Pre-glacial beds as occurring on the top of the Chalk bluffs, but this, as already mentioned, is a mistake   The fossiliferous sands there seen are merely patches of the ordinary Glacial deposits, full of the usual far-transported Boulder Clay stones, and without any trace of the common characteristic Crag fossils   The contortion of the Chalk appears to have forced it into the overlying beds, and compelled the Boulder Clay to mould itself to all hollows and open fissures; it has even, in some places, caused the Drift to underlie in mass the inverted anticlinal of the solid Chalk *   What becomes of the "Forest-bed" near the Chalk bluffs is not easy to make out; on the Sidestrand side of the northern bluff it can be traced to within 90 yards of the Chalk, quite undisturbed   The unseen 90 yards have always been a good deal hidden by talus, at least of late years, but it is quite possible that the Chalk has actually been folded so as to overlie Pliocene Beds as well as Boulder Clay   Between the two bluffs there is also undisturbed Forest-bed at the base of the cliff, though the foreshore exactly opposite, and only 130 yards from the cliff-face, consists of sharply undulating Chalk, mixed here and there with Boulder Clay.   The whole structure of the beds points to a long sharp fold with its axis parallel to the coast-line, and extending only a short distance into the present cliff, thus, when the two bluffs have disappeared, there will probably before long be a continuous section of the Forest-bed in the new cliff some yards south-west of the present face

In the upper part of the cliff at Trimingham there are also some very large contortions   One of these apparently causes the Boulder Gravel, as seen in the cliff face, to send an intrusive tongue for 270 yards into the Stony Loam   In reality the beds are curved and perhaps inverted, so that in the sloping cliffs the same bed appears twice.

FIG 10

Cliff section near Low Street, Trimingham (seen in a projecting point)

Scale, 100 feet to an inch.

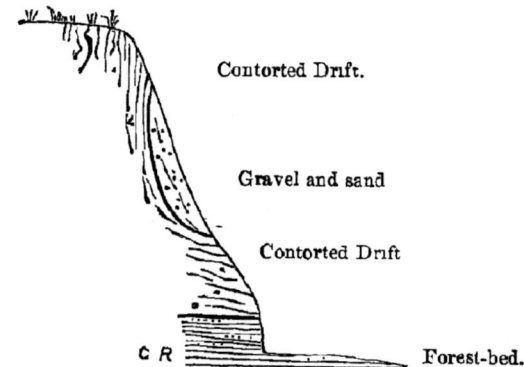

* See also p 116.

At several points the bed of reconstructed Chalk reappears in the middle of the gravel Notwithstanding its thinness, this bed is very important as marking a definite horizon, and also as pointing to conditions very different from those under which an ordinary marine gravel is deposited It may be a Boulder Clay, though I have not observed that any of the included flints are striated

Between the Boulder Gravel and the Stony Loam there are, generally, bedded sands, loams, and marls, probably representing the Middle Glacial; but here they are unfossiliferous

The lime-kiln at Low Street, Trimingham, is situated on a small hill of flint-shingle overlying a thick irregular mass of reconstructed chalk, which is dug for lime The contortions in the underlying loam and bedded marl are unusually sharp and angular, reminding one of those often seen in gneiss. Though contortions are much more conspicuous in the clay beds than in the overlying gravel, it is clear that the disturbance affects both, but in the incompressible gravels it often takes the form of faulting instead of contortion. These faults in the Glacial Gravels were particularly well shown in the railway cuttings near Cromer.

Notwithstanding all this contortion in the higher beds, affecting even their base, for more than a mile and a quarter the Pliocene deposits in the cliff opposite Trimingham village are quite undisturbed, the line of junction being sharply defined, and only rising and falling four or five feet in the whole distance Nearly a mile north of Low Street there is, however, a sudden change , for an exceptionally violent and complicated contortion cuts through the beds to beneath the beach line, and occupies the foreshore for fully half a mile. This is one of the few places where the nature of the underlying beds seems to have affected the composition of the Boulder Clay , for here were obtained from the base of the Contorted Drift several fragments of Forest-bed wood and bone, green-coated flints, fragments of *Tellina Balthica, Cardium edule, Cyprina Islandica, Astarte borealis, A sulcata*, and a nearly perfect specimen of *Pleurotoma turricula.* The drifts, in spite of their contortion, show a definite succession, though the beds are often nipped out , where complete, the order appears to correspond with that seen at Mundesley, patches of unstratified Boulder Clay very like the Till being preserved here and there at the base

It was found impossible always to separate these patches of Till, so both they and the stratified marls belonging to the Middle Glacial, have been coloured in the section as part of the Contorted Drift in the districts where the disturbance has so thoroughly mixed the beds

Notwithstanding this, it is probable that if the cliffs were continuously watched for a series of years by any one living on the coast, so that the whole could be examined free from talus, the succession of beds seen at Mundesley would be definitely traced at intervals as far as Cromer Though the whole mass of the Drifts appears to have been shifted after the beds were deposited, and the talus prevents a continuous section being seen, there is so great a similarity in the succession at various points that there is little doubt the beds were originally continuous.

Sidestrand.—Near Sidestrand the Pliocene Beds reappear, and for a mile and a quarter no contortion affects them The disturbance in the Drifts is very marked, especially in the upper part At the base, instead of contortion, there appears to have been a lateral sliding of the beds over one another; for they contain horizontal slickensides, and in one case the sliding has caused the same succession to be repeated, the Second Till and Sands being shown twice in a vertical section without inversion

Between Trimingham and Cromer the base of the Drifts should be carefully examined, for it appears at first sight to consist of evenly bedded Boulder Clay. On closer examination this laminated clay is seen to be full of horizontal slickensides, and apparently to be a clay-breccia, of which the broken fragments have been flattened out like dough under a rolling-pin. The appearance of bedding is very deceptive, for in this case it seems to be nothing but the effect of sliding pressure on the base of the moving mass, allied to slaty cleavage, and quite unconnected with a sedimentary origin

Fig. 11.

Section at right-angles to the Cliff near Sidestrand Church.

Scale, 60 feet to the inch

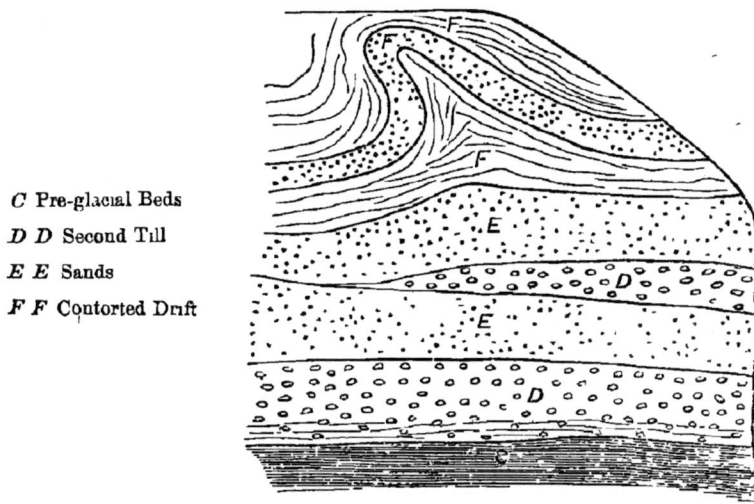

C Pre-glacial Beds

D D Second Till

E E Sands

F F Contorted Drift

Overstrand —About 600 yards south-east of Beck Hithe, the first of the transported masses of solid Chalk is seen   At the base of the Contorted Drift were two boulders of Chalk, each about 60 feet in length, one being within a foot of perfectly undisturbed Pliocene beds   A short distance further two more boulders occurred, and immediately north of Beck Hithe there was a fifth   west of that, no more were seen till Cromer was passed.

At Overstrand contortions and talus very much obscure the succession, and it was found impossible to obtain any accurate measurements of the thickness of the different beds   The Boulder Gravels must originally have been very thick, for where contortion has made them fill basin-shaped hollows, as at Kirby Hill, they measure over 100 feet   Great part of this thickness may be due to lateral compression, and a seaward dip, but, on the other hand, a good deal may have been lost by denudation

Cromer.—Between the Lighthouse Hill and the town, a large marl-pit has been dug in a mass of reconstructed Chalk, which is seen also in the cliff-face. The Chalk is very free from admixture with other materials, and, were it not for the occurrence of scattered quartz pebbles throughout, it might be taken for a very large boulder of the solid rock

In the cliff between the kiln and the Coast Guard station, good illustrations may be seen of the conformity between the Boulder Gravels and the Contorted Drift, for, however irregular the base of the Gravels may be, the lines of contortion always correspond and are not cut off   Mr. Alfred Savin states that several years ago he obtained from one of these gravel patches portion of the molar of an elephant, unfortunately not preserved   This is the only fossil known to have been found in these beds

Opposite the village, as the cliffs have been sloped, no section can be seen till the western end of the sea-wall is passed   Here the beds are very violently contorted, and just before the sandy part of the cliff is reached (called the Marram Hills) a contorted mass of laminated carbonaceous loam is seen included in the Boulder Clay   This mass, though no recognizable fossils could be found in it seems to be a boulder of the " Forest-bed " or associated deposits, caught up in the Boulder Clay, just as the Chalk boulders so common in the same neighbourhood have been. The Chalk-masses, being very conspicuous in the cliff from their contrast with the nearly black Boulder Clay, have long been known, but this mass of Pliocene Beds is the only boulder of that age yet found.

The large mass of gravelly sand a few yards further west seems to represent the "Middle Glacial," for it is not nearly so coarse as the Boulder Gravel in the immediate neighbourhood. Besides containing abundance of shell-fragments which may be derivative, it yielded a perfect *Dentalium* The other species are *Natica* sp, *Astarte compressa, Cardium edule, Cyprina Islandica, Mya ?* and *Tellina Balthica.* At its western end, the Contorted Drift is seen above as well as under the Gravel; an appearance probably due, as in the section at Trimingham already described (*see* Fig 10, p 98), to an inversion of the Boulder Clay. The great apparent thickness of this mass of sand is also deceptive, owing to the high angle of the bedding . the real thickness most likely does not exceed 20 feet

From this point to Runton Gangway the contortions are too intricate for description, and readers must be referred to the separate published Sheet of sections

Runton —The section at Runton will be best understood by reference to the folding plate at the end of this volume For half a mile the Contorted Drift is full of boulders of solid Chalk, varying in size from a few feet to over 180 yards in length.* These boulders correspond in character very closely with the Chalk seen on the foreshore in the immediate neighbourhood, but are separated from it by undisturbed Pliocene Beds At one point the Contorted Drift has ploughed into the solid Chalk, but only for a few yards. Long tongues of black Boulder Clay are seen in many of the Chalk masses, cutting across the lines of flints, and much resembling small intrusive basaltic dykes

At the point under Wood Hill where the Boulder Clay has cut down to the solid Chalk, it appears to fill a narrow channel sloping seaward , so that, while at the foot of the cliff there is still a little of the Pliocene Beds beneath the Contorted Drift, a short distance away, on the foreshore opposite, it can be seen to rest directly on the solid Chalk The bottom of this hollow, seen at the foot of the beach, contains a large collection of boulders of considerable size, and is the only place on the coast where far-travelled boulders are known to occur in quantity, or otherwise than scattered through the Boulder Clay, The deposit may be described as a very coarse gravel, a large number of the boulders exceeding a foot in diameter. At first sight it might be considered to be a heap brought by a single iceberg, which, stranding, cut a groove through the older deposits, and, melting, filled it with its cargo of rocks In the way of the acceptation of this explanation there are, however, several difficulties First, notwithstanding the irregularity of the overlying beds, the lines of contortion in the whole of the cliff above, here 160 feet high, seem distinctly connected with the outline of this hollow , secondly, no iceberg could well bring such a very miscellaneous collection of boulders, without calling at a number of widely separated localities, and picking up a few stones at each, in a way that neither icebergs nor shore-ice are known to do at the present day The boulders over a foot across were septaria (Kimeridge or Oxford Clay), earthy limestone (Lias ?), Coal Measure sandstone, Carboniferous Limestone, hard purple sandstone (Old Red ?), hard grits (Silurian or Cambrian ?), basalt, diorite, mica-schist, and gneiss; in fact, just such a mixture of rocks as might be obtained by washing a large quantity of the Contorted Drift May this channel be ascribed to the action of a subterranean stream, like those of limestone regions, which eroded its bed when the overlying Drifts were frozen, and on their thawing allowed them to subside into the hollows? At present there appears no other mode of accounting for the various difficulties

About 200 yards east of the small stream between Wood Hill and West Runton Gap is seen the contorted mass of gravel already mentioned as yielding a fauna corresponding in character with that of the "Middle Glacial Sands" of Yarmouth (*see* folding plate) This section is especially interesting as showing so markedly that the contortions are of later date than the deposition

---

* Some of these boulders have been figured and described by Sir C. Lyell, Mr. S V Wood, Dr James Geikie, and others

of the inter-glacial beds, and not (as has been stated) formed at the period of the Contorted Drift, and subsequently cut into by valleys afterwards filled with the "Middle Glacial Sands." The deposit consists of a mass of very chalky gravelly sand, with the lines of bedding nearly vertical, wrapped round, except at the top, by conformable sheets of Stony Loam   The shells found were generally crushed by the contortion, and could not be removed without falling to pieces, they were —

> *Littorina littorea* (fragments common).
> *Nassa reticosa* (one perfect specimen)
> *Natica Grænlandica?* (rare but nearly perfect).
> *Paludina glacialis?* (one worn specimen).
> *Purpura lapillus* (fragments).
> *Trophon antiquus*, reversed var (one fragment)⁻
> *Scalaria Grænlandica* (rare but nearly perfect).
> *Anomia* sp (one perfect specimen).
> *Astarte borealis?* (one fragment).
> —— *sulcata* (two fragments)
> *Cardium edule* (fragments abundant).
> *Cyprina Islandica* (small fragments abundant).
> *Leda* sp (two fragments).
> *Mya arenaria* (fragments common).
> *Nucula Cobboldiæ* (one small fragment).
> *Pecten* sp (two fragments).
> *Pholas crispata* (fragments common).
> *Tellina Balthica* (very common, and sometimes perfect)‿
> *Balanus* sp.
> Fish vertebra
> Rolled mammalian bone
> Wood.

Immediately east of West Runton Gap there is another patch of this shelly sand, resting for some distance directly on Pliocene Beds, though at the same time its position is clearly the effect of contortion, and not of erosion

Beeston —Towards Beeston the contortions become even more intricate than before, and again cut down to the Chalk, though for a distance of fully a mile no disturbance has affected the even junction of the Drifts and the *Leda-myalis* Bed. Between West Runton Gangway and Beeston Stream, a large mass of unstratified marl occupies the whole of the cliff for 160 yards. This marl has been extensively dug for lime, and being mixed with a small proportion of clay it forms a sort of passage between the pure reconstructed Chalk and the marly Boulder Clays. In it has been found a calcaneum of deer, now in Mr Savin's collection. The cliff-face shows very well-marked vertical jointing, like that of a limestone

From this point to Beeston Stream the Contorted Drift cuts to, or nearly to, the Chalk. A few yards west of the stream the line rises abruptly, and then continues at the same level as before. The sudden way in which all these scoops commence is very marked. The junction of the Drift and Pliocene Beds will continue at a nearly uniform level for a considerable distance, and then, without a gradual incline, the Contorted Drift scoops into the lower beds, often at an angle of 30° or 40°. Under Beeston Hill there is another small scoop, affecting the Chalk and squeezing it up into a boss (*see* Fig 12, p 115).

The Drifts in Beeston Hill are too intricate for description, and no definite succession is recognizable, though here and there a little of the Till appears to have been preserved over the Arctic Fresh water Bed. The Contorted Drift, when traced for a considerable distance, is found to contain more and more marl westward and nearer to the bare Chalk. West of Cromer the greater part of it would be more properly described as a marl than as a stony loam.

Sherringham.—The pinnacle of Chalk figured by Lyell in the Drift west of Sherringham has long disappeared, and at present Chalk boulders are only of occasional occurrence near this village. West of Skelding Hill several large masses of rock are seen in the cliff; but otherwise the complicated contortions call for no special remark, and attention need only be drawn to the extraordinary shape of the mass of sand which forms great portion of Skelding Hill (*see* Horizontal Sections, Sheet 127).

Weybourn —From Old Hithe to Weybourn the Contorted Drift may be described as a streaked marly Boulder Clay, with included masses of sand, gravel, and reconstructed Chalk No boulders of solid Chalk are now to be seen, but, the cliffs being low, they may have existed in the higher part long since lost by denudation.

For two miles and a half no disturbance has affected the Pliocene Beds, but at the cliff end, Weybourn, the Contorted Drift suddenly ploughs through the beds deep into the underlying Chalk.

Inland Sections.

General Description.

A study of the cliff sections will at once show that it would be a hopeless task to attempt to trace definite horizons in the Glacial Beds inland; for, even with a continuous exposure, the connection is often lost through the violent contortion of the different beds. In mapping the country it has therefore been necessary to keep to lithological divisions alone, for it is impossible in many cases to say to which of the various horizons an isolated exposure of sand or stony loam may belong. For this reason, after a general description of the deposits, the details will be given under the heads, "Contorted Drift," and "Gravels and Sands," with merely an indication of their probable equivalents in the cliff. It has not been thought necessary to insert in this Memoir full notes of inland sections, which are merely the counterparts of what is seen in the cliff-face, and which throw no fresh light on the Geology of the district; only the more important exposures of the beds will therefore be described.

Looked at broadly, the lowlands are occupied by the Contorted Drift, and the hills by Gravels and Sands; but contortions like those of the coast often cause bosses of marl and loam to occupy the top of the hills, while Boulder Gravel is sometimes seen at their foot.

The Contorted Drift of the southern and eastern portions of the district is generally a stony loam, the masses of reconstructed Chalk being almost entirely confined to the country north of Gunton and west of Trimingham.

The table land south of Weybourn and Cromer is formed by a continuation of the Boulder Gravels and Sands seen in the cliff. These beds can be traced from Sherringham Heath, by Felbrigg, Roughton, and Northrepps, to the coast at Sidestrand and Trimingham. Southwards they continue to Southrepps, Wilton, North Walsham, and Aylsham, forming the heath-lands of Marsham and Cawston, Abel Heath and Tuttington Heath, besides numerous small outliers; the deposit being probably continuous with the Boulder Gravel and Sand of Mousehold, near Norwich.

The Boulder Gravels and Sands replace each other laterally, so that while near the coast the boulders are principally at the base of the mass, near North Walsham and Aylsham, Mr. Woodward describes the Sand as being capped by Boulder Gravel. It is, however, impossible to say whether many of the inland sections of sand belong to the Boulder Gravel or to the Middle Glacial.

No definite traces of Chalky Boulder Clay occur in the area, although present about a mile west of Woodrow Farm, Cawston (in Quarter-Sheet 68 S.W.)

Inland Sections of Contorted Drift.

East of the Ant the inland sections are of little interest, consisting merely of pits in stony loam dug for bricks, or of shallow wells

Ingham —Just south of the Chapel a well showed :—

		Feet.
Glacial Drift { Brick-earth	- - - - -	10
{ Yellowish sand	- - - -	2

The Gravel-hole at its north end is entirely in gravel, but at the southern side there is a lenticular mass of brick-earth, clearly included in the gravel. This brick-earth is used for making drain-pipes and bricks. The total depth of the pit is about 30 feet, and the bottom, which must be near the level of the Alluvium, is always wet.

At the Brick-kiln three furlongs south-east of Ingham Church, there was.—

	Feet.
Gravel (irregular)	
Stony loam - - - - -	about 8
Fine false-bedded sand - - - -	5+

The well in the pit extends about 5 feet deeper.

Another Brick-kiln, a quarter of a mile east of the Church, showed —

	Feet
Pebble gravel (very irregular).	
Stony loam - - - -	4 to 10
Fine false-bedded sand with carbonaceous grains - -	4+

Witton.—In the Norwich Museum there is a last upper left molar of *Elephas primigenius*, which Mr. Gunn informs me was obtained "from Drift marl at Witton, near Bacton" Though no other specimens of mammoths' teeth have yet been recorded from the Boulder Clay of the country described in this Memoir, they are not uncommon in other districts.

Gimingham and Southrepps.—North of the North Walsham and Dilham Canal no sections of interest are seen till Gimingham is reached. Here, at a place called Lime-kiln Farm, is seen the first inland exposure of the reconstructed Chalk   On the opposite side of the stream there is another patch, and near Southrepps several more   None of these call for any further notice.

Roughton —At Roughton there are evidently large patches of marl, but the sections are not good.

Beckham and Upper Sherringham —Numerous marl-pits have been worked, showing that inland, as in the cliff, the beds become more marly when traced westward.

Overstrand.—All the inland marl-pits yet mentioned are in reconstructed Chalk, and not in Chalk boulders. At Overstrand, however, there is a pit which, though now only showing rubble, seems originally to have been dug in a transported boulder of solid Chalk, for Sir C Lyell gives an illustration, and describes it as showing distinct lines of flints *

No other sections of the Contorted Drift in the northern half of the map show anything but the ordinary Stony Loam or Marl   Numerous pits are opened, worked for a few years, and then ploughed over.

---

* Phil Mag., ser 3, vol. xvi , p 362.

The following notes relating to the south-west portion of the district are by Mr. Woodward :—

Marsham —North of the ʇ of Cambridge (on the map) 8 feet of stony loam was worked for brickmaking.

South of the *m* of Marsham (on the map) a pit showed .—

					Feet.
Glacial Drift -	Irregular brick-earth	-	-	-	3 to 4
Upper Crag -	Pebbly Gravel	-	-	-	3
	(*Water*)				

Brick-earth has been opened up above the *F* of Fengate (on the map), and east of Heath Farm.

Aylsham —At the Brick-kiln, about 1 mile south of Aylsham, the following beds were shown (the junction between them was even) .—

					Feet
Glacial Drift -	Stony loam	-	-	-	15 to 20
Upper Crag -	Buff sand	-	-	-	10

Near Warren House a section at the brickyard showed :—

	Feet
Buff false bedded sand and fine gravel - -	6 to 8
Brown sandy brick-earth (with chalky and flinty mass near top), passing down into greenish sandy brick-earth, with *Tellina Balthica, Cardium edule, Cyprina Islandica, Mya arenaria*, and fragments of *Inoceramus* - - -	8

Brick-earth has been worked N of Woodgate, and at the well dug for the little cottage further north, 25 feet of brick-earth was penetrated, so I was informed by Mr R J W Purdy   West of Woodgate Farm an old pit showed a boss of Contorted Drift, comprising brick-earth with a jamb of marl, surrounded by the sands which cover the higher ground of this neighbourhood

Sandy brick-earth has been dug by the *A* of Aylsham (on the map), to the depth of 10 feet   On the surface a pocket of buff sand was shown.

East of Woodbine Cottage, brick-earth has been dug beneath 8 or 10 feet of sand.   At the Railway station the well was sunk 25 feet through sandy brick-earth   Water was obtained at a depth of 18 feet.

A temporary well, sunk about half a mile west of the station, proved the following beds .—

					Feet
	Sand	-	-	-	10
Glacial Drift	Brick-earth and sand	,	-	-	10
	Blue clay	-	-	-	7

Immediately to the south-west of Spratt's Green, clay has been dug out.

Beneath the words " Wood House," of Aylsham Wood House (on the map) the soil is sandy, although brick-earth seems to have been dug there

The loamy districts around Aylsham and those forming the lower grounds of Banningham, Felmingham, Suffield, and Coleby, probably constitute the best land in what is sometimes called the Vale of Aylsham   From the general fertility of the soil, the numerous trees in plantations and hedge-rows, and the gently diversified scenery, the district round Aylsham has been termed the " Garden of Norfolk."

Blickling —6 feet of stony loam has been worked beneath 8 or 9 feet of sand at Whitetop Common.

Banningham.—The Brick-yard S. of the church showed 8 to 10 feet of brown loam resting on 6 feet of buff sand, the sand possibly occurring in a pocket.

Half a mile S. of the church, on the Aylsham road, a well sunk for the new Farm House (1879) showed :—

					Feet.
Loamy soil	-	-	-	-	1 to 2
Glacial Drift -	Sand	-	-	-	13
	Loam	-	-	-	4 to 5

The sand appears to rest in great hollows or contortions of the brick-earth, and to be interbedded with it.

Tuttington —Above the words " Ship Inn " (on the map), 6 feet of stony loam was exposed.

A little further to the south the following section was opened, showing:—

		Ft.	Ins.
Soil		1	0
Glacial Drift - { Pebbly and angular gravel		2	0
Stony loam		3	0
Upper Crag - Pebbly gravel		0	6 shown.

Skeyton —The Brick-yard N E. of the church showed 12 feet of brick-earth, overlaid by 10 feet of buff sand

Felmingham —By the last *e* of Waterloo Cottage (on the map) 5 feet of stony loam was opened up.

Brick-earth was also shown in excavations for the Rifle Butts east of the King's Head Inn

Suffield —East of the Rookery Farm, brown stony loam has been dug for the manufacture of bricks, tiles, ornamental vases, &c.

West of Lubbocks Alder Car, 9 ft of brown stony loam has been opened up

Westwick —Westwick Church is situated on brick-earth, beneath which is sand. The house is built on sand with a loamy soil on top.

Worstead.—East of the Obelisk in Westwick Park, a brick-yard showed —

		Feet.
Glacial Drift - { Buff sand		4 to 5
Stiff sandy clay with nests of buff sand near the top		20 (dug)

South-east of Penny Wood an old pit showed marl, brick-earth, buff and brown sand, confusedly arranged, and evidently part of the Contorted Drift

North Walsham —At the old Brick-yard west of the town about 15 ft. of brick-earth was dug

A well by some new cottages south of the word "yard" (on the map) was sunk about 40 feet, through brick-earth, into pebbly gravel, &c.

South of the *al* of North Walsham (on the map) brick-earth with nests of sand has been opened up.

H. B. WOODWARD.

Inland Sections of Gravels and Sands.

The only data for the inland mapping of the Gravels being the slope of the ground and the character of the vegetation, the boundaries on the map must only be taken as approximate, for the base line is so uneven and contorted that neither level nor apparent superposition can be accepted as a guide As the different Glacial Gravels are all mapped together, there are often near the base alternations of Gravel and Contorted Drift, which are mapped as one or the other according to the preponderance of pervious or impervious beds. Thus, with regard to these particular deposits, the Geological Survey Map in this district is essentially a lithological map, and does not always represent the relative ages of the various gravels and loams.

Ingham.—A pit north of Ingham Church showed:—

		Feet.
Gravel with large bouldered flints, seams of marl, and well-bedded pebbly sand		about 22
Fine sand and shingle		8

A few yards away the gravel is lost, probably in a contortion. This pit was deepened till water was reached.

Brumstead.—A patch of gravel occurs west of the Church, but there is no section.

Wayford Bridge.—The gravel at Wayford Bridge is remarkable for its coarseness, and the abundance of the large *Ostrea vesicularis* which it contains. Besides these oysters, so characteristic of the highest part of the Norfolk Chalk, it contains many of the porous flints only found *in situ* at Trimingham. The oysters are often covered with annular chalcedony (*Beekite*)

Witton and Edingthorpe.—In the large outlier extending from Crostwight to Knapton and Edingthorpe, pits have been opened at several places. One on Witton Heath shows about 15 feet of false-bedded sand and sandy gravel Another at Edingthorpe is in coarse boulder gravel and fine sand, contorted with the brick-earth.

Trunch and Trimingham.—Though very variable, the gravel between Trunch and Trimingham usually contains many large flints A pit at Middle Street, Trimingham, showed coarse false-bedded gravel, with obscure bedding, and a large proportion of the stones with their longer axes vertical.

Southrepps and Northrepps.—At these places there appears to be more sand than gravel, though the sands seem generally to have a gravelly base

The cuttings for the line between Southrepps and Cromer showed very good sections of gravelly sand, the boulder beds having died out. At the crossing west of Pit Farm, Southrepps, there was —

	Feet.
False-bedded rather loamy buff sand, with much carbonaceous matter, and lines of colour	25

The cuttings between this point and Cromer all show similar beds, but rather more gravelly.

The first cutting from Cromer Station is entirely in buff and orange sandy gravel, well-bedded, but not much false-bedded. The stones are mostly angular and sub-angular. Though these sands are evenly bedded for a considerable distance, at one point the bedding is tilted till for a few yards it becomes perfectly vertical, proving that some, at least, of the contortions are of later date than the deposition of the sands. Close examination often shows that these bedded sands, and the similar deposits in the cliffs, are full of small faults, though at a short distance the stratification seems undisturbed.

Roughton to Weybourn.—Similar beds extend over Roughton Heath, but the gravels appear to become coarser as they are traced westward, till at Weybourn they correspond in character with the "Cannon Shot Gravels" of Norwich

North Barningham.—A large pit on the west side of the church showed .—

	Feet.
Soil	1
Boulder gravel	8
Brown bedded gravelly sand	6 +

The following notes on the south-west portion of the district are by Mr. H. B. Woodward .—

Calthorpe.—S. of the church a deep and picturesque lane-cutting showed the junction beds of sand and brickearth. The northern portion of the outlier of sand and gravel at Calthorpe is partly formed of pebbly gravel.

Blickling—On Abel Heath from 6 to 8 feet of sand has been dug. Above the so of Mausoleum (on the map), sand and gravel has been opened up

Oulton.—East of the old workhouse, Oulton, about 15 feet of sand was exposed, containing pockets of brown loam, which looked like relics of Chalky Boulder Clay.

Cawston.—South-east of Woodrow Farm, sand and gravel has been opened up to a depth of 8 feet.

Aylsham.—S E. of Woodgate, and immediately east of the lane, sand was opened up to a depth of 8 feet.

The cutting at Aylsham station, and the foundation for the railway bridge, showed —

		Feet.
Irregular loamy soil		
Glacial Drift	Buff and yellow sand, with streaks of brown clay	10 to 12
	Sandy brick-earth with veins and nests of sand	3 to 5

About a quarter of a mile north-east of Bolwick Mill, a pit showed 3 feet of sand resting on 3 feet of pebbly gravel.

West of Spratt's Green, by the bridge, the following beds were opened up —

	Feet
Soil and reddish-brown clay - - -	3
Buff and brown sand with loamy veins - -	12

The sand seems to belong to the Crag series

By the plantation N E of Bolwick Mill a pit showed buff sands with seams of angular gravel, containing flint, quartz, and carbonaceous matter

Brampton —West of the church, and immediately south of the railway bridge, the following beds were exposed —

		Feet.
Glacial Drift	Fine angular and rounded gravel, and sand with large flints -	5 to 8
	Partly stratified brown brick-earth or stony loam, chalky in places - - -	3 to 5
Upper Crag -	Grey, white, and yellow sand - -	3

The beds were much disturbed, the brick-earth and overlying gravel occupying a sort of basin in the lower (or Crag) series of sands These latter, appearing as fine brown and white false-bedded sand, formed the mass of the cutting north of the bridge.

Burgh.—South of the *w* of New Barn (on the map) 10 feet of buff sand was exposed.

Skeyton.—North-east of the church a pit showed 6 feet of buff iron-stained sand, and fine gravel, with a number of large unworn flints.

Swanton Abbot —Several sand-pits have been opened on Swanton Hill, in one of which about 20 feet of stratified and false-bedded buff and brown sand was to be seen.

Westwick.—East of Old Woman's Plantation about 10 feet of buff sand was exposed.

Worstead.—Fine sections of the sand may be seen on Sandy Hill, by Bunns Hill Wood, and in the railway cuttings   In the cuttings of the Yarmouth and North Norfolk Railway 20 to 30 feet of false-bedded buff sand was exposed It contained scattered pebbles and lines of ferruginous gravel.

At the Almshouses 15 feet of buff sand was opened up

North Walsham.—East of the Great Eastern railway station the following beds were exposed :—

		Feet.
Glacial Drift	Irregular and somewhat contorted loamy and sandy deposit, with a few unworn flints and gravelly seams - - - -	5
	Coarse stratified boulder-gravel, chiefly flints, with a few quartz pebbles - - -	3

South of Field Mill, about 8 feet of coarse flint gravel, with pebbles and boulders of Igneous rock and Quartzite, was opened up A loamy and clayey soil occurred on top. These beds were also exposed in the cutting of the Yarmouth Railway, west of the Mill To the south, 15 feet of buff false-bedded sand, with a little gravel, was exposed in the railway cutting.

H. B. WOODWARD.

Transported Boulders.

Mention of the numerous large boulders scattered about the country has been reserved till the end of this Chapter ; for as they are almost always found loose on the beach, or placed by the road-side, it is often impossible to say from which of the different Glacial Deposits they have been derived. A person driving through the country might be struck by the abundance of boulders, though at the same time it is rarely possible to find a stone of over a foot in diameter in place in the cliff section This apparent abundance of large boulders is, however, quite deceptive ; they are in reality very rare, and those seen are the sole remains of the denudation of large extents of the cliff, or of broad inland valleys

Two reasons contribute to the large show of boulders often seen around farmhouses and by the road-side. The first is the high farming which has led to the removal of every large stone found on the fields, these being customarily placed in the conspicuous positions where they are now seen. The second is that brick being the general building material, no tools capable of breaking a large bouldered mass of hard rock are used in this district; therefore only the smaller stones, which can be broken by an ordinary stone-breaker's hammer, are used for road-metal, while the large masses are quite valueless, except as horse-blocks, or for the protection of ditches and the corners of houses Some of the boulders are used for building, but in the walls they are as well preserved as they would be in the fields, seldom being broken, but merely selected for their shape

Leaving out of account the transported masses of Chalk, which I believe have only travelled a short distance, the largest boulders consist of gneiss, mica-schist, garnetiferous-schist, hornblende-schist, hard metamorphic grits (Silurian or Cambrian ?), quartzite, Carboniferous Limestone, Coal Measure Sandstone, Old Red Sandstone, granite, diorite, and basalt. The smaller boulders are generally flints, hard Chalk, Oolites, Lias, and a very miscellaneous collection of igneous and metamorphic rocks of, at present, unknown origin.

During Easter of the present year (1882) the Director General of the Geological Survey went over this district with me, and examined many of the boulders, to settle, if possible, the country of their origin He informs me that a large number of them are in all probability Scandinavian. Of the metamorphic rocks many could not have come from any part of the British Isles nearer than the north-west of Scotland ; there is nothing like them in the southern Highlands, and marked and abundant south Scottish rocks are absent from the Norfolk Drifts. It seems therefore far more probable that these boulders are of Scandinavian origin, ·than that they have crossed from the north-west of Scotland without being mixed with a large proportion of the rocks from intervening districts.

The following notes include the larger boulders, the first two being the only ones I have seen measuring over 6 feet in length :—

Light-coloured quartzite, $7\frac{1}{2} \times 5 \times 4$ feet; on the foreshore at Sidestrand.
Apparently granite, but so rounded that it cannot be broken, $6\frac{1}{2} \times 4\frac{2}{3} \times$? feet; on the foreshore at Runton
Granitic rock, about $2\frac{1}{2}$ feet ; at Bessingham Church
Carboniferous Limestone, large Boulder at Happisburgh
White quartzite 4 feet long, Sexton's Wood, Felbrigg Park, in the path close to the high road.
Basalt, large mass showing portion of four columns , opposite the entrance to Broomholm Abbey, Bacton.

At Cromer, Beeston, and Bacton there are numerous boulders of meta-morphic, granitic, and basaltic rocks, commonly about 2 feet in diameter.

Black Meg, a large mass on the foreshore at Runton, has been described as a boulder of granite; but if this refers to the one now seen, it is a fallen mass, consisting of flint conglomerate cemented by lime and clay. Such masses are often formed in the Contorted Drift.

Mr. H B Woodward mentions that by the high road, north of Marsham Church, three boulders of veined grit may be seen, one of them 4 × 3 × 2 feet.

CHAPTER XIII.—ORIGIN OF THE CONTORTIONS.

Summary of the Facts to be explained.

A study of the cliff sections near Cromer brings out several facts as to the mode of occurrence of the contortions, which must be accounted for before we can pretend to understand their origin. At present so many difficulties stand in the way of every explanation which has yet been brought forward, that it will be advisable to give a summary of the facts and phenomena noted in detail in the last Chapter, drawing special attention to the points to be explained; then an outline of the different published theories, with a discussion of the facts which seem to support or oppose them; and finally a sketch of the view the study of the cliffs has led me to form. The latter is only brought forward tentatively, for the difficulties are so great, there is so much dispute as to important facts shown in the cliffs, and we are at present so entirely ignorant, except hypothetically, of the behaviour of ice in large sheets, that new discoveries may any day overthrow our most generally accepted theories.

The leading points brought out in the last Chapter are, firstly, that the so-called "Contorted Drift" consists of deposits of various ages, formed under very different conditions, and including large transported masses of Chalk, Pliocene beds, and of the various Pleistocene deposits formed before the contortion took place; secondly, that it is a deposit of very irregular structure, resting unconformably on any of the older beds, and eating into them in a peculiar manner at present unexplained, curiously like the replacement of stratified beds by sheets of basalt; thirdly, that these contorted beds, though often violently disturbed at their base, generally rest with a horizontal junction on the quite undisturbed deposits beneath; fourthly, that no contortion is cut off above by stratified beds deposited on its upturned edge, and that some of the large contortions affect the whole thickness of the cliff from the Chalk to the Boulder Gravel.

Old Theories.

The origin of these disturbances has long been a disputed question; for they are on so large a scale, are so complicated, and appear so unlike anything we have elsewhere in Europe, except in the Island of Moen,[*] that it is not surprising that great difficulty should have been felt in explaining their mode of formation.

---

[*] *See* Lyell, "Antiquity of Man," 4th edit., p. 388; and Johnstrup, Zeitschrift der Deutschen Geol. Gesellschaft, 1874, p. 583

The older writers referred these, like most other unexplained geological phenomena, to the action of the Deluge, and it was not till the publication of Sir C. Lyell's paper "On the Boulder Formation" in 1840 that any attempt was made to treat the matter scientifically.* Lyell speaks of the contortions as possibly formed in three ways : "firstly, by ordinary upheaval and subsidence, to which geologists are accustomed to attribute the bendings, inclination, and dislocation of strata; secondly, by landslips, or the sliding down of sea-cliffs, or the falling in of undermined banks of rivers, or of submarine sand-banks; thirdly, by the stranding of islands and bergs of ice. It is possible that all these causes of disturbance may have co-operated to produce the complicated movements which we now behold in the cliffs under consideration." After discussing the three explanations, Lyell adopts the theory that the contortions were formed by the stranding of icebergs and large masses of packed ice, and then describes similar though much smaller contortions formed at the present day in the Arctic Regions

In 1851 Joshua Trimmer brought forward the theory that the contortions had been formed by the melting of included masses of ice, which allowed the beds to subside into irregular cavities The Rev O. Fisher, in 1868, among other explanations, stated that "in attributing contortions in the underlying beds to the deposition of masses of matter upon the surface, I would go to the extent of suggesting that the remarkable bluffs of Chalk at Trimingham may have been upraised by some such action." Most other writers appear to have adopted the floating ice theory in some form, till in 1880 I suggested that the disturbance was caused by the pressure of the ice-sheet which, during the greatest intensity of the cold, probably filled the bed of the North Sea, and ploughed up large masses of Chalk, driving them laterally into the beds †

More recently Mr. T. Mellard Reade has tried to account for the transportation of the large Chalk boulders through the agency of submarine springs, the water of which, freezing in fissures in the Chalk, gradually forced up large blocks, and at last caused accumulations of ice sufficient to float the detached masses ‡

Objections to the received views.

To the first theory, that the contortions were caused by deep-seated disturbances, there is the fatal objection, as Lyell pointed out, that the beds beneath violent contortions are generally quite horizontal In the case of the Trimingham Chalk, about which Sir C. Lyell felt uncertain, subsequent observations by the Rev. O. Fisher, and others made in the course of the Geological Survey, have shown that its relation to the Boulder Clay and "Forest-bed" are such as can only be accounted for by a force acting

* Phil Mag., ser. 3, vol. xvi , p. 345
† Geol Mag , Dec II , vol. vii , p 55.
‡ Quart. Journ Geol Soc , vol. xxxviii., p 222.

from above, pinching up the Chalk and forcing the Boulder Clay into it. This disturbance at Trimingham will again be alluded to.

The second suggestion, that the contortions have been formed by the subsiding of the beds through landslips, is at once met by the difficulty that the materials appear to have been forced up, not let down. No landslips would account for the large masses of transported Chalk above, and separated by evenly stratified beds from, the solid rock, in places where the whole structure of the country shows that no pinnacles or cliffs of Chalk could have existed.

The theory which Lyell adopts, disturbance by icebergs and coast-ice, has been accepted by most writers without hesitation. To this hypothesis, however, there are several objections. The first difficulty is, that it would need a very large iceberg to contort beds 200 feet thick, as at Trimingham; and there is no evidence of any submergence sufficient to float such bergs. No trace of a contemporaneous marine fauna has been found in the Contorted Drift, though dredgings in the Arctic seas show that the marine boulder beds there forming, contain abundance of life. The second objection to the marine theory is, that we ought to find sedimentary Boulder Clays formed from the materials brought by the ice. Yet the only marine beds that do occur are the sands, which show no trace of glacial action. The associated Boulder Clays do not appear in any instance to be sedimentary, and there seems to be no stratified deposit formed contemporaneously with the contortion, unless it be the unfossiliferous Boulder Gravel which caps the hills. A third difficulty is, that the icebergs, to plane off such an even surface of Pre-glacial Beds as we see in these cliffs, must be flat-bottomed (not jagged as icebergs usually are), and all submerged to the same extent. The ice must move quite steadily, not rocking, and must be of great thickness, or else it would at once pack and form an irregular base. These and numerous other minor objections make it difficult, after an examination of the coast, still to accept the theory of the agency of floating ice in forming the Contorted Drift of Norfolk.

Trimmer's hypothesis, of the melting of included masses of ice which caused the beds to subside into hollows, is probably the true explanation of many of the smaller contortions, but it, of course, leaves undecided the origin of the Chalk Boulders and of the contortions in solid Chalk.*

The Rev. O. Fisher's theory of the forcing up of the beds by irregular deposition of masses of material on their surface, seems inadequate to the formation of contortions on so large a scale. It is doubtful whether anything less than a mountain piled on the surface at Trimingham would be sufficient for the contortion of two hundred feet of underlying strata; and even that would scarcely account for the inversion of the Chalk,—a phenomenon

* See also *ante*, p 82

R 1195. H

which seems impossible of explanation, except on the hypothesis
of a lateral thrust, or of a sliding pressure from above   This
inversion of the solid Chalk seems also a fatal objection to
Mr. Mellard Reade's theory.

The Land-ice Theory.

Taking all the facts into consideration, it appears probable
that the contortions must be accounted for by the agency
of the land-ice, shown by Scotch and Scandinavian geologists to
have covered so large a portion of northern Europe during part
of the Glacial Epoch   Various reasons have led my colleagues
Drs. Croll and James Geikie to consider that the ice-flow was
from the north-east; and it is interesting to find that the strike of
the larger folds in the Contorted Drift on the coast also points
to a force from the same direction *   The extreme shallowness of
the North Sea would cause it to be entirely filled with ice, which,
flowing over or abutting against the older Drifts, contorted them
in the way we now see.

A heavy ice-sheet flowing over the beds, in this higher land where
no water could collect beneath it, would drag the underlying
deposits.   When these beds happened to be alternations of clay
and sand, they would slide over one another, the sands saturated
with water acting as a lubricated surface over which more
coherent masses could readily be moved.   To this cause I am
inclined to refer the generally undisturbed state of the Pliocene
Beds , for we find that when clays occur immediately under the
Boulder Clay they are disturbed, but when sands they are generally
unaffected except for a few inches   Thus the dragging of the beds
over one another sometimes only affects the highest deposits in the
cliff, but, however low it may extend, its limit is always marked
by some continuous sandy bed

If this theory is correct it accounts for the repetition of the
deposits, as shown in Fig 11 (p. 100), and also for the bedded, or
rather flattened, structure so often mentioned as occurring in the
Contorted Drift.   It also explains the lamination at the base of
the Till in districts where that deposit has been affected by these
later movements.

Transportation of the Chalk Boulders.

The next point to be considered is the origin of the large Chalk
boulders, and the means by which they have been transported to
their present sites.

On the iceberg theory it is very singular that these transported
masses should be entirely confined to that portion of the coast on
which the solid Chalk is at a sufficiently high level to be occasionally
ploughed into by the Contorted Drift   It is also curious that the
boulders, as before mentioned, correspond with the Chalk in the

---

* Croll, " Climate and Time," 1875 , J. Geikie, " Great Ice Age," 1874. [Ed. 2, 1876.]

immediate neighbourhood, that is to say, to beds which, if there had been a sufficient submergence to float large icebergs, would be entirely out of reach beneath the sea level.

I believe that on the coast can be seen boulders of Chalk in every stage of manufacture, and that none of them need have been moved more than a few hundred yards from their original bed. In Figs. 12 and 13 are shown what appear to be two stages of the formation of a boulder.

The first, taken under Beeston Hill, shows the Contorted Drift scooping down to the Chalk, and driving it up in a boss or ridge The second is a section of the north-western Chalk bluff at Trimingham, as seen in the projecting point at right angles to the cliff. The third stage is represented by the enormous boulders at Runton (see folding plate).

If the ice-sheet, instead of flowing over the beds, happens to plough into or abut against them, it would bend up a boss of Chalk, as at Beeston. A more extensive disturbance, like that at Trimingham, drives before it a long ridge of the beds, and nips up the Chalk, till, like a cloth creased by the sliding of a heavy book, it is folded into an inverted anticlinal A slight increase of pressure, and the third stage is reached,—the top of the anticlinal being entirely sheared off, the Chalk boulder driven up an incline, and forced into the overlying Boulder Clays

This bending of the solid Chalk can scarcely have taken place suddenly, but must have occupied several years, or at least months. The extent of the disturbance at Trimingham also points to the employment of enormous force, as well as a steady pressure. Though much has yet to be explained as to the cause of the flow of an ice-sheet, the acceptation of this agency seems the only way of accounting for these phenomena. By continental geologists the theory has already been applied to the explanation of the even greater disturbances seen in the Island of Moen in Denmark *

The masses of reconstructed Chalk so common in the Contorted Drift are probably nothing but a later stage of the transported boulders, in this case so shattered and mixed with clay that they form a sort of transition to an ordinary Boulder Clay. From the very marly character of the Contorted Drift when traced westward,

FIG. 12.

Section of the Base of the Cliff under Beeston Hill

Scale, 50 feet to an inch

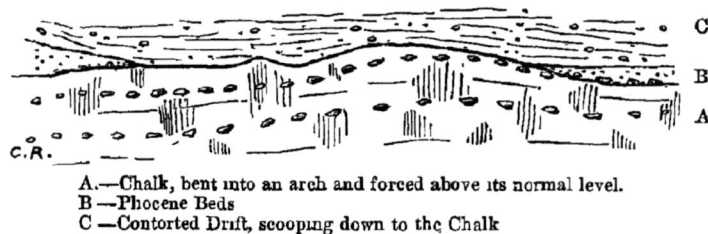

A.—Chalk, bent into an arch and forced above its normal level.
B —Pliocene Beds
C —Contorted Drift, scooping down to the Chalk

* See Johnstrup, Zeitschrift der Deutschen Geol. Gesellschaft, 1874, p 533.

FIG. 13.

Section at right-angles to the Cliff through the westerly Chalk Bluff at Trimingham.

Scale, 200 feet to an inch.

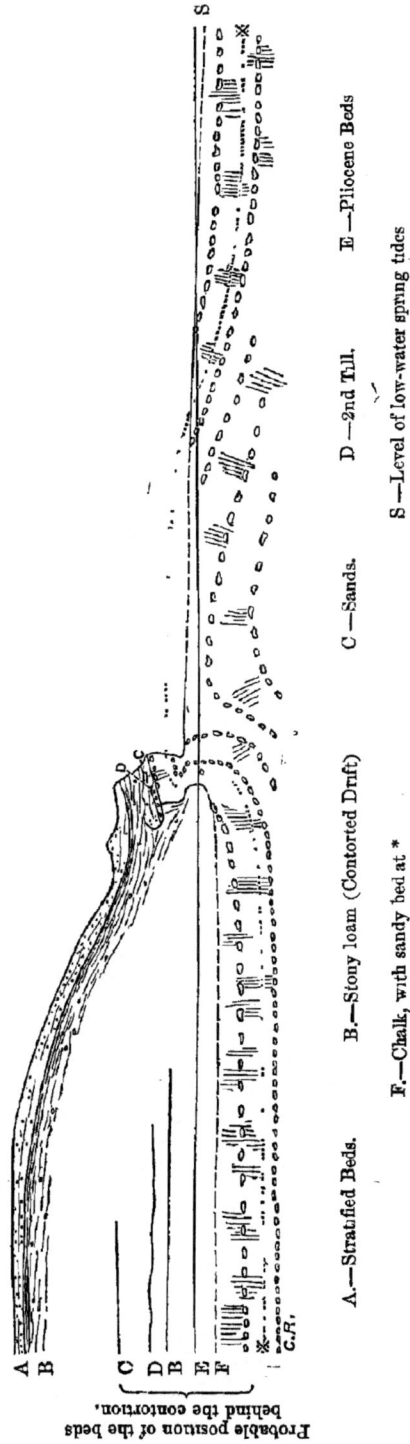

A.—Stratified Beds.　　B.—Stony loam (Contorted Drift)　　C.—Sands.　　D.—2nd Till.　　E.—Pliocene Beds

F.—Chalk, with sandy bed at *　　　　　　S.—Level of low-water spring tides

it seems not improbable that that portion of the deposit is continuous with and passes laterally into the Great Chalky Boulder Clay. The general structure of Norfolk and Suffolk appears to show that the whole of the contortions are of one age, that of the greatest glaciation, or of the Great Chalky Boulder Clay, and it is probably to this period that the disturbances on the coast may be referred (see also Norwich Memoir, p. 137).

Effect of Contortion on the apparent Thickness of the Beds.

If the beds have in reality been subjected to a powerful lateral thrust, as above suggested, the height at which any particular deposit is now found is no criterion for its original position. It is clear that the Trimingham Chalk has been squeezed up, and driven far above its normal level; and, as the same contortions have still more violently affected the newer beds, these also have probably been raised, and their apparent thickness much exaggerated by the lateral compression. Taking the depth of the little disturbed beds at Mundesley as a scale, and supposing the measurement at Cromer originally to have been about the same, contortion has increased the thickness from 150 feet at the former place to about 250 feet at the latter.

Origin of the Boulder Gravels.

The origin of the unfossiliferous Boulder Gravels still remains to be explained. From their structure they seem more like the deposits of a turbulent lake or flood than ordinary marine shingle; for though the flints are often thoroughly rounded, in many places they are quite unworn. This peculiarity, in addition to the fact that the stones have often the longer axes vertical, points to the agency of strong currents, and not of the regular surf of a beach. There is also a marked limitation in the distribution of the Boulder Gravels, which may be connected with their mode of origin. They commence just where the Chalky Boulder Clay ends, the two deposits only being known to occur together at one or two localities, where, for a short distance, the gravel extends over the Clay.* This peculiarity has already been noticed by Messrs. Wood and Harmer,† who described these beds as " Cannon Shot Gravels "; and I am inclined to agree with them, that the Gravels may be "a local modification of the clay due to the action of some powerful current over this part of Norfolk"; or they may have been formed in an ice-dammed lake, liable to sudden floods, and to the heavy waves caused by falling masses of ice. The term " Flood Gravel " is used by Mr. Skertchly for beds of this description (Geology of the Fenland, pp. 196, 208). It is noticeable that, if derived from the Boulder Clay, or from the same source as the Boulder Clay, nearly all the softer rocks must have been destroyed, the deposit now consisting almost entirely of flints.

---

* See " Memoir on the Geology of the Country around Norwich," p. 129
† " Supplement to the Crag Mollusca," Pal Soc., Introduction, p. xxvii.

CHAPTER XIV—ALLUVIAL DEPOSITS— PLEISTOCENE FOSSILS.

The Post-glacial Beds in this district consist entirely of valley deposits, without, so far as is yet known, any trace of marine beds like those seen at Hunstanton or in the Nar Valley. As these deposits are of small extent and of very similar origin, they will all, notwithstanding their different ages, be included in the present Chapter, except the Shingle and Blown Sands, which will be more conveniently described in the Chapter on Denudation

Older Valley Deposits.

Bacton.—On each side of the Coal Gap, and also about a quarter of a mile north-west of the Coast Guard Station, just above the beach, there is seen some gravelly and sandy Alluvium, and at the latter place a patch of stiff blue carbonaceous clay

At Bacton Green there commences a thick deposit of valley gravel, overlaid at the Gap by a little peaty loam The gravel consists of little worn flint and other stones washed out of the Boulder Clay It rests, with a very irregular base, on the eroded surface of the Glacial or Pre-glacial Beds, cutting at one or two places to beneath the beach-level, but generally capping a low cliff. The thickness of the gravel varies from 5 feet near the Gap to upwards of 45 feet about half a mile to the north-west At its base, a few yards from the point where it is thickest, a jaw of *Elephas primigenius* was found, coated with moss, and evidently long exposed in the cliff face From the pervious nature of the gravel the jaw had entirely decayed, leaving only a soft clayey substance However, three molars were obtained, and are now in the Museum of Practical Geology The section given by Lyell, as showing regularly stratified Glacial Gravels resting on the truncated edges of the Contorted Drift, appears from his description to have been taken at the north-western end of this deposit, and therefore is only evidence of Post-glacial and not of Glacial denudation.[*]

Inland these gravels are continued (in local patches) as an old river-terrace connected with the Bacton Valley, rising to nearly 50 feet above the present Alluvium One outlier has been mapped immediately east of Bacton Church ; and there is perhaps, trace of another overlying the "Forest-bed" gravels on Crostwight Heath. The latter, however, is too uncertain to be mapped.

At Dilham Long Common and Smallburgh Hill the gravel reappears, and is of very considerable thickness At a large pit at the latter place. about 250 yards east of the parsonage, there was —

	Feet
False-bedded, coarse, angular flint gravel, with large scattered flints and a little laminated loamy sand - - -	20 +

A good many of the porous flints, so characteristic of the Trimingham Chalk, are seen in the gravel , and in one place there is a little brick-earth overlying it, probably a wash from the Boulder Clay Mr. Gunn informs me that bones have been found in this pit, but only elephant could be recognised.

Mundesley —The next section of valley deposits exposed in the cliff is the well-known one at Mundesley (*see* Folding Plate). Here, between two beds of Valley Gravel which coalesce at the edge of the basin, there is a thick lenticular mass of peaty loam with plant remains, shells, bones and elytra

---

[*] Phil Mag , Ser 3 , vol. xvi , p 351, Fig I., and "Antiquity of Man," 4th edit , p 262, Fig. 35

of beetles This deposit, as already mentioned, was confounded by the older observers with the "Forest-bed," and was accepted by them as proving the interstratification of fresh-water beds with the Glacial series.

Lyell in 1840 described the section, and gave a long account of the character of the deposit and the included fossils; among the latter he mentions and figures the *Hydrobia marginata* (given as *Paludina minuta*), a shell now extinct in England The woodcut accompanying his paper shows fresh-water beds dovetailing into the Boulder Clay, though at the same time Lyell states that during his earlier visit in 1829 he "inclined to the conclusion that the Mundesley formation . . . . might, as a whole, be considered as the deposit of a lake or hollow excavated in the drift "*

In 1861 Prof Prestwich pointed out that two quite distinct fresh-water deposits had been confused, and gave a carefully drawn section of the beds, in which was shown the basin in nearly the same state as now † Other writers have since restated that the bed is intercalated in the Boulder Clay, or, as Messrs Wood and Harmer describe it, it undercuts that clay ‡ Though at the present day there is no trace of this intercalation at Mundesley, it is quite probable that such may have been seen a few years ago The Boulder Clay is much inclined to slip into a valley, even when the sides are less steep than those of the old Mundesley river In this way it may cover part of the peat, and afterwards be covered by a continuation of the same No section on the Norfolk coast shows this interbedding, but I have lately seen in Holderness an exposure of alternating Valley Gravel and Boulder Clay undoubtedly formed in this manner, though the clay, unless closely examined, seems quite undisturbed.

Several interesting additions have recently been made to the fauna of the Mundesley "river bed," as it is often called, and it now possesses a distinctive character which makes it of special interest to the geologist Among the fossils is a molar of *Elephas antiquus*, found in making the gangway, and now deposited in the Norwich Museum In the same Museum are the remains of a water tortoise, *Emys lutaria*, obtained as long ago as 1863 by Mr. C W. Ewing, but not recorded till 1879 § *Emys lutaria* had only once previously been found in England, and this locality was also in Norfolk, being near East Wretham. In the course of the Geological Survey a large portion of the skeleton of a bird, the red-throated diver, *Colymbus septentrionalis*, was found at the base of the loam Probably the missing parts of the skeleton had been washed away by the sea, for some of the bones projected from the face of the cliff Among the shells is *Hydrobia marginata*, now extinct in England, but living in the south of France || A seam of peat at the base of the loam is full of leaves of willows, and scattered throughout the deposit is abundance of *Ceratophyllum demersum*.¶

The lowest part of the hollow cuts a few feet below the beach line, and near this spot the details of the section are —

								Feet
Soil - - - - - - - -								3
Gravel and a little sand - - - - - -								8
Peaty and sandy loam, full of fossils, and with a seam of peat at the base								30
Clayey gravel, penetrated by roots - - -								4
Gravel (bottom not seen)								

---

* Phil. Mag , Ser. 3 , vol. xvi ,p. 352. *See also* "Antiquity of Man," 1st edit , p 224.

† Geologist, vol. iv , pp 68, 119

‡ Supp to Crag Mollusca.

§ E T Newton, "On *Emys lutaria* from the Norfolk Coast." Geol. Mag , Dec. II , vol. vi , p 304. *See* also note by H B Woodward, Trans. Norf. Nat Soc , vol. viii., p. 36.

|| Dr Sandberger, however, has described the Mundesley shell as a distinct species under the name *Belgrandia nana*, Sandb , in Palæontographica. vol xxvii , p 88 , but it is very close to the recent *H marginata*

¶ For full list of fossils see table at the end of this Chapter Prof Prestwich suggested that the Hoxne bed, yielding Palæolithic implements, might be of the same age as the Mundesley bed, Phil Trans , Part II , 1860, p 308 , but up to the present time no Palæolithic implements have been found at Mundesley.

Runton —No Post-glacial deposits occur between Mundesley and Runton, but at West Runton Valley Gravels again cap the cliff (*see* folding plate). Though no fossils have been found, this section is of special importance as being the most northerly locality where, up to the present time, Palæolithic implements have been found in stratified beds   In 1878 Mr. Alfred Savin, of Cromer, obtained at this place an axe of the ordinary type,—the only one, as far as I am aware, yet found on the Norfolk coast.

Sherringham —At Lower Sherringham a similar gravel is seen, but no fossils have been found in it.   It can be traced across the common to the foot of the hills.

Weybourn —There is a patch of little worn flint-gravel on the top of the cliff near the Coast Guard Station, apparently of Post-glacial date

Bure Valley —Mr H B Woodward mentions that " between Aylsham and Brampton traces of Valley Gravel fringe the marshland , and by the letter *M* of Mucklands (on the map), the ditch sections showed an indurated gravel or conglomerate " No other Post-glacial deposits are known in that district, except the recent Alluvium, which will be treated of in the next section.

Alluvium.

Palling and Eccles —Between tide marks at Palling and Eccles there is one of the so called " submerged forests," though in reality it is merely a continuation of the Alluvium seen on the landward side of the sand dunes This alluvial deposit is a peaty clay penetrated by roots, which originally was protected from flooding at high water by the sand hills Thus trees were able to grow on it though the surface was slightly beneath the level of spring tides Roots may penetrate much below the sea level, as long as the flow of the land-springs is seaward, and can keep out the salt water The mere occurrence of the smaller roots near the level of low water is no evidence of submergence. This deposit, which contains fragments of bone, and I have been told, antlers of deer, has constantly been mistaken for the much older " Cromer Forest-bed "*

The Alluvium of Palling and Eccles is merely portion of the stretch in which Hickling and Calthorpe Broads occur The whole of the country near Palling is very flat, and it is often difficult to say exactly where the Alluvium ends

Another long strip of Alluvium extends from near Bacton, to the Ant Valley at Honing, then continuing down that valley with a width of about half a mile, to Stalham, where it passes out of the map to which this Memoir refers.

A narrow strip of Alluvium occurs on either side of the Dilham Canal , and Mr. Gunn has stated that " About the year 1824, when the Dilham Canal was being excavated, a bed of peat was cut through, which was found exceedingly rich in mammalian remains, chiefly those of the red deer. Bones of the ox [*Bos primigenius*], sheep, &c , were plentiful, and associated with the remains of man   These were met with at a depth of 12 feet from the surface."†

In the south-west portion of the map Mr. H. B. Woodward observes that " The alluvium occupies but a narrow strip on either side of the Bure and its tributaries in the area The upper portions of the valley of the Cawston Beck show about four feet of bog earth resting on gravel. To the north of Heath Farm a fine skull of *Bos primigenius* was obtained in 1876 in clearing out the bed of the stream, by labourers in the employ of Mr. R. J. W. Purdy. This was presented by him to the Norwich Museum "

Dredged Fossils

Though not strictly within the district described in this Memoir, the dredged fossils are so constantly mixed with those from the " Forest-bed " that it will be desirable to point out the districts from which they have been obtained, and the probable age of the deposits out of which they were washed.

---

* Prestwich, Quart Journ. Geol Soc , vol xxvii , p 464,
† Norwich Mercury, 25th July 1868

The Happisburgh Oyster bed has already been mentioned as yielding numerous "Forest-bed" fossils; but mixed with these are a few of later date, probably derived from the destruction of higher beds in the old cliff, like those in which the jaw of a mammoth was found at Bacton.

Further from the land, the trawlers often obtain teeth and tusks of the mammoth, as well as other large bones, scattered over the bed of the North Sea. The principal locality for these Pleistocene fossils is the Dogger Bank, a shoal under 10 fathoms, 120 miles north-north-east of Cromer, and about 80 miles from the nearest land; though similar fossils appear occasionally to be dredged over a much wider area.

Mr. William Davies has published an account of the Dogger Bank fossils, with a list of the species (most of them collected by the late Mr. J. J. Owles, of Yarmouth) now in the British Museum.* In this paper he clearly separates the dredged Pleistocene fauna from the very different Pliocene one of the Norfolk coast. The species mentioned are :—

Ursus, sp.	*Bos primigenius*, Boj.
Canis lupus, Linn.	*Bison priscus*, Boj.
Hyæna spelæa, Goldf.	*Equus caballus*, Linn.
Cervus megaceros, Hart.	*Rhinoceros tichorhinus*, Cuv.
„ *tarandus*, Linn.	*Elephas primigenius*, Blum.
„ *elaphus*, Linn.	*Castor fiber*, Linn.
„ sp.	*Trichechus rosmarus*, Linn.

Fossils, though originally abundant, are now seldom found, as the whole surface of the Dogger Bank has been gone over again and again by the trawlers, and every loose mass has already been brought to the surface.

Succession of the Deposits.

From the fact that certain of the old valleys have been cut considerably below the sea level, it is evident that during part of the Pleistocene period the level of the land must have been much higher than at present. If we consider that the section at Mundesley was then much further from the sea, it is clear that the sea level must have been lower, or there would be no sufficient fall to allow this small river to scour out its channel. This period of elevation is probably represented by the lower Gravel at Mundesley, and the Valley Gravel with *Elephas primigenius* at Bacton, both of which could only have been formed when the land was higher.

Afterwards some change caused the stagnation of the Mundesley stream, and the silting up of its bed with 30 feet of peaty loam. On this loam was deposited a newer Gravel. The intermediate peaty bed only being known at Mundesley, it is impossible definitely to correlate the Palæolithic Gravel at West Runton with either of the beds at Mundesley. At present too little is

* Geol. Mag, Dec. II, vol. v., pp 97, 443.

known of the fauna and flora of the deposits to admit of any satisfactory analysis. With regard to the physical geography, it may be observed that an elevation sufficient to allow the mammoth-bearing beds at Bacton to be formed, would also bring above the sea-level the Dogger Bank with its similar fauna. This points to conditions very like those under which the Pliocene Upper Fresh-water Bed was deposited, and a re-extension of the Rhine estuary over the shallow southern portion of the North Sea. An advance of the estuary in Post-glacial times would allow of the return of the animals and plants into the area as the climate ameliorated, and account for the re-stocking of the rivers with fish, and also for the occurrence of such species as the water-tortoise in the little stream at Mundesley.

TABLE OF PLEISTOCENE FOSSILS FOUND NEAR CROMER.

	Pliocene.	Arctic Fresh-water Bed.	Boulder Clay	Glacial Gravel	Old Valley Deposits	Prehistoric Alluvium.	Authority.
PLANTÆ.							
Hypnum turgescens, Jens		M					Nathorst.
*Carex, sp	?	M, Ost					Carruthers.
*Cyperus, sp	?	Ost					Carruthers
*Juncus, sp.	?	M.					Carruthers.
*Potamogeton, sp.	?	M, Ost.					Carruthers
Nuphar luteum, Sm.					M		Lyell.
*Ceratophyllum demersum, Linn.	×	M, Ost			M		Carruthers.
*Hippuris vulgaris, Linn.	×	Ost					Carruthers
*Betula nana, Linn					M		Carruthers
*Salix polaris, Wahlb.		Bees., M, Ost.				?	Nathorst and Carruthers.
*——, sp.							
CIRRIPEDIA.							
*Balanus porcatus, Da C.	×			R			
*—— crenatus, Brug.	×			M ? R			
ENTOMOSTRACA.							
*Candona candida, Müller.		Bees.					G. S. Brady

* These species have been examined in the course of the Geological Survey of the district For explanation of Contractions, see p. 127.

Table of Pleistocene Fossils found near Cromer—*continued*

	Pliocene.	Arctic Fresh-water Bed	Boulder Clay	Glacial Gravel	Old Valley Deposits	Prehistoric Alluvium.	Authority.
COLEOPTERA.							
*Byrrhus ?							C. O Waterhouse.
Copris lunaris, Linn.					M.		Lyell
*Donacia crassipes, Fab	×				M.		C O Waterhouse
* ——— sericea, Linn.					M.		C O Waterhouse.
* ——— lœtitris ? Hop.					M.		Lyell
Harpalus, sp.					M.		Lyell.
*Lacon murinus, Linn					M		C O. Waterhouse
*Notiophilus palustris, Duf. or N. aquaticus, Linn.		Ost.					
							C. O. Waterhouse.
LAMELLIBRANCHIATA.							
*Anodonta cygnaea, Linn.	×			R.			
*Anomia, sp.	×			R			
*Astarte borealis ? Chemn.	×			R.			
* ——— sulcata, Da. C.	×			Cr.	M		
* ——— compressa, Mont.	×		passim	passim			
*Cardium edule, Linn.	×		passim	passim			
*Cyprina Islandica, Linn.	×			R			
*Leda, sp. (L. oblongoides ?)	×						
*Mya arenaria, Linn.	×		passim	Cr , R			

* These species have been examined in the course of the Geological Survey of the district

Table of Pleistocene Fossils found near Cromer—*continued.*

	Pliocene.	Arctic Fresh-water Bed.	Boulder Clay.	Glacial Gravel.	Old Valley Deposits	Prehistoric Alluvium.	Authority.
Nucula Cobboldiae, Sow.	×			R.			
Pecten, sp. ...	?			R.			
Pholas crispata, Linn.	×		Hap.	R.	M.		Lyell
Pisidium pusillum, Gmel.	×				M.		
Sphaerium corneum, Linn.	×			passim.			
Tellina Balthica, Linn.	×		Hap.				
* lata*, Gmel. ...	×						
GASTEROPODA.							
Bythinia tentaculata, Linn....	×				M.		
Dentalum, sp.	?			Cr.	M.		
Hydrobia marginata, Mich.	×				M.		
Limnaea peregra, Muller	×		Hap.	R., Cr.			
Littorina littorea, Linn	×			R			
Nassa reticosa, Sow.	×			Cr, R			
Natica Groenlandica? Beck	×			R,			
Paludina glacialis? S. V. Wood	×				M		Lyell.
Planorbis albus, Muller	×	M					
* complanatus*, Linn.	×						
* vortex*, Linn.	✓		Trim.	R	M,		Lyell.
Pleurotoma turricula, Mont...	×				M.		
Purpura lapillus, Linn.	×			R			

* These species have been examined in the course of the Geological Survey of the district

Table of Pleistocene Fossils found near Cromer—*continued*

	Pliocene	Arctic Fresh-water Bed	Boulder Clay	Glacial Gravel	Old Valley Deposits	Prehistoric Alluvium	Authority
*Scalaria Grœnlandica, Chemn.	×						
*Succinea putris, Linn.	×	M. M.		R.	M.?		
* —— oblonga, Drap.	×						
*Trophon antiquus, Linn., reversed var	×			R			
*Valvata piscinalis, Muller	×				M.		
* —— cristata, Muller	×				M.		
PISCES							
*Esox lucius, Linn	×				M		E T Newton
Perca fluviatilis, Linn	×				M		Lyell.
Salmo, sp					M		Lyell.
Cyprinus or Carpo					M.		Lyell
REPTILIA.							
*Emys lutaria, Merr.					M.		E. T. Newton.
AVES.							
*Colymbus septentrionalis, Linn					M.		E. T. Newton.

* These species have been examined in the course of the Geological Survey of the district.

Table of Pleistocene Fossils found near Cromer—*continued.*

MAMMALIA	Pliocene	Arctic Fresh-water Bed.	Boulder Clay.	Glacial Gravel.	Old Valley Deposits.	Prehistoric Alluvium.	Authority.
Arvicola, sp.	?	..	..	..	M.	..	Gunn.
Sus scrofa, Linn.	×	..	..	..	M.	.	Green.
Bos, sp.	?	..	..	..	M.		Prestwich.
Cervus megaceros, Hart.	?	.	..	..	M	Dil.	Green.
* — *elaphus*, Linn.	?		Bees ?	..			Gunn.
* *Elephas antiquus*, Falc.	×	.	...	..	M.	.	Gunn.
* — *primigenius*, Blumb.	×	..	Bac., Small bro'.	Cr ?	..	Dil	Gunn and E. T. Newton.
* *Homo*		..	..	..	(An implement) W.R.		Savin.

* These species have been examined in the course of the Geological Survey of the district.

Bees. = Beeston.   R = Runton.   Cr. = Cromer.   Trim. = Trimingham.
M. = Mundesley.   Bac. = Bacton.   Ost. = Ostend.   Hap. = Happisburgh.

CHAPTER XV.—DENUDATION.

Marine Denudation

The whole of the coast described in this "Memoir is being rapidly denuded by the sea; the rate being perhaps as much as two or three yards a year, though, without a longer series of observations, it is impossible to give an accurate estimate. The following account of the waste of the land has been to a large extent taken from a paper by Mr. Redman,* and from Lyell's Principles of Geology, supplemented by observations and measurements made in the course of the Geological Survey.† During the time I have studied the coast the rate of denudation has been extremely variable. A single storm on 30th January 1877 carried away about a yard along the whole of the coast; and for three furlongs, from the Life-boat Gap at Bacton to Walcot Gap, a strip of land was lost averaging about fifteen yards in width.‡ Since that time this part of Bacton has only been touched by one tide sufficient in height to clear away the blown sand, and probably the loss on the whole of the remainder of the coast has not exceeded a yard.

At Weybourn the Chalk cliffs are protected by a shingle beach about seventy yards in width, which only allows the cliff to be touched by very exceptional tides. Since I have known the coast very little has been lost here. Between this place and Old Hithe a foreshore of Chalk with flints appears at low-water, though at Weybourn the tide rises and falls entirely on shingle.

Lyell mentions that at Lower Sherringham "it was computed, when the present inn was built, in 1805, that it would require seventy years for the sea to reach the spot; the mean loss of land being calculated, from previous observations, to be somewhat less than one yard annually. The distance between the house and the sea was fifty yards; but no allowance was made for the slope of the ground being *from* the sea, in consequence of which the waste was naturally accelerated every year, as the cliff grew lower, there being at each succeeding period less matter to remove when portions of equal area fell down. Between the years 1824 and 1829 no less than seventeen yards were swept away, and only a small garden was then left between the building and the sea. There was, in 1829, a depth of twenty feet (sufficient to float a frigate) at one point in the harbour of that port, where, only forty-eight years before, there stood a cliff fifty feet high, with houses upon it !"

---

* " The East Coast between the Thames and the Wash Estuaries," Proc. Inst. Civ. Eng., vol xxiii , p 186, 1865
† See also S Woodward, " Geology of Norfolk ", Gunn, " Geology of Norfolk," and Athenæum, 1867, p. 455 , Hewitt, " An Essay on the Encroachments of the German Ocean along the Norfolk Coast," 8vo., 1844.
‡ Geol. Mag., Dec. II., vol. iv , p 186.

Groynes have recently been constructed at Sherringham to protect the village; but at the same time they have caused denudation to progress much more rapidly than before on the leeward side. The beach drifts to the east and south-east on this coast, as is proved by the banking up of the shingle on the west side of the groyne at Sherringham. I believe that even as far as Weybourn the movement is in the same direction, though further west, as stated by Mr Redman, the movement is in the opposite direction.*

At Beeston Hill Mr. Redman estimates the loss of land between 1838 and 1863 at the rate of two or three yards annually. Between Sherringham and Cromer the foreshore consists to a large extent of bare Chalk with numerous layers of flints. The large unworn flints have a tendency to collect into irregular lines or "scars," often at right angles to the coast, or inclosing pools of water, used as harbours for the small boats. Some of these ridges rise to a height of about four feet above the Chalk floor, and form permanent features for a series of years, keeping up the beach like natural groynes. The shifting of these scars often leads to the entire obscuring of sections which have been exposed for many years, or, on the other hand, to the discovery of quite new beds. A large ridge of flints at Wood Point having increased lately, the beach has been banked up, and it is not improbable that no good sections may be seen at West Runton for several years.

After the storm of 1877 there was an enormous accumulation of unworn flints at Runton, and it is probable that the rate of denudation on this part of the coast is to a large extent governed by the rapidity with which the flints can be worn into sand. The stones were too large to be moved by ordinary waves, and therefore for a long while formed ridges to protect the coast. After the storm the tints of the beach appeared a good deal darker than usual, and on examination this change was found to be due to the enormous number of flint-pebbles which had been broken or chipped by the violence of the waves, instead of showing merely their ordinary battered greyish coat.

Near Cromer the coast has been artificially protected by groynes, without which it is probable that the portion of town between the church and the cliff would have been destroyed, for it projects beyond the general cliff line. South-east of Cromer the waste is very great, especially as the defensive works at the town prevent the beach from travelling. The cliffs near the Lighthouse are constantly slipping; for, besides being undermined by the sea, the beds are full of water, which often causes very extensive shoots. Another mode by which the cliff is denuded is well illustrated during the east winds of spring. The dry wind blows away the sand in the contortions, till the clays are undercut and fall.† Both the wind and springs appear to play merely a subordinate part in the denudation of this coast; for the rate depends on the extent to which the sea can cut away the unweathered

* "The East Coast . . ," Proc. Inst. Civ. Eng., vol. xxiii, p 186
† Noted by Sir W C Trevelyan, Edin. New Phil. Journ, vol xl, p 207, 1846

R 1195

base of the cliffs, and the beds beneath the sea-level. Whether the
cliff is brought down by land-springs or merely undermined by the
sea, will make little difference, for in either case denudation cannot
proceed till the talus has been cleared away.

Near the Coast Guard Station, Trimingham, the cliffs have
receded 50 yards since the Ordnance Map was made,—equal to
a rate of a little over a yard a year. At Mundesley Church
Mr. Redman states the mean loss at 4¾ yards per annum. The loss
at Bacton during the storm of 1877 has already been mentioned
Between Ostend and Happisburgh the cliffs have been destroyed
at the rate of about 3 yards annually. At Happisburgh Mr. Redman estimates the encroachment at 2¼ yards, but quotes the
"North Sea Pilot" as giving a higher result, viz., 2·83 yards per
annum.

"Since the Conquest the villages of Shipden, Keswick, Clare,
Wimpwell, Eccles, and Ness, or the greater part of them, have
been washed away."*

The churches of Beeston Regis and Sidestrand are now near the
cliff, and lately the latter has been dismantled, for in a few years
it will be reached by the sea A long account of Eccles Church,
now washed by the sea, will be found in Lyell's Principles of
Geology.† The sand-hills, which in 1839 surrounded the tower,
have now moved inland, and left it on the foreshore, several
yards below high-water mark. This portion of the coast is now
protected by groynes.

Besides the ordinary action of the waves on the coast, it is
evident that submarine denudation must go on rapidly up to a
certain depth; for there are now several fathoms of water at places
to which not long ago the dry land extended. A very remarkable
instance of this submarine denudation has been mentioned in
Chapter V. (p. 44), where it was noticed how a storm scoured out
a channel 15 fathoms deep, and the sea tore up slabs of ironstone
from at least 10 fathoms, and threw them on the beach at
Happisburgh. Not only does this mechanical action of the water
erode to a considerable depth, but where the set of the currents
prevents sand from accumulating on the rock, organic action helps
the waste. To as great a depth as the *Laminaria* or oar-weed
extends, rocks are torn from their bed by the action of the
currents on the wide fronds of the plant. Even beyond the
range of the *Laminaria*, any bare Chalk or other soft rock will
be bored by annelids, molluscs, or sponges till it is quite honey-
combed and crumbles away.

It seems doubtful whether any part of the bed of the North
Sea is really beyond the reach of submarine denudation, for even
the deeper parts, like the "Well" in the Wash, only exist because
they are constantly scoured out by the tides. It is therefore
unsafe to consider the North Sea as necessarily entirely formed by

---

* S Woodward, Geol. Norfolk, p 17 The pipes of old wells are frequently
exposed in the cliff
† 12th edit., vol. 1, p. 518.

subsidence; for at the present rate ordinary marine action might denude the shallow-water bay which forms its southern half in less than 100,000 years.

Subaërial Denudation.

Subaerial denudation in the district here described does little beyond carrying the material from the higher lands, and depositing it on the alluvial flats, or in the Broads. From the recent date of the submergence which formed the Broads*, and is now causing them to be silted up, the materials washed down by the sluggish streams are generally deposited long before they can reach the sea. Probably, if it were not for human agency in clearing the channels and tilling the land, little solid matter would be carried away by the rivers of East Norfolk.

Wind denudation, as already mentioned, undermines the cliff, often at the same time depositing sand on the edge above. Thus, near Cromer many parts of the cliffs are capped by Blown Sand, full of land shells. Near the Old Lighthouse the cliffs are covered by five or six feet of this sand, which only extends a few yards inland.

At Skelding Hill the blowing away of the sand and soil at the edge of the cliff has laid bare a number of flint chips and flakes, pieces of rough pottery, and the remains of shell-fish used for food. The Hill appears to have been fortified at more than one period.

One indirect effect of the waste of the cliffs remains to be mentioned,—the decrease of the drainage area through the destruction of the land. This may seem a very small point; but when we consider that most of the streams rise near the coast, and flow inland to join the Bure, it is evident that the loss of a strip of land two or three miles wide since the time of the Romans, may have materially affected the amount of water in the Bure, and consequently made it more sluggish.

---

* See also "Geology of the Country around Norwich," pp 3, 143, 146, 148

CHAPTER XVI.—ECONOMIC GEOLOGY.

Soil.

The most important practical bearing of geology in this district is certainly its connection with agriculture. There are no mines, and no minerals of economic importance, except the materials dug for lime, bricks, or road-making

A rich loamy and marly soil extends over most of the area coloured on the map as Contorted Drift, except where the surface is covered by a wash from higher sand-hills The land around Happisburgh and Bacton is considered by many to be the best in Norfolk, though its exposure to the north-east winds makes the crops late. A considerable portion of the district, especially near Cromer, is covered with sand and gravel, forming heaths, as yet only partly cultivated Much of this heath land near Cromer has been planted with trees, the woods seldom extending beyond the area of the gravel The portion under tillage, though forming a very light soil, is often of fair quality ; near the sea, however, it is not uncommon for the easterly winds of spring to blow away from a field the whole of the top-soil with the seed, heaping it against a neighbouring bank.

Good sections of the soil can be seen in the cliffs, and attention may be especially drawn to its unusual thickness on the flat lands near Bacton and Happisburgh It often exceeds 3 feet.[*]

Lime.

Pits have been opened at numerous localities in the reconstructed Chalk; and I have been told by farmers that this impure material makes a better lime for agricultural purposes than pure Chalk[†] In the Bure Valley, pits have been dug in the undisturbed rock.

Road Metal.

Reconstructed Chalk is often mixed with the road metal, and where this is done, and the stones properly broken, the roads are very good. In the district near the sea, the roads are generally made with small stones from the beach ; these, being rounded, never bind properly, and cause the roads to be uneven, and always covered with loose pebbles Inland, stones are obtained from the ploughed fields, or from the gravels.

---

[*] See also Trimmer, "On the Geology of Norfolk as illustrating the Laws of the Distribution of Soils" Journ Roy Agric Soc, vol vii, p 444, 1847.

[†] Mr. Marshall gives a good account of these "chalk-marl" beds in his "Rural Economy of Norfolk," 1787, vol 1, pp 4–30 See also "Memoir on the Geology of the Country around Norwich," p 134

Building Materials.

Brick is the principal building material, except in the churches, where squared flints are used In the parts within easy reach of the sea, large flints and miscellaneous boulders from the beach are often employed, and many of the inland farms are partly built of boulders obtained on the land

The bricks made in the district are usually very bad, more from careless selection of the materials than from the absence of good brick-earth The bed usually dug is the stony loam, corresponding in character with the well-known Norwich brick-earth For temporary purposes, numerous brick-pits have been opened in the shallow soil, which is even worse for brick-making than the stony loam. Where care is taken in the selection of the materials, very fair bricks, pipes, and flooring-tiles can be made Among the more permanent brick-yards may be mentioned those at North Walsham, Suffield, Skeyton, Blickling, East Runton, Ingham, and Ostend, the last being in clean loam or marl without stones, belonging to the Intermediate Beds of the Till.

Peat

Peat has been dug at a few places on the alluvial flats near Dilham, but not in sufficient quantity to call for further notice

Minerals

A considerable quantity of jet is thrown up on the beach, especially after east winds Though generally in small pieces, the quality is fair, and a good deal is manufactured into ornaments by local lapidaries This jet occurs, as derivative fragments, in the "Forest-bed," and is associated with abundance of a shaly lignite or brown coal. It is decidedly different from the Liassic and Oolitic jets found near Whitby, and I believe that it was in all probability originally derived from Lower Tertiary beds under the North Sea, a few miles from the present coast. Mr Savin estimates the average annual find of jet near Cromer at from 10 to 20 lbs. Lady Buxton has an exceptionally large mass from this coast.

Amber also occurs, though the annual yield is considered to be only 3 lbs or 4 lbs. It is generally found in collecting the sea-weed for manure. One piece, now in Mr. Savin's possession, weighs 11½ oz., and was found at Overstrand . the usual size is, however, much smaller. Mr. Savin informs me that he has found both amber and jet in a black bed west of Melbourne House, Cromer, and also directly under the Boulder Clay at Overstrand zigzag, apparently in a disturbed mass of the "Forest-bed" Most of the Cromer amber is cloudy; and the only specimen containing insects, of which I have been able to learn, is one which was some years ago in the possession of Mrs Savin. Probably the jet and amber originally came from the same bed.

Though scarcely belonging to Economic Geology, the other minerals obtained in this district are so few that they may be mentioned here. Agates and carnelians are often found on the beach; but being derived from the Drifts, they can scarcely be considered as Norfolk stones. Pyrites occurs in the Chalk and "Forest-bed"; Calcite in the Chalk fossils; Quartz crystals, in the flints; Beekite (annulated Chalcedony) on fossils in Glacial Gravels; Selenite, in the "Forest-bed" at Sherringham and Bacton; Vivianite (phosphate of iron) stains the Chalk at Trimingham, and is also found in small concretions in the Upper Fresh-water Bed of Ostend, and in Post-glacial Alluvium at Dilham*; concretions of Race (Carbonate of lime) also occur in the Pre-glacial soils, and Oxide of Manganese often fills small fissures in the Chalk.

The occurrence of Iron slag near the ancient earthworks on Beeston Heath was noted in 1868 by the Rev. A. R. Abbott †; but I cannot learn what ironstone was smelted there, though it may have been some of the very ferruginous sand which is now and then found in the Glacial Deposits. The ironstone may, however, have been brought from a distance, as was often the case in well-wooded districts.

It may be useful to mention here the masses of porous slag, so constantly thrown up by the sea, both at Cromer, and other parts of the east of England. These look like pumice, and, unless their origin is known, might be taken for a natural product, especially after they have been some time in the water, and are covered with seaweeds. In reality they are clinkers thrown overboard by passing steamers the denser slags fall at once to the bottom, and only the very porous masses float.

Mineral Waters.

Ferruginous springs are often given out by the Glacial Gravels, but I do not know of any other class of mineral waters in the area. In many places, especially near Overstrand, red stains are seen in the face of the cliff, marking the spots where ferruginous water oozes through the Boulder Clay. The following account of Aylsham and other spas is by Mr. H B. Woodward :--

"About 200 years ago, Aylsham was noted for its Spa, a chalybeate spring situated a little less than a mile south of the church, and now commemorated in the name of the Spa Farm. Probably the same spring trickles along the road-side, issuing from the Glacial Sands and Gravel that cover the rising ground east of the Farm, being thrown out by the Brick-earth (Contorted Drift) beneath. The Spa, it is said, was formerly much resorted to by invalids afflicted with asthma and other chronic diseases It is mentioned by B. Allen in his 'Natural History of the Chalybeate and Purging Waters of England,' 1699, (p. 23,) and by Dr. J. Elliot in his ' Account of the Nature and Medicinal Virtues of the principal Mineral Waters of Great Britain and Ireland, 1781, (p. 127).

* Letter of S Woodward to C B Rose, 30th Nov. 1826
† Norwich Geol Soc, Norwich Mercury, 16th Sept. 1868

"Blomefield also observes, in reference to Oulton (Olton), ' Here is a fine spring called the Spaw, being a strong *mineral*, much frequented formerly, before the Spaw at Aylesham had gained its reputation" (History of Norfolk, vol. iii. 1769, p. 617.)

"In Chambers' 'General History of the County of Norfolk,' (vol. ii., p. 1333,) mention is made of a mineral spring discovered at Mundesley in September 1823 "on the estate of F. Wheatley, Esq. The well which has been sunk is not more than 600 yards from the edge of the cliff, and is 56 feet deep" I can obtain no particulars of the spring indicated by the ' Spa Common,' about a mile east of North Walsham."   H. B. W.

Water Supply.

The greater part of the area is supplied with water from shallow wells, sunk till a spring is met with in the contorted beds This water, though probably wholesome, is hard and generally ferruginous, so that, till one is accustomed to it, the taste is very unpleasant. A few springs are given out at the base of the Boulder Gravel, especially near Mundesley. There are not so many of these as might be expected, for the contortions prevent the underlying beds from holding up the water, as each vertical bed of sand forms a sort of pipe to conduct the water to a lower level. From this cause the only bed that can be depended on to yield a large and constant supply is the Chalk, and lately the town of Cromer has succeeded in obtaining abundance of water from this source.

According to the engineer the surface at the Cromer waterworks well is 117 feet above high-water spring-tides. The well was sunk for 81 feet, then a bore-hole was carried to a depth of 400 feet from the surface After numerous delays a copious supply was obtained from a spring in the Chalk; continuous pumping 10 hours daily for three weeks being insufficient to reduce the level of the spring. The details of the beds passed through are given below, the upper part being taken from my own measurement, and notes,[*] the lower portion from a MS. section belonging to Mr. E R. Priest The beds being contorted, the two sides of the well give quite different results

		S side. Feet	N side. Feet.
Soil 1 foot	- - - - - -	1	1
Contorted Drift, 112 feet	Brown brick-earth with a few scattered angular flints, and flint and Chalk pebbles, occasional thin seams of lead-coloured clay Fragments of *Cyprina Islandica, Tellina Balthica,* and *Cardium edule.*	6	8
	Buff fine sand, rather loamy - -	4	$2\frac{1}{2}$
	Brick-earth as above - - -	$1\frac{1}{2}$	1
	Sand - - - -	$1\frac{1}{2}$	5
	Light lead-coloured Boulder Clay -	8	$4\frac{1}{2}$
	Sand (water at base bad) -	$5\frac{1}{2}$	6
	Blue clayey loam, with very few fossils	$14\frac{1}{2}$	14

---

[*] See also Proc. Norwich Geol. Soc., vol. i , p 129.

		Feet.
	Sand (with a little water) - -	thin seam
	Blue-black clayey loam with a few stones	18
	Soft mud and clay (water at 61 feet and at 69 feet)	19
Contorted Drift, 112 feet.	Wet blue clay and running sand - -	3½
	Stiff clay - - - - -	4½
	Very firm clay - - - -	6
	Do lighter colour - -	6
	Do darker ,, - -	5
	Do hard, with flints - -	1
	Soft wet sandy clay - - -	1½
	Hard blue earth (water level at 111 feet) -	6½
Pliocene Beds, 29½ feet	Soft blue earth - -	4
	Wet sandy earth with flints - -	7
	Running sand with flints - - -	5
	Hard small gravel with a little lignite (described as like concrete).	13
	Flints - - - - -	½
	Chalk - - - - -	3
	Flints - - - - -	¾
	Marl, Chalk and blue clay mixed (the clay probably fallen from above when the bore was enlarged.—C R.)	26
	Chalk - - - - -	11
	Flints - - - - -	3½
	Chalk - - - - -	24
	Large flint - - -	1½
	Chalk (spring at 210 feet) - -	20
	Flint - - - - -	⅛
	Chalk - - - - -	20
	Flint - - - - -	¾
	Chalk - - - - -	3½
	Flint - - - - -	½
Chalk, 258½ feet	Chalk - - - - -	19
	Flint - - - - -	1½
	Chalk - - - - -	5
	Flint - - - - -	½
	Chalk - - - - -	15
	Flint - - - - -	⅔
	Chalk - - - - -	4
	Flint - - - - -	½
	Chalk - - - - -	7
	Flint - - - - -	⅔
	Chalk - - - - -	35
	Flint - - - - -	½
	Chalk - - - - -	37
	Flint - - - - -	1½
	Chalk - - - - -	2
	Flint - - - - -	⅖
	Chalk - - - - -	13⅙
		400

The following analysis of the water from this well has been published by Mr. Sutton, F.C.S. :—

County Analyst's Office and Laboratory,
London Street, Norwich, November 11th, 1880

	Grains per gallon
Total dissolved solids - - - - -	21·2800
Free ammonia - - - - - -	·0056
Ammonia from organic matter - - -	·0028

				Grams per gallon.
Nitrogen as nitrates or nitrites	-	-	-	none
Chlorine	-	-	-	2·2400
Equal to common salt	-	-	-	3·7100
Lime	-	-	-	7·2800
Magnesia	-	-	-	·6050
Sulphuric anhydrid	-	-	-	1·4400
Equal to gypsum	-	-	-	2·4500
Oxygen required to oxidise organic matters	-	-	-	·0760
Natural hardness	-	-	-	15 degrees
Hardness after boiling	-	-	-	3 8 do.

(Signed)   FRANCIS SUTTON.

REMARKS.—This water is undoubtedly to be ranked as a water of high-class purity, and in all respects is admirably adapted for dietetic purposes. The organic impurity is practically *nil*, and the mere trace which is found to be present is unquestionably mainly derived from vegetable sources of a perfectly harmless description. The hardness is also very moderate, and well within the limits which have been practically found conducive to health, at the same time, it is quite sufficient to prevent any absorption of lead from metal pipes. By simple boiling the hardness is reduced to one-fourth of its original amount I consider it an admirable water, both for domestic and general purposes

(Signed)   FRANCIS SUTTON.

It may be remarked that this well appears to have passed through an exceptional number of alternations of clay and sand In most places the section would be simpler, but it is impossible beforehand to say what will be found in a well sunk in these contorted beds

Missing Page

INDEX.

U.

Unio-bed, 31, 32.
Upper Boulder Clay, 82.
  „ Crag, 17, 105, 106, 108.
  „ Erratics, 82, 94.
  „ Fresh-water Bed, 11, 13, 22, 24–27, 30–43, 55, 58, 62–67, 71–80, 134

V.

Valleys, Denudation of, 109, 131
Valley Gravel, 118–127.
Vivianite, 134.

W.

Walcot, 20, 41, 87, 128
Walsham, North, 2, 103, 106, 108, 133, 135.
Waterhouse, C O , 67, 124.
Waters, Mineral, 134, 135.
Water Supply, 135–137.
Wayford Bridge, 107.
Wells (Water), 135–137
Westleton Beds, 8, 9, 21
Westwick, 106, 108.
Weybourn, 3, 11–13, 24, 66, 68–70, 73, 74, 103, 107, 120, 128, 129.

Weybourn Crag, 8, 9, 11–19, 46, 54, 58, 59.
  „   „ Lists of Fossils from the, 16, 18, 65–75, 78
  „ Sands, 8, 9
Wilton, 103.
Witton, 104, 107
Woman Hithe, 26, 27.
Wood Hill, 15, 27, 47, 129
Wood, S V , 54, 93
  „ jun., 8, 9, 17, 21, 50, 82, 94, 101, 117, 119.
Woodrow Farm, Cawston, 104, 107
Woodward, H. B., 2–4, 7, 10, 11, 16, 17, 49–53, 56, 60, 97, 103, 105–108, 110, 119, 120, 134, 135
  „ Samuel, 3, 7, 20, 44, 81, 128, 130
Worstead, 50, 106, 108

Y.

Yarmouth, 3, 56.

Z.

Zones in the Crag, 19, 44, 48, 60.

LONDON:

Printed by George E. B. Eyre and William Spottiswoode,
Printers to the Queen's most Excellent Majesty.
For Her Majesty's Stationery Office.
[14208.—375.—11/82.]

Missing Page

93 SW THE GEOLOGY of the CARBONIFEROUS ROCKS NORTH and EAST of LEEDS, and the PERMIAN and TRIASSIC ROCKS about TADCASTER By W. T AVELINE, A. H. GREEN, J. R. DAKYNS, J C WARD, and R. RUSSELL. 6d (Out of print)

95 SW, SE - The GEOLOGY of the COUNTRY around SCARBOROUGH and FLAMBOROUGH HEAD By C FOX-STRANGWAYS. 1s.

95 NW - The GEOLOGY of the COUNTRY between WHITBY and SCARBOROUGH. By C FOX-STRANGWAYS and G BARROW

96 SE - The GEOLOGY of the COUNTRY around NEW MALTON, PICKERING, and HELMSLEY By C. FOX-STRANGWAYS 1s

98 SE - The GEOLOGY of the NEIGHBOURHOOD of KIRKBY LONSDALE and KENDAL By W. T AVELINE, T McK. HUGHES, and R H TIDDEMAN. 2s.

98 NE - The GEOLOGY of the NEIGHBOURHOOD of KENDAL, WINDERMERE, SEDBERGH, and TEBAY By W. T. AVELINE and T McK. HUGHES. 1s 6d

101 SE - The GEOLOGY of the NORTHERN PART of the ENGLISH LAKE DISTRICT. By J C. WARD. 9s

THE MINERAL DISTRICTS OF ENGLAND AND WALES ARE ILLUSTRATED BY THE FOLLOWING PUBLISHED MAPS OF THE GEOLOGICAL SURVEY.

COAL-FIELDS OF ENGLAND AND WALES.
Scale, one inch to a mile

Anglesey, 78 (SW).
Bristol and Somerset, 19, 35.
Coalbrook Dale, 61 (NE & SE)
Clee Hill, 55 (NE, NW).
Denbighshire, 74 (NE & SE), 70 (SE)
Derby and Yorkshire, 71 (NW, NE, & SE), 82 (NW & SW), 81 (NE), 87 (NE, SE), 88 (SE)
Durham, 103 105
Flintshire, 79 (NE & SE).
Forest of Dean, 43 (SE & SW)
Forest of Wyre, 61 (SE), 55 (NE)
Lancashire, 80 (NW), 81 (NW), 89 (SE, NE, NW, & SW), 88 (SW, NW).
Leicestershire, 71 (SW), 63 (NW)
Northumberland and Durham (N. part), 105, 106 (SE), 109 (SW, SE).
North Staffordshire, 72 (NW), 72 (SW), 73 (NE), 80 (SE), 81 (SW)
South Staffordshire 54 (NW) 62 (SW)
Shrewsbury, 60 (NE), 61 (NW & SW),
South Wales, 36, 37 38, 40, 41, 42 (SE, SW)
Warwickshire, 62 (NE & SE), 63 (NW & SW), 54 (NE), 53 (NW)
Yorkshire, 86 (NE, SE), 87 (SW), 92 (SE), 93 (SW)

GEOLOGICAL MAPS.
Scale, six inches to a mile.

The Coal-fields and other mineral districts of Lancashire, Northumberland, Durham, Yorkshire are published on a scale of six inches to a mile, at 4s to 6s each MS Coloured Copies of other six-inch maps, not intended for publication, are deposited for reference in the Geological Survey Office, 28, Jermyn Street, London

Lancashire.

Sheet		Sheet	
15	Ireleth	87	Bolton-le-Moors
16	Ulverstone	88	Bury Heywood
17	Cartmel.	89	Rochdale, &c
22	Aldingham	92	Bickerstaffe, Skelmersdale
47	Clitheroe	93	Wigan, Up Holland, &c
48	Colne, Twiston Moor	94	West Houghton, Hindley, Atherton
49	Laneshaw Bridge.	95	Radcliffe, Peel Swinton &c
55	Whalley	96	Middleton Prestwich, &c.
56	Haggate	97	Oldham, &c
57	Winewall	100	Knowsley, Rainford, &c.
61	Preston	101	Billinge, Ashton, &c
62	Balderstone, &c.	102	Leigh, Lowton
63	Accrington	103	Ashley, Eccles
64	Burnley	104	Manchester, Salford, &c
65	Stiperden Moor	105	Ashton-under-Lyne
69	Layland	106	Liverpool, &c
70	Blackburn, &c	107	Prescott, Huyton, &c
71	Haslingden.	108	St Helen's, Burton Wood
72	Cliviger, Bacup, &c	109	Winwick, &c
75	Todmorden	111	Cheadle, part of Stockport, &c.
77	Chorley	112	Stockport, &c
78	Bolton-le-Moors	113	Part of Liverpool, &c
79	Entwistle		
80	Tottington		
81	Wardle		
84	Ormskirk, St. Johns, &c.		
85	Standish, &c.		
86	Adlington, Horwick, &c.		

Durham.

1.	Ryton.	3.	Jarrow.
2	Gateshead	4.	S Shields.

Sheet		Sheet.	
5.	Greenside.	23	Eastgate
6.	Winlaton	24	Stanhope
7	Washington.	25	Wolsingham.
8	Sunderland	26	Brancepeth
9		30	Benny Seat
10	Edmondbyers.	32	White Kirkley.
11	Ebchester	33	Hamsterley
12.	Tantoby.	34.	Whitworth.
13	Chester-le-Street	38	Maize Beck.
16	Hunstanworth.	41.	Cockfield
17	Waskerley	42	Bishop Auckland
18	Muggleswick.	46	Hawksley Hill House
19	Lanchester	52	Barnard Castle.
20	Hetton-le-Hole.	53	Winston
22	Wear Head		

Northumberland.

44	Rothbury	81	Earsdon	98	Walker
45	Longframlington	82.		101	Whitfield
		83	Coanley Gate	102.	Allendale Town.
46.	Radcliffe and Broomhill	87.	Heddon on-the-Wall	103	Shiley
47.	Coquet Island	88	Long Benton	105	Newlands.
54	Longhorsley	89.	Tynemouth.	106	Blackpool Bridge
55	Ulgham	91.	Greenhead	107	Allendale
56	Druridge Bay, &c	92.	Haltwhistle.	108.	Blanchland
		93	Haydon Bridge.	109.	Shotleyfield
63	Netherwitton.	94.	Hexham	110	Wellhope
64.	Morpeth	95	Corbridge	111	Allenheads
65	Newbiggin	96	Horsley	112.	
72.	Bedlington	97.	Newcastle-on-Tyne		
73	Blyth				
80.	Cramlington				

Cumberland.

55	Sourness.	70	Grange
56	Skiddaw	71.	
63	Thackthwaite.	74.	Wast
64	Keswick	75.	Stonethwaite Fell.
65	Dockray, &c	76	
69	Buttermere		

Westmorland.

12.	Patterdale.	25	Grasmere	38	Kendal.

Yorkshire.

5.	Romaldkirk	116	Coniston Moor	260	Honley
7.	Redcar	133.	Kirkby Malham.	261.	Kirkburton
9.				262	Darton.
12.	Bowes	184	Dale End.	263.	Homsworth.
13	Wycliffe	185.	Kildwick.	264	Campsall
20	Lythe	200.	Keighley	272	Holmfirth.
24.	Kirkby Ravensworth.	201	Bingley	273	Penistone
25.	Aldborough.	202	Calverley	274	Barnsley
32	Whitby	203	Seacroft	275	Darfield
33		204	Aberford.	276	Brodsworth.
38	Marske.	215	Peake Well	281.	Tankersell
39	Richmond	216	Bradford	282.	Wortley
46.		217	Calverley	283	Wath upon Dearne
47	Robin Hood's Bay	218	Leeds	284	Conisborough
53.	Downholme	219.	Kippax	287.	Low Bradford
68	Leybourne.	231	Halifax	288	Ecclesfield
82	Kidstones	232	Bristal	289	Rotherham.
84	E. Wilton.	233	East Ardsley	290	Brentiwell
97	Foxup	234.	Castleford	293	Hallam Moors.
98	Kirk Gill.	246	Huddersfield	295.	Handsworth.
99	Haden Carr.	247	Dewsbury	296.	Laughton-en-le-Morthen
100	Lofthouse	248	Wakefield	299	——
115	Arncliffe	249.	Pontefract.	300	Harthill.
		250	Darrington.		

MINERAL STATISTICS

Embracing the produce of Tin, Copper, Lead, Silver, Zinc, Iron, Coals, and other Minerals By ROBERT HUNT, F.R.S Keeper of Mining Records. From 1853 to 1857, inclusive, 1s 6d each 1858, Part I, 1s 6d., Part II, 5s 1859, 1s. 6d 1860, 3s. 6d., 1861, 2s , and Appendix, 1s 1862, 2s 6d 1863, 2s 6d., 1864, 2s 1865, 2s. 6d. 1866 to 1881, 2s each.

CPSIA information can be obtained at www.ICGtesting.com
Printed in the USA
LVOW131937290212

271010LV00010B/72/P